WARTIME IN WEST SUFFOLK

THE DIARY OF WINIFRED CHALLIS,
1942–1943

Photograph of Winifred Challis, taken c.1942 when she was forty-six. © *John Boorman*

WARTIME IN WEST SUFFOLK

THE DIARY OF WINIFRED CHALLIS, 1942–1943

Edited by

ROBERT MALCOLMSON and PETER SEARBY

The Boydell Press

Suffolk Records Society
VOLUME LV

A Suffolk Records Society publication
First published 2012
The Boydell Press, Woodbridge

ISBN 978–1–84383–702–2

Issued to subscribing members for the year 2011–2012

The Boydell Press is an imprint of Boydell & Brewer Ltd
PO Box 9, Woodbridge, Suffolk IP12 3DF, UK
and of Boydell & Brewer Inc.
668 Mt Hope Avenue, Rochester, NY 14620, USA
website: www.boydellandbrewer.com

The publisher has no responsibility for the continued existence or accuracy
of URLs for external or third-party internet websites referred to in this book,
and does not guarantee that any content on such websites is,
or will remain, accurate or appropriate

A catalogue record for this book is available
from the British Library

Papers used by Boydell & Brewer Ltd are natural, recyclable products
made from wood grown in sustainable forests

Printed in Great Britain by
CPI Group (UK) Ltd, Croydon, CR0 4YY

CONTENTS

ILLUSTRATIONS

ACKNOWLEDGEMENTS

It is a decade since we came upon Winifred Challis's diary in the Mass-Observation Archive at the University of Sussex, and we are indebted to many people and institutions for assisting us as we edited it. To two people we offer our special thanks: John Boorman and Dorothy Sheridan. Dorothy, who was at that time in charge of the MO Archive, was able to put us in touch with Winifred's kin, whose sanction was needed for us to publish the diary under Winifred's actual name. During the editorial process she and her colleagues at Sussex were of great help to us, not least in providing copies of the typescript diary (we are grateful to Anna Kisby for doing much of this work). Without those copies our task would have been impossible.

John Boorman is Winifred's nephew. He appears in the diary as a schoolboy, and the span of his years since then – he is now retired – is a measure of the distance that separates us from the events described in the diary, remote yet still within our reach. John responded to our initial approach with kindness and enthusiasm, and has constantly supported our efforts. This volume has been enriched by his detailed knowledge of the Challis clan in the last 150 years, and his loan of evocative family photographs and the very few surviving letters from Winifred's hand.

In the last ten years we have many times tramped the streets of Bury St Edmunds, noting the ways they have altered since Winifred Challis was writing her diary; among the many surprises has been our witnessing the elegant restoration of some of the dilapidated and ramshackle premises she described. The difficulty in tracing one-time lineaments beneath changes wrought during the prosperity of the post-war epoch has been challenging; fortunately we have many times been enlightened by Clive Paine, whose incomparable knowledge of Bury's topography has been placed at our service.

We offer our warm thanks to the staffs of the West Suffolk Record Office in Bury St Edmunds, and the university libraries in Cambridge and Kingston, Ontario, for assisting us in our researches. We are grateful to the Suffolk Records Society for bearing patiently with our elongated editorial process, and to its co-ordinating editor, David Sherlock, for guiding us through its last stages before publication. We hope that he, and the many others whose help has been invaluable to us, will welcome this addition to our wartime knowledge of the Home Front and the Suffolk county town that was one small part of it.

Robert Malcolmson, Nelson, British Columbia
Peter Searby, Swaffham Bulbeck, Cambridgeshire
December 2009

INTRODUCTION

'Written history is always merely an expression of a point
of view.'   Winifred Challis, 8 May 1945

The Diarist and her Diary

In November 1942, Winifred Challis began her diary for the social research
organization Mass-Observation, whose mission was to promote a 'science of
ourselves' – a sort of social anthropology of contemporary Britain.[1] We do
not know why she chose to start writing for Mass-Observation at this time,
when she was living in Bury St Edmunds, working as clerk to the county's
public assistance committee, and living by herself in a very spartan two-room
flat (it lacked electricity) at 62 Guildhall Street. Winifred in 1942 was in her
mid-forties, unmarried and had no children.

No diarist who wrote for Mass-Observation was in any way typical.
Diarists at any time see and must see the world from a subjective perspective. Each diarist experiences the world in his or her own distinctive way;
each perceives and interprets external facts and events through a subjective
lens; and each, when recording feelings and thoughts – sometimes in depth
and frequently at other times only in passing – is bound to write personally, though some diarists are much more self-disclosing than others. There
is certainly much that is personal, even idiosyncratic, in Winifred Challis's
diary. But – and this is crucial – it is not always inward-looking. For Winifred
was, when she wanted to be, an excellent observer of life around her. She had
a reporter's eye for detail, a good grasp of some facts (though not of others),
and a questioning mind; and she was a clear, vivid, and sometimes witty
writer. Her diary, then, is a document of social life in wartime that deserves
a wider audience.

Winifred Mary Challis was born on 17 February 1896 in Myrtle Cottage,
Doris Street, Newmarket (Plate 1). In June 1982, at the age of eighty-six,
she composed for her nephew, John Boorman, a personal history, mainly
prior to her twenties, and this autobiography of childhood and adolescence
is sufficiently revealing and informative that we have reproduced most of
it as Appendix B (below, p.176). Furthermore, much of her understanding

---

[1]   For further details on Mass-Observation, its purposes and those who volunteered as
      'observers' see Appendix A, below, p.173.

1. *Winifred's birthplace and family home, Myrtle Cottage, Doris Street, Newmarket, c.1900. The infant pictured is probably Winifred, who would have then been four years old. The house still stands, largely unaltered.* © *John Boorman*

2. A Challis family photograph taken c.1916. Standing are Arthur (1902–83), George (1898–1989), Winifred (1896–1990), Florence (1899–1927) and Lilian (1911–18); seated are Edith (1904–94), Alfred (1868–1938), Nancy (1870–1926) and Harry (1907–96). © John Boorman

of herself in old age is akin to the personality that she had disclosed four decades earlier in her diary.[2]

Winifred was the eldest child of a small builder who was originally a bricklayer. Eight children were born to her parents, of whom three boys and three girls survived to adulthood (Plate 2). Winifred portrays herself as a child sometimes at odds with authority, and not inclined to deference. Clearly, she was something of a free spirit, which did not well suit what was expected of young women in the early twentieth century. 'Being a female is a tragedy because one gets split in two', she wrote in March 1944. Her leanings were decidedly intellectual, and she would have received an academic schooling suited to her talents had she accepted her parents' offer to pay her fees at Bury County School.[3] However, whether from restlessness, perversity, or some other reason, she declined this opportunity, stayed in the elementary school and left it at thirteen. 'At the age of 17', she recalled in her late forties, 'I'd have liked to learn all sorts of things and develop myself. I was curious

---

2   See Appendix B. We are very grateful to John Boorman for allowing us to see and make use of his aunt's autobiographical essay, which was sent to him as a long letter.

3   The County School was, in modern British parlance, a grammar school.

3. Winifred Challis c.1920 aged twenty-four. © John Boorman

about almost everything in the world except sex and I'd have liked to become an artist or an authoress and to travel all over the world. Actually, of course, I did neither, but just travelled round in a comparatively small circle as a shorthand typist, relieving the monotony by changing jobs, until it wasn't so easy to get one [in the 1930s] and I found unemployment looming ahead because I was over 34, and was only willing to work my brain and not merely my body. That was far worse than the lack of success in love affairs.'[4] She was, it seems, regularly searching for satisfaction, which was elusive, and she often found little of it, certainly from her mid-thirties, and probably during some of her twenties as well (Plate 3).[5]

---

4   MOA, Directive Reply, March 1944.
5   'I know there is a superfluity of females,' she wrote after the war, when she was fifty,

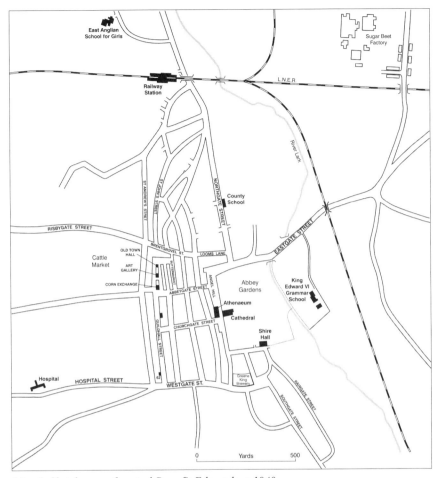

Map 1. Sketch map of central Bury St Edmunds, c.1940.

Between her early teens and mid-forties Winifred probably held about twenty-five jobs, most of them as a shorthand typist. She once worked in Australia House – and did not like it (24 May 1946). For many years, job

'but some women could marry a dozen times a year, whereas the longest anyone ever tried to pay me attention was three weeks, and he was young and out of experience. As a female, nobody on earth could be a bigger failure! Fortunately I don't want to get married now and prefer solitude. The period 19 to 30 was the worst, when I was self-conscious about being an "unwanted female". During that period it was a real tragedy to have been a woman instead of a man' (24 June 1946). On the other hand, she had previously written that 'during the last war I was extremely happy in Dunstable and Luton [where she worked in munitions], and on the whole I was happy in Bexhill in 1939' (23 August 1943).

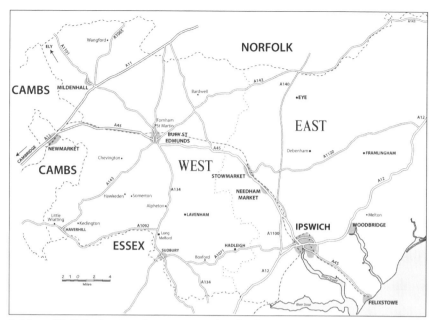

2. Map of Suffolk showing places mentioned in the diary.

security did not concern her, for she preferred 'risk and adventure to getting bored' (2 March 1943). She also trained as a nurse in the early 1930s but practised this profession (for which she had many harsh words) only briefly. In 1938 she opened a small office in Bexhill-on-Sea, East Sussex, in the hope of attracting orders for typing – she was not very successful – and during her stay there she met and befriended Hans Martin Luther, a refugee from Nazi Germany who was then less than half her age. During the war he was interned on the Isle of Man and figures prominently in Winifred's diary as 'my internee'.

Winifred moved to Bury St Edmunds shortly after war began, sometime in 1940. Bury, a town of about 17,000 people when war broke out, was the administrative centre of West Suffolk and the meeting place of both the county council and the town council. (In 1888 Suffolk had been divided into two, a division that lasted until 1974. East Suffolk was administered from Ipswich.) It was an ancient town, with many reminders of its proud history: ruins of one of the largest monasteries in England were prominent in the town centre; houses dating from the sixteenth and seventeenth centuries stood in many streets, including Guildhall Street where Winifred lived; and guide-books drew attention to the numerous distinguished Georgian and Victorian buildings, a legacy of Bury's place at the heart of a prosperous agricultural region. This was the town that tourists were drawn to. But between the two world wars Suffolk agriculture suffered. There was much poverty in Bury and its neighbourhood, and some of the historic properties (such as Wini-fred's house) were badly in need of repair. Industry also had a presence in Bury. The Greene King brewery was one of the biggest enterprises in East Anglia, and there was a large factory for the refining of sugar from sugar-beet. Typical, perhaps, of many smaller concerns was the ice-cream manufac-tory of Alderman Robert Ollé, Winifred's landlord.

While in Bury Winifred often reflected on her life. 'Until I went nursing, 1930–33, I revelled in facing life', she wrote on 6 May 1945, just before war in Europe ended. 'It was after I went to college in 1936–7[6] and came out to find myself too old to be accepted on the labour market as I was 40 that I became afraid. Tramping London looking for jobs with one's capital evapo-rating takes the guts out of one, I suppose. Bexhill revived me a bit and then came the war with its badly paid jobs and its housing problems. I ought to have got about, given up these rooms, sold the furniture and somehow made some money, but I let the years of opportunity go lingeringly by without profit. Dreary, dark, imprisoned years.'

While her diary is full of such passages of gloom and regret, there are also many occasions when, in her writing, she is looking outward, not inward, when she is describing and recording external facts. These are entries where she portrays people in her workplace or in public places; where she recounts conversations both private and public; where she describes her everyday life and the everyday lives of others in Bury; and where she reports details concerning eating out in British Restaurants, diet, the behaviour of soldiers, rumours, prices and wages, health and illness, poverty and privilege, sexual mores, the lack of shelter, public meetings, and proposals for social reform. Sometimes, too, she offers informed opinions about a particular subject, such as housing. In these many passages she casts much light on everyday life in wartime Britain. Our task as editors has been, in particular, to highlight this material of social observation, to shape it into (we hope) a striking portrait of life in West Suffolk in 1942–43, and to reinforce and enlarge upon Winifred's testimony by drawing upon other contemporary sources.[7]

---

[6] This was Hillcroft College in Surbiton, Surrey, established in the 1920s as a residential college for women's adult education. 'The aim of this working women's college', according to an authority on its history, 'was not for specific vocational training, for promotion, or any form of go-getting. It was simply to equip its students for a fuller and better life, whether they returned to their former occupation in factory, shop or home, or launched out into something more congenial.' The college's goal was 'to broaden the students' outlook and increase their powers of service to the community'. See Margaret Joyce Powell, *The History of Hillcroft College*, 1964, pp.4 and 33. It offered a one-year programme, emphasizing a liberal education, for around twenty-five to thirty students.

[7] We have tried to tilt the process of editorial selection to emphasize what Winifred wrote about public and domestic life in West Suffolk and to de-emphasize her writing about herself, especially when she was unhappy. We have also omitted much of what

from W. M. Challis, 62 Guildhall Street, Bury St. Edmund. Sunday, 31/1/43. Doing housework in these 2 rooms is like running round in circles: by the time the kettle are filled the oilstoves & lamps want oil, & by that time it is washing-up & the emptying of bowls into pails & the cleaning & putting away of the bowls & other paraphernalia, & then it is time to get ready for a meal, etc. etc. Everything has to go in & out. One can, for instance, if one has a kitchen, leave things in it, but it looks terrible to have wiping-up cloths & so on in the drawing-room! My food I store in a chest of drawers as the mice can't get in it, though for some reason I haven't heard a mouse since Xmas. I've a nice white patch on the ceiling now. I thought the plaster was falling so got a tin tray & a poker to help it down, but it was only 2 layers of ceiling paper dropping off. The last paper put on is grey, the previous one whitish, & the ceiling itself a glaring white & apparently quite firm. This would be a marvellously light room if it had a white ceiling. If it were my own place I'd whitewash it, but it isn't & I might be quitting any week. It is a pity because both rooms are a nice size & cold, with the furniture I have, look lovely. I'd like to be back in my Bexhill place for the summer — the only trouble there was that I spent much more than I earned, because I earned next to nothing. I wouldn't have minded whitewashing that place, because I'd got a very nice landlord, & a helpful one.

4. *A characteristic page from Winifred Challis's manuscript diary.* © Trustees of the Mass Observation Archive, University of Sussex

Public Assistance

The Poor Law, dating from Victorian times, was dismantled in 1929 when its functions and buildings were transferred to county councils, including West Suffolk. Elected 'guardians' had previously been responsible for administering the Poor Law; these were abolished and most of their duties were taken over by public assistance committees nominated by each county council.[8] These public assistance committees – PACs, for short – provided means-tested relief for the destitute and others in distress, including the elderly, children, and the ill and disabled (but not the able-bodied unemployed).[9] Many persons in need were 'relieved' at home, but others were accommodated in a variety of establishments – hospitals, asylums, training centres, orphanages, and old people's homes. As a contemporary authority on the subject pointed out, 'The Minister of Health is charged with the central direction and control of all matters relating to the administration of poor relief, but has no power to interfere in any individual case for the purpose of ordering or varying the amount of relief.'[10] These decisions were to be made locally – and they could and did range widely. On 2 June 1944 Winifred mentioned allowances for the poor in Sudbury, and added, 'This only relates to Sudbury, as other districts in the county have different prices, varying according to the generosity or niggardliness of the respective committees.' A very basic form of health care was also a part of public assistance. 'In addition to providing assistance in cash, or by admission to an institution, public assistance authorities also are required to afford medical relief where necessary in the form of the services of a medical practitioner and the supply of requisite drugs and appliances. … Persons in receipt of outdoor relief, and others who are without the means of providing themselves with medical attention, are entitled to the services of the district medical officer.'[11]

Winifred's job as clerk to the public assistance committee of the West Suffolk county council gave her an inside view of many issues relating to

---

she wrote about office politics and gossip, another favourite topic; internment; detailed matters of local government; and the iniquities (as she saw them) of the nursing profession. Our selections for Part One (November 1942 to January 1943) represent a little less than half of what she wrote during these months; the selections for Part Two (February to June 1943) represent considerably less than half.

8 Confusingly, the name 'guardians' continued to be used for the county councillors who administered the 'institution', as the workhouse was now called.

9 Aid to employable people who were unemployed was the responsibility of the unemployment assistance board, which was set up in 1934 to administer the National Insurance Acts of 1911 and 1920 and their later modifications. Of course, by the time Winifred started to write for Mass-Observation, few able-bodied unemployed people existed in Britain; the war and conscription had taken care of that.

10 Herbert W. Marshall, 'Public Assistance', in William A. Robson, ed., *Social Security* (London, 2nd edn, 1945; first published 1943), p.43.

11 *Ibid.*, p.55.

wartime welfare and poor relief, and she writes a lot about them, not only as matters of administration and policy, but also in terms of the treatment and circumstances of life of specific distressed and disadvantaged individuals. Her job provided an excellent vantage point to record happenings that were largely unknown to outsiders – and she made good use of this unusual opportunity. She was, as often happened during the war, a woman doing a 'man's job'; and perhaps she took notice of things that a man might not have noticed. The man who had held this job would (she mentions several times) be able to reclaim it when he was demobilized, a prospect that much concerned her. She felt, as she had often felt, that her position in life was alarmingly insecure. In 1942 her annual salary was £170 plus a six per cent wartime bonus.

THE DIARY OF WINIFRED CHALLIS
1942–1943

Diarist 5271 in the Mass-Observation Archive
at the University of Sussex

PART ONE

November 1942 to January 1943

The diary that Winifred Challis produced for Mass-Observation begins abruptly and without ceremony.

Tuesday, 3 November 1942

Guardians committee clerk: 'Have you Iris Brown's case-paper?' Public assistance case-paper clerk: 'Yes, I've been writing to East Suffolk because her foster mother would like to keep her at school until she is 15'. G.C. clerk: 'Our (West Suffolk) committee thinks she might as well go to domestic service'. C.-P. clerk: 'Well, East Suffolk [will] pay for her, but I don't suppose they'll let her stay at school, they're a frightfully mean lot'. 'Worse than us?' 'Yes.' Children's boarding-out clerk: 'East Suffolk has lots more money than West'. C.-P. clerk: 'Well, they have bigger towns'. G.C. clerk: 'We may have more aristocracy'. C.-P. clerk: 'What difference does that make?' General laughter. Politically this may be interesting, because East Suffolk is Labour and West Suffolk Conservative.

The whole of the staff at _____ [unnamed] public assistance institution have applied for more wages and we have appointed a sub-committee of four to deal with it. One is a very careful retired farmer who never moves from this district. The second is a retired insurance agent who thinks a great deal of every sixpence. The third, an old lady between 70 and 80, is kindly but thinks it terrible workpeople should charge so much that persons with limited incomes (herself) cannot afford to have things done. The fourth is a new, mediocre lady member.

It might be well to have one committee to deal with staff questions for the entire county. The Shire Hall salaries are perhaps lowest because the Shire Hall people are apathetic and permanent but the law of supply and demand operates in the Institutions etc. with the result that an office-boy at one place may be paid 10s. a week and the same at another place 30s. We attempt to level them up now and again but salaries are perpetually changing, and we always endeavour to get each individual as cheaply as we can, so levelling is almost impossible. Besides, a lot depends on the generosity of the committee in the particular town. We do try, but in vain, to keep the emergency hospital salaries at the Shire Hall level. For months now the medical officers have needed a secretary and we have spent a lot advertising for her – we get lots and lots of excellent applications but they all ask for from £3 10s. to £6 a week, whereas we can only pay £143 a year inclusive of cost-of-living bonus.

If it were a cook instead of a secretary we should probably pay what she asked, even if double that amount of £143.

The Shire Hall people don't bargain individually regarding salaries – they have a salary scale and leave the rest to NALGO [National Association of Local Government Officers] which they hardly trouble to support. Most of them don't approve of trade unionism. There was a comparatively good attendance at their last meeting – over 30. My salary (it's a *man's* job) is £170 a year plus 6 per cent bonus. For about nine months now NALGO has applied to the county council for increased bonus for all, suggesting the present national scale, and at this meeting the council offered another 4 per cent to persons such as I. *All* [those in] the clerk's department present wanted to say 'Thank you very much and if later you can spare some more we shall be pleased to accept it.' *All* the public assistance department present voted solidly for the national scale, which did win the day. I hear that as a result the council has now withdrawn its offer and we have to go to arbitration about the national scale. Much the same thing happened in our Institution for Mental Defectives,[1] but there the attendants accepted the Public Assistance Committee's lower rate of wages, bringing up the salaries of the non-resident married men to about the rate of the farm labourer's present wage of £3 a week.

My sister's husband [in Staines, Middlesex] was a co-operative society's furniture manager but is now a soldier, so she is very hard up because his pay is not made up by his employers. This making-up of pay acts very unequally. My brother also is a soldier but as a civil servant his pay is made up and so he and his wife have no monetary troubles.

Since her husband joined the army my sister-in-law, a school-mistress, has decided to have a child. I suppose it is an instinct, possibly a good one, to have a child in case the father does not return. Personally I do not understand women with responsibilities and under present conditions retiring from the stress of life to have a baby – it seems rather selfish and rough luck on the baby; but then, I am a spinster.

I wonder why emoluments are not subject to income tax? We supply one of our officers with a good house and value it as 15s. a week emoluments. Therefore he gets a house worth 30s. for 15s. and pays no income tax whereas if we paid him the 15s. he would spend 30s. and in addition pay income tax on the 15s. Nurses, too, though drawing high salaries, usually escape payment of income tax.

This billeting business is very rough on householders. We get nurses and sisters whose pocket-money is £3 or £4 a week and they are billeted at 21s. a week payable by the authorities, and expect a daily bath and good food for it. The ordinary typist with £1 a week pocket-money has to pay 30s. (a

---

[1]   This public assistance institution was in the former workhouse in Kedington, near the Essex border.

reasonable figure for the landlady) out of her 50s. a week salary and is not half the trouble a nurse is.

There is also a billeting payment of 5s. a week which does not cover food. I pay 5s. for each empty room so if a nurse were billeted on me I'd have to provide her with furniture, firing, light, and pay the laundry bill, all for nothing. This must very often happen. She would not get a bath as I have no bathroom, and all water has to be brought upstairs and taken down again, as well as heated upstairs on oil-stove or open fire.

The salaries of nurses are very high now. The conditions under which they work are as a rule very bad, owing to unsuitable buildings, 'hospital etiquette', deplorable sanitary conditions, lack of organisation, a two-shift instead of three-shift system, tradition, 'seniority', an excessive number of probationers to trained nurses, [and] insufficient staff, particularly at night. By means of their present co-operatives nurses have taken salaries into their own hands but they have done nothing to improve their working conditions.

There seems to be no contact between the nurse and the committee which governs her institution.

Today I wrote from one public assistance officer to another that they must agree it was almost impossible to find an ideal married couple as master and matron – one would practically always be better than the other. Yet all these places still try and get masters and matrons instead of a clerk and steward and a matron who is not his wife. Habit, I suppose, for there can be nothing to recommend it save, perhaps, a little saving in emoluments. Marriages of convenience, too, where the man has to find a trained nurse before he can become a master on the strength of it.

Nursing always makes me feel as if I've dropped out of the present century back into the middle ages.

Tomorrow I must get ready for Sudbury House[2] and boarded-out children's meetings and Bury St Edmunds area guardians meeting. I must also file many papers and make out agendas for the emergency hospital meeting and the hostel meeting. This will be all right if I don't get too many phone calls and enquiries and the public assistance officer [Thompson] doesn't want me as his typist. I cannot say that the county council pays me for nothing – I do 40 times the work I did in the Wool Control [her previous employer], but I have more freedom so prefer it. The only disadvantage is that now I have no time to knit and had I remained in the Wool Control I'd have learned another language by now. Still, one can't have everything, and I got very bored there. Pure wool could not by its very nature prove very exciting.[3]

---

2   Winifred is probably referring to the former workhouse in Sudbury, whose name had been changed to the Public Assistance Institution following the 1929 Act of Parliament.

3   The Wool Control office of the Ministry of Supply was in 6 Hatter Street, Bury St Edmunds. During the war the government regulated the supply and use of many raw

Don't know yet if the Home Office will grant me permission to visit my internee Xmas week. Nor do I yet know if he wants to see me. I think Fleetwood a ghastly place but Douglas feels a happy place. I'd have to risk getting a boat and I'd nearly die if I had to remain stranded in Fleetwood for Xmas. I think I told the internee, though, to expect me if he sees me, so probably he won't say whether he'd like me to go or not, but will merely 'bow to the inevitable'. So long as he is painting eight hours a day I don't mind to any degree, because the interest and occupation will make his confinement endurable.[4]

Wednesday, 4 November

I see that East Suffolk *is* willing for that child to remain at school until she is 15. Just as well because, like most of the boarded-out children, she is somewhat mentally deficient.

A Los Angeles letter, from an attorney friend of my internee. He is interesting on the subject of American divorces and writes humorously on other topics. Belvoir Castle, built in Saxon times, was the home of his ancestors. I must tell him that the name brings to my mind only the subject of beer. I

---

materials, of which wool was one. Three months later (24 February 1943) Winifred would write about this office. 'The job of Wool Control here is to send out census forms to farmers, who complete and return them. All the wool is sent by the farmers to the seven or eight warehouses, where it is appraised and sent off as directed by the Bradford headquarters. The Wool Control keeps a copy of the warehouse records and makes a return or two to Bradford about the quantities available. I was there about 18 months.' Earlier in this day's entry she has noted that 'it is only on rare occasions that wool has to be appraised, and there are very few wool farmers in the Eastern Area'.

4   Hans Martin Luther, a refugee from Nazi Germany whom Winifred had met in Bexhill in 1938, was born in 1917 or 1918. She became very attached to him, and during his later internment seems to have adopted him as her personal cause. He was one of some 71,000 German and Austrian nationals who were living in Britain in September 1939, of whom around 70 per cent were listed as 'refugees from Nazi oppression', many of them Jewish (he was not). About 350 were initially regarded by Whitehall as security risks because of their Nazi sympathies and interned. With the critical threat to Britain's security in the late spring and summer of 1940, many other Germans were interned, most of them Jews and others eager to assist Britain's war effort. Internment was carried out hastily and with little discrimination, and internees suffered considerable hardship. There were almost 20,000 internees in various parts of Britain by July 1940, of whom Hans Martin Luther was one (Italians had by then joined Germans and Austrians); by far the largest number, close to 11,000, was held on the escape-proof Isle of Man. Thereafter many were released and by the summer of 1942 there were fewer than 5,000 internees on the Isle of Man.

The main sources on internment are François Lafitte, *The Internment of Aliens*, a Penguin Special published in November 1940 (2nd edition, 1988, with new introduction); Peter and Leni Gillman, *'Collar the Lot': How Britain Interned and Expelled its Wartime Refugees* (London, 1980); and Miriam Kochan, *Britain's Internees in the Second World War* (London, 1983).

wonder if there is a brand of ale, or something, with that name? His father's ancestors were English, his mother's Scottish. Says I can share his letters with the internee if I don't find them too frightful. But is it wise to send to an internment camp a letter which says gasoline is rationed and in Los Angeles they have no cellars as protection from bombs?

Another letter which tells me not to visit the internee at Xmas – everybody says, don't do anything, keep quiet, or the Home Office will get annoyed and refuse to release him. Personally I don't see it would, or should, have any bearing on the matter. Still, as Bloomsbury House[5] tell me to leave it to them, and they don't like my attitude any more than the Home Office does, I may as well *not* go at Xmas. I don't know why they keep him interned all these years, but we are both entirely in Home Office hands and there is nothing to do but await their pleasure. It is damnable. Trust in God, I suppose – a hard thing to do. Funny that in years gone by I thought I was free, and now we must not criticise, or talk (or above all write) or even throw a piece of paper down in the street, for fear of imprisonment. A queer life, plus black-out and possible bombs, and despite it life goes on much the same, fortunately.

The Adelphi Players are returning here December 18 and 19, but their prices will not be so abnormally low this time. In the summer they gave me the only week really worth living that I've had since the war started. ENSA concerts don't interest me – I much prefer poetry and acting to music.[6]

A few parsons at the British Restaurant today. The Bury St Edmunds British Restaurant seems to attract that class rather than the poor. The helpings are all too dainty for my complete satisfaction, but it does lessen my shopping and cooking even though I still have to cook additional vegetables to be adequately nourished.[7]

---

5 Bloomsbury House was the headquarters of all the main organizations concerned with refugees in the United Kingdom. It was set up in a hotel in Bloomsbury (hence its name) leased for this purpose in 1939.

6 ENSA – the Entertainments National Service Association – founded in 1940, promoted concerts and entertainment of all kinds for the forces and civilians.

7 British Restaurants, which began in early 1941, were designed to provide affordable hot meals for people who were unable, or found it a challenge, to prepare food at home. They were cafeteria-style and run on a non-profit basis, and depended heavily on volunteer labour, often supplied by the Women's Voluntary Services. British Restaurants were intended to supplement, not replace, commercial catering establishments. By late 1942 there were almost 2,000 of them throughout the nation. A full-course hot meal in a British Restaurant usually cost around one shilling. The name 'British Restaurant' had been suggested by Churchill himself, partly because he did not care for the name 'Communal Feeding Centre', which was often used initially. The British Restaurant in Bury was located in the old St Mary's Infants' School in Crown Street and had been opened in early May 1942. It was to be open daily from 12.30 to 2 p.m., serve a hot three-course meal for 11d., and accommodate up to eighty people at a time (*Bury Free Press*, Saturday, 9 May 1942, p.2.) At the time it opened there were already around forty British Restaurants in Suffolk, with more approved or under consideration. It

I shall have to look at that ¼lb cheese I bought four or six weeks ago – I don't like being without cheese but unfortunately it won't keep indefinitely. I've bought my ration of margarine and cooking fat lately because since shell eggs became non-existent I've needed cakes made with powdered egg to fill the gap and each time I make one for myself I also send one to the internee. I've now, however, neither box nor brown paper to send another. No use buying cakes even if obtainable, because they would be mouldy before he got them. I'm no economist – I put 2s. worth of fresh walnuts in one recently.

The county's adopted children who are old enough are simply overjoyed at the idea of joining the Forces. After the prospects of eternal domestic service *they* will feel drunk with freedom. It is expected they will produce many illegitimate children, but they cannot all be banished into mental deficiency homes just out of fear of that. The adolescent is a very big problem in wartime. St Mary's Church here did, however, provide some excellent lectures on sex and parenthood last winter. Where the brain is slow, though, the animal nature undoubtedly acts first.

A lot of kleptomania about and things keep vanishing from the shire hall. Lost my best fountain pen last week – shouldn't have left it on my desk, I suppose. The solicitor lost his gloves today.

I *thought* we needed a more comprehensive committee for wage questions. Gooch [chief clerk] in the office *acted*. I found him floundering in figures, making comparisons in wages of the various classes of employee at the various Institutions, and he has fixed up with the public assistance officer to have a committee formed from *all* the county committees concerned and for the masters and clerks and stewards to be present to represent their staffs. This will be good, and may do something to allay the dissatisfaction which is evident in most of the Institutions, if not all.

The wireless has been on downstairs [at 62 Guildhall Street] all the evening. Mine won't go because the Electricity Company won't let me have a meter because I'm not in a self-contained flat. I have to share the lavatory and water-tap downstairs, in other words. So as no gas is laid on, I burn paraffin in lamps and stoves.

I really *must* get up in time to cook bacon for breakfast tomorrow – or *that* will be bad, being already a week old. The tomatoes I got to eat with it went into a stew last weekend.

I've now some washing wants doing, but now there is a tenant downstairs I've nowhere to hang it to dry. She is far too fussy to look at a linen-line stretched across her two square yards of back garden. It *might* dry in the cupboard where the plaster has vanished and the wind blows from outside through the laths.

---

was said that 'In the smaller country towns, British Restaurants are doing valuable work. Newmarket caters for 350 meals a day, Sudbury for 160, Haverhill for 110 and Lavenham for 80' (*South-West Suffolk Echo*, Saturday, 2 May 1942, p.2.)

Thursday, 5 November

Is this Guy Fawkes' day? I think so, by the date, but I've heard no mention of it. There are poppies in windows ready for the 11th – Armistice Day of the last war, with its poignant memories.

A few years ago one of my landladies bought a second-hand wardrobe, chest of drawers and washhand-stand from London dealers for 30s. The price of a similar wardrobe (minus the chest) today is between £9 and £10 in this district.

Books seem to be about the only cheap things to buy – why, I know not. I've here 1270 pages (and 1292 poems) for 8s. 6d. and the other week I bought *Masterpieces of British Art* [edited by W. Leon Soldes, 1940], with 100 good colour plates in it, for 12s. 6d. It is really a lovely book, originally priced at two guineas [i.e., £2 2s.].

I've been in Sudbury all day, mainly dealing with cases of boarded-out children. The Sudbury people (why, I know not) always have about five times as many of these children as Bury St Edmunds does. Perhaps the committee rounds them up more thoroughly.

It is possible that, owing to petrol shortage, in future the county health visitors only will visit these children and the committee members lose their job. The public health people demand a higher standard of home, but you can't board children out in good homes if the good homes aren't there. The members have been most interested in the children and even if they don't know asthma from whooping cough they have probably done very good work, but there may be overlapping.

For the average child we pay 12s. a week plus 40s. a quarter for clothing and possibly many working-class mothers take the children to help make ends meet. When we allow relief to a family it runs to about 5s. or 6s. a child, and I myself think it should be the same as for the boarded-out child, particularly as in most cases the relief children have more character and better mentality, which to my mind should be helped to develop and not fade away owing to malnutrition.

Big newspaper headline today about Germans being in full retreat in the Western Desert. As the number of prisoners stated as taken is only 9,000, I didn't pay any attention to it. My boss, however, thought it might be a turning point in the war and said that the end of the last war came when the Germans were in retreat. I said 'Yes, but wasn't France a different proposition?' thinking that the Western Desert was only a small part of the present war area and we'd yet got to conquer most of Europe, whatever happened in the East. He said that coupled with the fact that the Germans had not taken Stalingrad things looked black for them, and I agreed they would not appreciate the idea of another Russian winter. Later one of the women committee members remarked 'Isn't the news lovely?' and some of the men said we mustn't say too much about successes, remembering Libya.

5. *Diners in the British Restaurant, North Street, Sudbury. Originally these restaurants catered for evacuees but then opened their doors to the general public. Sudbury's restaurant was housed in the Technical Institute which also served as the town library. At the time the photograph was taken, the Sudbury restaurant was serving about 135–40 meals a day. From an archive copy of The Suffolk and Essex Free Press, 10 July 1941, p.3. © The Suffolk Free Press*

Mr Spencer, who is chairman of NALGO, has been taken to hospital with another attack of haemorrhage. In courtesy, brains, unselfishness, courage and personality, he altogether outshines most of the big-salaried Shire Hall people and it is a very great pity he has tuberculosis. Burchill, though without the charm of manner, also has brains and will probably carry NALGO business on in his absence.

I had lunch at Sudbury British Restaurant today [Plates 5 and 6]. They do not serve soup as at Bury St Edmunds but they have a much more abundant supply of cabbages and the meal is more satisfying. I think this is in part due to the fact that Sudbury caters more for the poor and also each person gets about the same amount, whereas in Bury they look at you and decide how much to give according to your sex and size and whether you are still growing. I, therefore, being a woman aged 46, get less than most. It does not *really* matter, as I can always come home directly after and have something else if I wish.[8]

---

8   The British Restaurant in Sudbury was set up in January 1941, so it must have been one of the first in Suffolk to open. It was located in the Technical Institute on North Street, which also housed the WVS office. 'The majority of the diners are evacuees,'

6. The Technical Institute, North Street, Sudbury, which housed the British Restaurant during the War. The site is now occupied by the entrance to North Street car park and the Argos store. © Sudbury Museum Trust

My boss's wife and various others went to Cambridge today to see the film *Gone with the Wind*. Neither the Odeon nor Bostock (the menagerie man who employs the secretary downstairs in the Home Guard) I hear would have the picture in Bury St Edmunds. Bostock owns lots of cinemas and is teaching

---

it was reported in mid-1941, 'for whom the scheme was primarily intended. Now, anyone may go to the Sudbury Centre for a meal. Amongst those who patronise it are lorry drivers who, being unable to stay, take their meals with them. We understand that meals to take away are served.' It was serving 135 to 140 meals a day, at a cost of 9d. (or slightly more) for a full meal. (*Suffolk and Essex Free Press*, 10 July 1941, p.3.) This report is accompanied by an excellent photograph of the interior of Sudbury's British Restaurant. (See Plate 5.) The photograph is captioned 'Eatanswill Restaurant?' Eatanswill is the name of the borough in which Mr Pickwick and his friends witnessed a pre-Reform election. It is thought that Charles Dickens had Sudbury (Suffolk) in mind – a notoriously corrupt constituency.

Evacuees, who were prominent in West Suffolk, had other needs as well, and one of these was noted in the *Suffolk and Essex Free Press*, 29 May 1941, p.7: 'An appeal for the gift or loan of perambulators, push-chairs and the like is made by the Women's Voluntary Services. These "prams", which can be loaned or given, are required for the use of evacuated children whose mothers have lost their baby carriages and find it hard work carrying their children about.'

the secretary how to run one so that she will have a job after the war. He seems to treat his employees with *extreme generosity*.[9]

I thought this morning in bed, how easy it would be for the average person to bear a grudge against an internee. If, for instance, I were not positive that my internee is on the side of England and craving to help us, would it not be a *possible* thing to feel aggrieved and to say 'Why should my brothers bleed to keep a foreigner while he learns to paint pictures?' As it is, of course, I am truly thankful that he *is* painting pictures, just to keep his mind employed.

Today we allowed a baby to be adopted in a home where an Italian is living and it was rather amusing to hear the remarks that the Italian was quite all right because the police would keep an eye on him. The members seemed to have implicit reliance on the police. Actually, from what I saw of the police at Bexhill, I think they were most vigilant about foreigners *before* the war. I take it, however, that all their records were swept aside as useless when the bulk internments of friends and foes took place.

I will tell the internee I will not visit him at Xmas I think. Then I can buy the Dutch picture he wishes me to sell for him. He must have money now he can earn none and I don't want to live in these rooms if they are going to be half bare – the mice and dim lighting and dirty wallpaper make them dismal enough as it is. And my landlord is such a skinflint that I absolutely won't have the place redecorated for his ultimate benefit – besides, I'd move any time I could find accommodation with the use of a bathroom and garden big enough to sit in. Not much hope of finding such things, though. Expect the war will end first and – what then?

Friday, 6 November

The county council, after many months of pressure from NALGO, have increased my earnings to the value to me (deducting income tax) of about 1s. 4d. a week. They are now trying to make us work another six hours a week without pay – presumably to earn the 1s. 4d. at less than 3d. an hour. I don't know what will happen. We are but serfs, when all is said and done, and the only hope seems to be trade unionism; though it is extremely difficult to get employees to combine like their employers do. A woman in the Forces says they also give something with one hand and take something else away with the other hand. That is her remark, not mine. Perhaps Bury St Edmunds people are especially mean. There are a few quite nice people on our Bury Public Assistance Committees, but on the whole the Bury committees are by far the meanest-spirited in the county. The Relief Meeting this morning here was unusually good. The public assistance officer was in exceptional form and forced relief upwards for a good number of cases, and there was a very

---

9   Douglas Bostock was the owner of a chain of cinemas in East Anglia.

good attendance of women, which was definitely to the good. So far as my experience goes, women (whatever their faults) are more generous than men are. Some of these women are no good on the committee, but others are. When they are few in number the men squash them, even by rudeness. A Mrs Greene has recently come on and improved the tone of the committee and the men treat her, for some reason or other, with respect. She is very definitely an acquisition. This morning they even increased relief to a penniless widow and seven children to 50s. a week and 3s. a week for coal, an increase of 8s. a week plus the coal money, as she had been getting 42s. She has no rent to pay but has already sold most of her furniture to keep away from poor relief, so she will certainly need the 50s. for food, clothing and household goods. The women on the committee realise what household expenses are and how much food costs, but most of the men know nothing about that and care less. We have a large number of retired army officers aged between 70 and 80 on this committee, and one of them says repeatedly that with free milk a baby costs nothing at all and the cost of living has not gone up. Possibly the cost of cheese has not, but I recently bought a 6d. tin tray for 2s. 6d., bed linen is more than four times its pre-war price and yesterday I saw a second-hand wardrobe which in peace-time would have fetched twenty shillings, marked up at *£9 18s*. But of course, in the opinion of such men, the poor don't want bedclothes or wardrobes or tin trays, but only the roughest of food with nothing to cook it in.

A rather unusual case today of a man who had been ill about nine months and now said he was in debt and wanted money for himself, wife and child to live on. The committee knew him as a respectable, careful plate-layer on the railway and concluded he should have saved enough from his wages, being a thrifty person, to carry him over an illness. So they gave him about one-seventh of what he would have received had the committee not known him....

I *did* look at the newspaper today but I'm sure I don't know what was in it. Because I don't know of a better, I let the man leave me a *News Chronicle* – its chief fault is that it contradicts itself so much. I wonder why it boosts Beaverbrook so much? I had an idea (maybe a mistaken one) that he was pally with such people as William Harrison (Inveresk man) and Beverly Baxter and that they were in opposition to Lloyd George, and yet this paper seems to be a Liberal one and I hear is largely owned by Cadbury's. Sounds an awful mixture! The paper, however, whoever directs the ingredients, loves Beaverbrook. I myself know nothing about Beaverbrook, whether he comes from our aristocracy or out of the gutter, or what his politics (if any) are – I fancy he had something to do with Fleet Street, but what, I have no idea.[10]

---

[10] William Harrison was chairman of Inveresk Paper Company and had a controlling interest in a number of publications; Winifred had once worked for him. Beverly Baxter had been editor-in-chief of Inveresk Publications in 1929 and editor of the

I am sending the Mass-Observation papers to Los Angeles – that attorney may find them interesting as an account of a wartime organisation.

Saturday, 7 November

Can write as I drink cocoa made with powdered skim milk – milkman probably forgot to call again. If I clean these rooms (it is only light enough at weekends), dress and go out to tea, also call on other friends, collect laundry and get groceries and meat, do some washing, cook, wash-up and bath myself, I'll require lots more energy than I've got, and spend the whole weekend working, which, after a week of intense work, is not too good.

Increasing our working hours will please the county council but, like most of their actions, is somewhat shortsighted. During the whole war most of their staff have done ARP [Air Raid Precautions] work at night and helped in canteens and hospitals, on farms and elsewhere, all most happily, and much of this must perforce drop if they are compelled to remain in their offices more hours a day. It will also have the effect of making the staff more bored and apathetic owing to lack of variation in their activities. The war does not necessarily get won by turning workers into non-thinking slaves.

Amusing! The Archbishops have after all these centuries decreed that women need not wear hats in church.

Monday, 9 November

The newspaper today looks as if we really might have cleared something up in Egypt.

County council meeting today – I counted 30 cars and there were others round the corner. A very long discussion as to our working hours and then they referred it to the Finance Committee with power to act.[11]

I called on my friend the borough health visitor on Saturday.[12] She said

---

Daily Express, 1929–33, which was owned by Lord Beaverbrook. Winifred's vagueness about Beaverbrook, hardly an obscure personality in British public life, testifies to her wobbly knowledge of current affairs. Beverly Baxter was at this time MP for Wood Green.

[11] The Ministry of Labour had suggested that the appropriate number of hours per week for clerical workers was forty-six, and the West Suffolk County Council was considering this suggestion. It rejected any increase from the current total of thirty-nine. At this meeting, Councillor Ollé, Winifred's landlord, and others argued that the total should be raised, for, they said, senior officers were already working forty-six hours and fairness required that the working week should be lengthened for others (*Bury Free Press*, 14 November 1942, p.11). The finance committee seems to have held the total to thirty-nine hours.

[12] Health visitors at this time were usually appointed by the welfare departments of local authorities, and normally had trained in public health or nursing or midwifery, or some

she had given up belonging to NALGO because the College of Nursing did everything necessary for her wellbeing and also because there was talk of NALGO amalgamating with the trade unions. I said I didn't see that the latter made much difference, it was the present tendency and she knew what the borough council was like. She said she did know and her cost-of-living bonus was less than mine, being 3s. a week. Which of course isn't much when you consider that the rent of the house I am in has probably trebled itself owing to the war. (I don't know this but if any person paid more than 7s. 6d. for this house pre-war, he or she was being robbed.) But, she continued, when the borough was underpaying her, the College of Nursing got it altered, and though it perhaps did not matter to clerks, it was lowering to professional women like nurses to belong to a trade union. I laughed, for being both clerk and trained nurse myself, I can cope with the snobbery of the average nurse towards what she considers the 'lay people', and from a long experience of nurses and clerks I consider the latter far superior people, speaking generally. I did not, however, know anything actually about the College of Nursing, so questioned her and found she was a founder member, and that it really was, as its name implied, a college. I had wondered recently why we had to apply to it for permission for one of our hospitals to become a training school for nurses. I had often heard the place mentioned by our sister-tutor when I was training and rather imagined it had something to do with our nursing examinations, but I just concluded it was a bunch of silly old matrons who were no good to anybody. I remember once when I was training there was talk of some trade union for nurses (it was a London County Council place) and then immediately the LCC said 'Don't join that, join ours', and as there didn't seem to be much point in joining what our employers *desired* us to join, I think there was no response at all – I never heard of any. Probationers are pretty ignorant of everything, including trade unions.

In talking to the public assistance officer this afternoon Gooch said he didn't see why the county council here should always do what the brewery did instead of taking a lead. (It works the other way too, for what the brewery does not do we don't either.) The mayor is the brewer and with my landlord

---

combination of these. 'It was the function of the health visitor to see each child as soon as practicable after it had left hospital or when the doctor or midwife had stopped calling, and to revisit at regular intervals … The number of cases each visitor had to deal with varied from authority to authority but it was not uncommon for a visitor to supervise more than 1,000 infants, perhaps scattered over a wide area; she would have to make visits from door to door in all weathers and this in addition to her other duties. The competent health visitor needed to be a trained observer, a teacher of mother-craft, an adviser on health matters for mother and child, and a social worker. She was able to detect complaints that needed skilled attention from family doctor or local hospital but perhaps her most important duty was to advise on hygiene, feeding and minor ailments' (Sheila Ferguson and Hilde Fitzgerald, *Studies in the Social Services* (London, 1954), pp.145–6). The senior health visitor in Bury was Miss C.A. Osborne.

(late mayor and ice cream manufacturer) is on the county council as well as borough council.[13]

Tonight I called in a tiny general shop for some paraffin and a very pleasant little man served me. Something was said about sunshine and I said we didn't get any in the Shire Hall, not my part of it anyhow. This led to other topics and he told me that Bury St Edmunds could have become an industrial town but the brewer and his clique (the place was run on cliques) prevented it, except for one particular factory on the outskirts. I said I could not imagine how the people of the place would exist at all without that factory, and he said it was previously just agriculture. I said I knew nothing about the mayor [E.L.D. Lake] but heard he was very pompous and he said this one's father had been mayor in the last war in the hope of a title he didn't get and that was what this one was after, and probably he wouldn't get it either. I said that not being used to mayors I was greatly amused when my landlord spoke from a platform about the mayor in such a way that it made royalty appear comparatively unimportant, and he said that was the sort of way he would talk and the brewer was commonly known as the Uncrowned King of Bury St Edmunds.

The general shop man said he knew a few places in this town on which he would *like* Hitler to drop a few bombs, for nothing else would wake up some of the people here. I said that the common people of the place seemed very apathetic and afraid of the others, and he agreed. (On the other hand, a friend of mine from Bournville said she found the *very* poor here had a sturdy independence she could not find in Birmingham; though of course the people I meet and now call the common people are about on my own level.) I was not surprised at this man's remark about cliques, because remarks by other people have suggested it strongly. I must say that I believe the clerk of the county council stands outside the cliques and does no underhand business. I do know, however, that some people here seem to be able to do exactly as they like. I was also surprised to hear that the town used to supply electricity but sold out to a private firm, and the late mayor (I don't know when the sale

13 Major Edward Lancelot Dewé Lake (1880–1946), managing director of Greene King brewery since 1919, was a Conservative councillor from 1937 and the mayor of Bury throughout the Second World War. He was one of six brothers who had fought in the First World War. The brewery, on Westgate Street, was one of the largest businesses in East Anglia, and had over 500 tied houses in 1942–43. Today there are over 1,400. Greene King flourished during the war, thanks in part to a robust demand for its products from soldiers, airmen (many of them American), and workers at aerodromes. Details are provided in R.G. Wilson, *Greene King: A Business and Family History* (London, 1983).

Robert Ollé (1890–1975), owner of the Bury St Edmunds Pure Ice Co. Ltd, 6 St Andrew's South Street (near where Winifred lived), had been mayor of Bury in 1936–37. He lived at 60 Fornham Road. (Winifred always omitted the accent from the spelling of his surname, which the editors have here and in other places restored.)

was made) told me, when I said I could not get a meter from the Electric Company, that they would let him have one for me as he was well-known to them. For all I know, it may be customary for borough councils to sell their electricity undertakings, but at least it seems to me to be a step backwards, not forwards. I have heard from many quarters that my landlord when in office made an extremely good mayor. The borough office people I understand are paid worse than the county council ones but they have quite a nice modern town hall. They have built council house places without bathrooms but there is one very good Central School, whoever built that.[14] The roads are bad, the paths are dirty, houses unpainted and falling to bits through long years of non-repair; the billeting officer the most unpopular man in the town. The borough education officer is arranging for the Adelphi Players to return for a couple of days, so I am much obliged to him. I believe that is everything I know about the borough of Bury St Edmunds. My landlord is pally with my boss.

I ought to be chopping prunes and wood nuts for a cake to send to the Isle of Man. The forced reduction in prices got me some excellent pastry today for 1s. 2d.

Tomorrow we do a bit of rest centre work[15] and also attend the Newmarket guardians meeting, going by motor-car. My boss's petrol hangs out pretty well.

The emergency hospital office staff all want more money and how we are going to keep them and still keep their money anywhere near as low as the Shire Hall staff is a problem. As it is, we usually give them free meals because that does not *look* like a rise.

Our office-boy will soon be in the Forces – we shall miss him very much. I thought a boy of 14 might help if engaged but am told that to lick stamps in the Shire Hall a boy must have the school certificate. It is unlikely that there will be a replacement and Gooch (a chartered secretary and holder of the relieving officer's certificate or whatever it is called, earning £5 a week) has already worked out what part of the office boy's job *he* will do.

Coupons for Nurses' Clothing. Gooch is going all over the county showing the various masters and matrons how to fill up forms for extra coupons for nurses' clothing. He usually gets the jobs in the department which nobody

---

14 No school in Bury was formally designated the Central School, a name given to certain higher elementary schools which were to an extent 'selective', though they were not secondary or grammar schools under the aegis of the county council. Winifred probably meant the Silver Jubilee School in Grove Road, opened in 1936, the only senior elementary school in the borough, intended for pupils aged eleven to fourteen.

15 In May–June 1941 almost 200 rest centres 'for the relief of distress in time of war', particularly for people made homeless, had been identified in West Suffolk. These premises included schools; chapels; reading rooms; and village, town, church, and 'Victory' halls. There were fourteen rest centres in Bury St Edmunds (Suffolk Record Office, Bury St Edmunds Branch, EF505/1/69/36).

else is capable of doing, and hospital people are no good in filling up forms – some of them can't even keep a record of unemployment cards. The clerk and steward and almoner at Newmarket is an exception, being extremely capable, but unfortunately some of the clerical work there has to be done by the medical and nursing side of the place, who probably look down on figures and don't know how to deal with their intricacies, anyhow. I don't see why they want extra coupons, for when they are wearing out uniform they are not wearing out mufti. Perhaps they do need some for overalls (dresses and aprons are most unhygienic) which should never be worn off the wards, but surely the coupon business could have been made simpler? As it is, there is one rule for one section of nurses, and other rules for other sections. Reminds me of when I told our matron we wasted so much time because there was no uniformity in the hospital and although we were taught in the school-room the *correct* way of making a poultice, when we got on the 18 wards the 18 sisters wanted poultices made in *their* way, irrespective of right or wrong way, and all their wards were different. She said that of course all the sisters thought their own way was best. Nursing always is like that, with no organi- sation about it. Perhaps all the sections want their own methods, too.

Lord Woolton [Minister of Food] has earned my profound thanks by allowing most groceries to be collected monthly – I now need only to fetch bacon (if wanted) and matches weekly, which unfortunately are sold at two different counters. I'll have to ask for time off on Wednesday to fetch my laundry – the place is always shut when I am free, and shops shut so early Saturdays that I had no time to get there on my afternoon off. When I had to fetch butter, sugar, etc. each week, shopping was really terrible, and some- times I had to stand an hour at the grocer's to get served. It really is much better now. I can dispose of my monthly points in one go and also collect the month's soap ration in one lot, too, and as there are no shell eggs I need not call at all for them. Collecting my weekly joint is rather a nuisance but cannot be helped as I *must* cook my own meals weekends, unfortunately.

I told the old man at the Institution who cleans the board-room, lights fires, etc. etc., that if he could find my lost fountain-pen I'd give him 2s. 6d. and I wondered why he was then so anxious to find it – I quite think it was picked up in the Shire Hall, but there was a bare chance I left it in the board-room. I heard today that his earnings are 2s. 6d. a week, so now I understand the keenness.

Wednesday, 11 November

In the middle of the morning someone mentioned it was Armistice Day. Later Blossom came round selling poppies, and that was all.

The public generally seem more hopeful now about the war, some wondering if the news can be true and others what will be the next step. Somebody said tonight she wondered if Wendell Willkie were a Fifth Columnist. To cover my ignorance of Wendell Willkie [Republican US presidential candidate in 1940], I said it was difficult to know who was and who was not.

Suppose it was because of my youth in last war, but that one seemed so comparatively simple. Then if you were English you fought on one side and if German on the other, and you knew where you were. But now it seems to be mixed up with a revolution and it is mighty difficult to know friend from foe, whatever the nationality, or social position.

I am making a cake with a packet of 'sweetened almond-flavoured cake flour', which I think was considerably dearer than flour. When mixed it tasted very flat so I added a fair amount of sugar to wake it up. It is only for my own consumption so I put in dripping from mutton and one duck's egg. (There was one duck's egg only on the ration this week, after several weeks without, but I still have a tin of dried egg in stock. I like ducks' eggs but never feel that ration eggs are fresh enough to be boiled.).

Billeting. I heard two people say today that when they got out of favour with billeting people, they were paid out by having persons billeted upon them, which brought to mind a tale, not necessarily a true one, I heard yesterday. A wife of a certain country clergyman takes it as her duty to condole with persons who have lost relations in the war. A woman in the place let rooms to a certain lord who had lost someone in this way (though he only stayed there at intervals). Hearing of his arrival, the clergyman's wife went early one morning to condole and had an altercation with the landlady, whose orders were not to call his lordship (who is reputed to be more often drunk than sober) until 11 a.m. The landlady won the battle and the other was unable to condole, but soon after that arranged for the landlady to have evacuees billeted upon her, to leave no room for the lord. The landlady, however, boarded out the evacuees whenever his lordship was due and eventually managed to get them settled elsewhere permanently.

Music. The present downstairs tenant in this place is the only person I've lived near in this town who listens to classical music on her wireless. It may be because she is about 40 years old – it seems to be the younger folk who enjoy that noisy jazz, swing, etc. Music which probably does stir their blood and makes me have visions of naked, writhing bodies of niggers and savages, which I personally don't like.

V.D. Paper today says 'Medical officers of health given powers to compel treatment of V.D.' and adds that Dominions, USA, Russia and several other countries have laws for compulsory treatment. I wonder why it is we always follow other countries in such matters. Do we *ever* lead? Or is it that when we lead we hear nothing about it? These diseases are certainly horrible enough to stir people to action. A curious fact is, however, that very often it is not the cause of the disease, but the disease itself which is abhorred. Hundreds of girls in this town indulge in sexual intercourse before marriage and probably with more than one man, but that is more or less overlooked. Yet one girl who used to lodge in this house once had syphilis and ever since the town has looked upon her as if she were a leper. These things were supposed to be kept secret but I myself was told about this girl by five different people, and I mix with very few.

Friday, 13 November

Church bells to ring on Sunday to celebrate Egypt. Was dreaming about them last night, muddled with door-bells, air-raid hooters and door-keys. Mrs A. today laughing about the idea and saying it was stupid when this was our first victory but probably it was just to test the bells to see if they *would* ring for an invasion.[16] Noticing that evacuated children are returning from Canada and USA. I am wondering if it is thought that Great Britain is now more secure. Don't know anybody who has really at any time considered invasion probable. Some of us feel the war has now begun; others think it is practically at an end.

Committee. A few weeks ago Mrs B. said that when paying a workman one could not take into consideration whether married or single. Today a lady technician was engaged. Medical superintendent said she had given him her budget and the minimum she could live on was £3 10s. The clerk said they had to consider what the job was worth, not the conditions under which the employee had to live. Then it was found that the more experienced head technician was having £3 10s., so as they had no demand before them for that to be increased, it was agreed that the other one must have £3 only. The clerk's 'what the job is worth' really meant 'what we can get anybody for'. The masseuse may be worth no more than the secretary, but she will get three times as much because she is part of an association which lays down the amount of her salary. The clerk's attitude is, in my opinion, the attitude of the majority of employers. There is no sense of justice.

Kleptomania. It is astounding what a terrific lot of stealing has gone on everywhere since the war started – people even steal pillow-cases from hotel beds, tables, jugs, cutlery, toilet rolls and towels. It is nearly like an epidemic, and if a sign of the times a very bad one. They steal electric light bulbs too; in fact, anything they can lay their hands on. So far, too, I've never known a thief to be cured, which certainly suggests it is a disease, for they will do it when they know it means disaster.

Both the medical superintendent and the clerk and steward of the emergency hospital stick up in their respective ways for their staff, against the county council.

---

[16] On 13 June 1940, when an attempted invasion seemed likely, the ringing of church bells in normal circumstances was banned; henceforth they were to be rung by the army or police to warn of an airborne invasion. In November 1942, when the threat of invasion had receded, they were rung to celebrate the British victory over Rommel's Afrika Korps at El Alamein.

Captain King of Newmarket has been made vice chairman of the county council. He is comparatively young and has a very good reputation in Newmarket. The chairman has been ill for about two years. I asked if he was likely to get better and was told 'Some would say, "I'm afraid not", some would say "I care not", and others would say "I hope not"'. So Captain King looks like having a pretty free hand and we *hope* for improvement in the council.[17] Actually I think the chairman, clerk, accountant and public assistance officer and even county medical officer have got along very well together, and some of the members too like the chairman. The chairman is an accountant by profession, and I should say is useful in keeping down the rates or trying to. That may, of course, recommend him more to the council members than the staff, though the saving may be more apparent than real.

A[lfred] M[cLelland] Burrage the author applied for our medical officer's secretary job but his application was not even submitted to the committee. One girl applied but wanted £260 a year, so the job is still vacant.

The clerk and steward doubts that any comparable hospital in England is run with such a small office staff as the Newmarket Emergency Hospital.[18] I believe that as master of the same place years ago he ran it more economically than any in England, but he is a particularly capable, enthusiastic man with a sound knowledge of very many things, and he probably did it by good management. The cost of running many of these places seems to be entirely out of proportion to what the inmates receive, which is largely discomfort, often cruelty....

Monday, 16 November

A curious weekend. For no reason, except perhaps that on Friday I went to bed after midnight and then lay awake for hours listening to mice as they scratched and bumped into things, I was 'fed up' on Saturday. Shopped all the afternoon which meant leaving housework until Sunday – the only day of the week when I can do it in daylight. Then the tenant downstairs asked if I would only go through her rooms to the water tap and lavatory once a day, at 8.45 a.m., as she liked to be private. Felt very annoyed and said I'd do what I could but could make no definite promise. At her request I have already put my bicycle up at the office. I do not share her kitchen and oven because I don't want to, and I should no longer be able to hang out laundry in the bit of back yard because I know it would offend her vision. I also have nowhere

---

[17] Captain Herbert R. King, JP, lived at Graham House, High Street, Newmarket. On Monday, 9 November 1942 he 'presided at the West Suffolk county council meeting ... in the absence of the chairman, Ald. A. Oliver Usher.... Capt. King was elected as vice-chairman in succession to the late Alderman Lord Loch' (*Bury Free Press*, 14 November 1942, p.6.). At the end of the war King was chairman of the West Suffolk County Council.

[18] The former Newmarket workhouse (from 1929 the Public Assistance Institution) was now an emergency hospital for evacuees and members of the armed forces.

to shake rugs – unless out of the front windows into one of the town's main thoroughfares! And passers-by might object to that, particularly if I used the attic window, in which case the window-frame with its remnants of glass (it is at present tied together with string) would possibly drop into the roadway with the dusts from the rugs.

I don't imagine the tenant herself is so anxious not to see me, and her little boy of eight years will be quite sorry, but the man who visits her some weekends is most anxious that they should not be intruded upon. To talk to she seems quite a wise and unselfish person, but she may have too much sympathy with the male sex. Her husband, she says, a political agent, was a charming man and they were happy, but at his death she was nearly swamped with bills for his drink and gambling. Then she became engaged to a boilermaker and made him presents but found his manners and morals began to grate on her sensibilities so gave him up. She has more or less lived with the present man for a few years. His wife was older than he and they started a laundry business with her small capital and it thrived and thrived. He has a son aged 21, and is at present upset because the son won't write to him. Sometimes the downstairs tenant sends the man home to see if he can put up with his wife, but it never works, and the wife refuses to divorce him. The man has left the money with the wife (he is an officer himself) and the tenant downstairs says she will never allow the man to keep her but only to pay his own share of expenses. She really seems intent on working not only now but after the war. I cannot quite understand her refusal to let him keep her – is it she objects to the term 'kept woman'? I could understand it if he were merely a friend, but as she sleeps with him I see no reason why he should not keep her.

The little boy downstairs is rather charming and friendly. He weeps occasionally, always for the same cause. He has lived with relations and has also been evacuated, and has only just returned to his mother, who considers he has been spoilt. Whether through his upbringing or because of some physical disability, the child wets his bed and also his trousers by day. She slaps him each time at present but he seems to forget his tears quickly. If a disability, it is a terrible one. One of our Poor Law youths had the same trouble and that, coupled perhaps with mental dullness, made him incapable of holding down a job, and in consequence he is now put away in an institution for the mentally deficient. The child downstairs is intelligent.

Sunday morning I was still 'fed up' so stayed in bed thinking perhaps I ought to put up with a cat to clear the mice up and that I'd better do the housework and make an afternoon call at the next door house to ask if they would take me as a boarder and make room for my furniture. Still in bed at 11 a.m. when the bells were rung for the Egyptian victory. I had expected a wedding peal but the only ones which sounded in my bedroom were like a toll. Wrote to my internee and told him I was 'fed up' and had sent him a cake, flour and suet, and told him how to use the two latter. I felt rather as though a storm of some sort were brewing – a kind of tension. Perhaps it *was* the weather, for certain other people had seemed upset on Saturday morning. The master and matron of the Bury St Edmunds Public Assistance Institution (soon, I think, to be renamed 'St Edmund's Hospital') were so generally 'fed up' that they were both threatening to resign and the public assistance officer said 'I just left them and let them get on with it'.[19]

When I looked at my tidy and (except for the dirty ceiling and wallpaper) very charming sitting-room, I felt better, and when I came into the back room and caught sight of my internee's photograph and portrait and the landscape by Dr Leonard Adam, I felt that life might eventually be worth living, after all.[20]

(It may surprise you, but this 'diary' is the sort of stuff I have ever since June 1940 been sending to internment camps – I'm quite *sure* some of the censors have cursed me.)

I decided to call on the neighbour after tea, so got the housework done in comfort and after tea went out. Moonlight. Walked up and down looking at people's houses and endeavouring to pluck up courage and knock on her door. Then standing opposite realised that her house was only two-thirds as big as this one (hardly two houses are alike in this town) so she couldn't possibly squeeze my furniture in. Decided I'd come in and get the internee's letter ready for post and post it on my way to St Elizabeth's Moral Welfare Home – the only place I could walk into without waiting for the door to be answered. Left a lamp alight so that I shouldn't tumble into things in the dark on my return and went – to find that after black-out they now lock their door!! The household consisted of a black lurcher, a sandy small cat, a tiny superintendent and her matron who was a missionary in India and looks almost Indian herself, and three young, robust, pregnant girls. The girls and I knitted and we sat round the fire and talked and at 8 p.m. had soup, and the wireless was on most of the time.[21] After the *News* Herbert Morrison [the Home Secretary] spoke. I'd never heard him before and thought his a queer accent, perhaps a bit Scottish. Personally I prefer very much the BBC announcer type of voice to the voices of *most* politicians, or well-known men. I'm not so keen on accents and like culture, when it is real and not merely society affectation, which after all is only another form of accent. I

---

[19] The former workhouse in Hospital Road, Bury, was renamed the Public Assistance Institution as a consequence of the Act of Parliament of 1929.

[20] No trace has been found of Leonard Adam, including in Suffolk sources. He may, then, have been an amateur artist. Sarah King of the Victoria & Albert Museum provided helpful research assistance on this matter.

[21] St Elizabeth's Moral Welfare Home, 11 Lower Baxter Street, accommodated unmarried mothers and their babies, and young women 'at risk'. It was run by the Anglican Diocesan Moral Welfare Association, and had a close association with the Poor Law authorities and their successors, the public assistance committees. Its superintendent was Miss D.E. Westell. Winifred often went there to have a bath.

also wondered why people who could afford good dentists couldn't procure false teeth which would permit them to sound the letter 'S' without whistling.

Now I am definitely prejudiced against Morrison for his 18B and for the fact that after all this time his department has my internee still interned, so the following remarks must be taken bearing the prejudice in mind.[22] I think that he must be an awful turncoat and merely engaged on making his own way, when I hear him urging others to fight and patting them on the back for doing so (the letter you [Mass-Observation] were good enough to send me and which I got today says I need not be afraid I am 'informing' etc., but of course Morrison has the power to seize this letter I now write as it goes through the post and to imprison me without trial, so it really *is* very dangerous to write and talk these days) and realise that when he himself was of an age to fight he was a conscientious objector. I do not see how any conscientious objector in the last war could possibly be keen on war in this one, except for his own benefit. I also get annoyed when I read of Morrison at this or that social function, because I think he ought to be at work supervising the clearing up of the internment camps muddle. I laughed when I read (though the newspaper report was probably an exaggeration) that when he went to a garden party at the governor's house in Douglas he was accompanied by a strong police contingent – or whatever they are called. I went to Douglas alone and walked past most of the camps before I got to my internee's 'P' Camp, I sat with internees, drank tea and ate biscuits made by internees, and never felt a qualm of fear, and there was Morrison, on an island packed with Forces, [who] had to take his own police escort. Perhaps it was to give the police a free trip.

I am much more of a rebel than the St Elizabeth's people are, though we are friends. I think that they are more like the German populace in that they would believe unquestioningly in whatever government we might happen to have. I find that women are much more like that than men are. Still, I suppose the nation swallows the Christian religion or the Church of England whole, whereas I can only digest the odd morsel here and there.

The camp commander has sent me a receipt for £10 which I sent in part payment for my internee's Dutch picture (he wanted it sent to Sotheby's for sale so I preferred to buy it myself). I got the receipt this morning and the address is changed from 'P' Camp to 'Hutchinson's Camp'. I'd only just got over the fear that they might have handcuffed internees in 'P' Camp and now comes the new fear that he may have been moved from 'P' Camp which, so

---

[22] Regulation 18B (which preceded Morrison's appointment as Home Secretary) provided the legal basis for executive detention; it permitted the government to imprison anyone who was thought to be a threat to national security without charge or trial and for an indefinite period of time. The history of 18B is examined in A.W. Brian Simpson, *In the Highest Degree Odious: Detention without Trial in Wartime Britain* (Oxford, 1992).

far as buildings and space and privacy are concerned, is the only decent camp in Douglas. If 'P' stands for 'Pioneer (Corps)' they may have moved him since he can never now join the Pioneers,[23] but I hope he is still there because in the others the men are just like animals on view in London Zoo cages. It is impossible too to give him any moral support through letters, owing to the fact that the spies resident in the Camp act as censors.

I have written elsewhere (not to you) of my disillusionment when I found that three of our British spies were apparently of a very low and common Jewish type. One of them looked as if in his blood there might be strains of Negro, German, Spanish, and Italian ancestry, so I concluded he was an enigma, probably Jewish. Not at all a nice type, and when he flashed his glance on me I loathed and feared him. He had the audacity, too, to look at me as if I, not he, were the despicable worm. In two days he would have had me flinging things into his ugly mug or weeping in hysteria and fear. I watched my internee watching him. The internee, I could see, did not like him and watched his actions intently, but he was not afraid of him, as I was. The internee does not hate as I hate, which perhaps is as well.

Nevertheless, despite the possibility of a change of camp, I have felt more light-hearted today than during the weekend....

I am compelled to make cakes for my internee because it is not allowed to send any rationed goods. Sugar, fruit, jam, chocolate, milk and eggs are *all* rationed, so I have to put them into a cake – cakes are *not* rationed. Very little in these days is labour-saving.

Remark from a woman in a little shop regarding the war: 'Well, the government got us into this mess; the government must get us out of it, that's all *I've* got to say.'

Girl at Shire Hall: 'Suppose I'm made that way, but to my mind it's as bad to think that Germans are being slain as to think that British are.' She has spent holidays in Germany.

At St Elizabeth's: 'I'd like to kill Germans myself.' Same person: 'Well, that Lutheran parson who preached tonight may be a German, but he can't help where he was born; any of you could have been born in Germany, it was only luck that you were born here'.

A lot of newspaper jabber about Montgomery treating his captured German general with courtesy. But it usually is the soldiers who treat the enemy with the most sympathy. Most of the soldiers in 'P' Camp were very nice to internees. One on my internee's first visit to Douglas lent him 3s. 6d. to buy food, whereas the policeman who took him prisoner asked if he could have some coins and to gain time for packing the internee let him help himself to

---

23 The Pioneer Corps was employed mainly on construction jobs and other forms of manual labour requiring little skill. Many were middle-aged men, some of them veterans of the First World War. One way for an internee to be released was to join the Pioneer Corps, and around 4,000 had done so by the end of 1940.

what he wanted, regardless of value. Policemen vary, of course, and another when collecting an internee warned him not to take articles of value, which was as well because they were robbed of everything on the hell ship *Dunera*. It was a voyage lasting over two months, packed below like sardines, with the person in charge of the boat calling them 'rats' and with no change of clothes all the time or the use of a toothbrush.[24] My internee enjoyed the trip back, being free on the boat and getting friendly with Australian seamen, and rather expected to be released on arrival, but was taken back to Douglas and has been a prisoner there since last February again. There is no reason why, except government department slowness. They had suddenly got him switched from Class C to Class A, but that was either to protect themselves when they sent him to Australia, or through some confusion which they have never yet tried to unravel.[25]

The first post my internee received in Australia was 29 letters. These had been written when he was in Douglas and on board ship – and they were *all* from me. I bet he looked through and through them in the hope that *somebody* else had written him!! Still, being interned, he was doubtless glad to get even 29.

Tuesday, 17 November

Another remark by the St Elizabeth's Home lady was 'that we shouldn't get out of this war as easily as the present time might suggest to some of us; that we had not yet felt the war; it was the people on the Continent who were doing that; and apart from the few people who had been bombed, to us war meant glory and excitement and a "good time"; and unless we come to see and feel the other side of war there will be yet another war at the end of the next twenty years.' We all talk with apparent inconsistency, and in another mood she would be quite capable of saying that Germans are solely responsible for this war!

A friend of mine recently expressed her appreciation of our (apparent) intention to invade the Continent, she being of opinion that we had sat still long enough while Russia bled and Europe starved, and she asked if I didn't feel a louse to belong to a country which always got jam on its bread and butter. Can't say I do. For one thing, I think this climate necessitates jam and

---

[24] Over 2,500 internees, some of them unrepentant Nazis and others fiercely anti-Nazi refugees, sailed for Australia on the *Dunera* in July 1940. Life on the ship was even harder than Winifred suggests. By the end of 1943, the internees in Australia were either released or had returned to Britain, some of them, like Hans Martin Luther, facing continued internment. A guide to the entire episode is Peter and Leni Gillman, '*Collar the Lot!*', chapter 22.

[25] Enemy aliens were placed in three classes, A, B, or C: As were considered the most dangerous and interned, Cs the least dangerous (or not dangerous at all) and usually at liberty by 1942. It is not clear why Martin Luther's classification was changed.

butter. Secondly, I don't see that our starvation would necessarily fatten other nations. Thirdly, Russia can afford to lose more men than we can and she is fighting for herself and not necessarily for us. Fourthly, though I am sorry for Continental people at this juncture, they have, on the whole, asked for what they have got: France and Belgium could have fought with us if they had wanted to. This war showed us that we had extremely few friends; and it was perhaps good for us to realise that we must stand alone. America has joined us now but she did not do so to preserve our ideals and democracy (whatever democracy signifies) but merely to destroy the power of Japan which threatened to injure her economically. So here we all are. I don't know why we are fighting, except to save the Jews from barbarous treatment. Last time it was to save Belgium, or we thought so.

I wondered last night what effect this war will have on the mentality of children now growing up. My nephew aged 16 is now pleased to belong to some officers' cadet corps (I think that's the name).[26] To him Germany must be the enemy to be destroyed and the vital object in the life of a male Briton must be to fight Germans. If the war lasts much longer he will be fighting and that may make him think, but if he does *not* experience the combat and see the horrors, isn't he going to bring up his own children mainly as fighting animals, fighting from a sense of unreasoning patriotism?

We English are queer people, and sometimes I think we do not talk enough. I have seen no real reason given anywhere for our treatment of India and it *looks* as if all the right is on the Indian side, not ours. Yet I remember Ireland. She flooded our country with her literature showing how very badly we had treated her, and as a child I got very sympathetic. But when I got working in London with Irish (Southern) nurses I learned that it was they, not us, who were 'top dogs'. We gave them their 'Home Rule' and ever since, instead of gratitude, they have given us stabs in the back or bombs under our feet. So far as my personal experience goes, they do not understand quietness and courtesy and merely despise us because we do not rule them with whips. But we never trouble to explain this sort of thing in writing; and wouldn't understand it if we did....

Wednesday, 18 November

Curious how each day brings up oddments to write about. Today has been uneventful and packed with work, nevertheless topics have arisen.

Black Market. Somebody today offered to get me certain articles of clothing without coupons, which suggests [the] Black Market is still in operation here. I thanked her for the offer but as I do not like fattening human rats and am not especially interested in obtaining more than my share of clothing, the offer holds no temptation.

---

[26] She is probably referring to the OCTU – the Officer Cadet Training Unit.

Rates of Wages in Suffolk on 13 November 1942.

Carpenter & Bricklayers:	Bury St E.	1s. 8½d./hour	Labourers:	1s. 4½d./hour
	Newmarket	1s. 9d./hour		1s. 4¾d./hour
	Sudbury	1s. 7d./hour		1s. 3¼d./hour

Stokers are normally paid labourers' rates with addition of ¾d. per hour for government work. I can see no reason for differences.

Typist. One of the two typists who works for me (we have three typists in our public assistance department) gave a month's notice today. Her RAF husband has been moved and has found her a job near him with some government contractors....

Spain. At the time I saw no reason why we should take part in the Spanish revolution, but sometimes now I half wish we had and that we had destroyed Franco. Newspaper today says Spanish Republicans who had been living in Vichy France now handed over to Spanish authorities; also that Spain is mobilising its forces, and the Spanish Cabinet had decreed that no foreign power would be permitted to enter Spanish territory. These news came mainly from German reports, but below them we say 'Assurances have already been given to Spain and Portugal by the Allies'. If the last bit is right, are we daft or crooked? Or am *I* daft? I can understand we might say we would not, to gain our own ends, invade them, but why make such a promise knowing that Franco is hand and glove with Hitler and Mussolini and that Spain is needing liberation from Franco perhaps more urgently than France needs it from Hitler? There will probably be more in the papers about this.

France. I don't know anything about Darlan or Mr E. Granville [M.P.] (Ind. Eye) but I like the latter's speech: that whatever might be going on behind the scenes, Darlan must go. We were playing for high stakes in North Africa but we had to play with clean hands. The prize was the French fleet and the cooperation of the French armed forces. We had landed not the prize, but Darlan. He hoped this would not set back the clock of revolt in France and Italy. The American and British press had flown the Darlan kite and it had come to earth labelled 'Quisling'. He wanted to know what had happened to the De Gaulle prisoners captured in North Africa, and to the Spanish Republican prisoners kept there. He hoped they would be released immediately.[27]

---

[27] Admiral François Darlan, foreign minister and vice-premier of the Vichy government, had a few days before defected to the Allies and been appointed by them as high commissioner for French North Africa. Many people found this *volte face* and sudden alliance with a previous enemy hard to understand. Edgar Louis Granville, MP for the Eye division of Suffolk, who sat as an Independent between February 1942 and April 1945 (before and after these dates he sat as a Liberal), argued on 17 November that 'we have to ask ourselves whether we can discriminate between military necessity and the cause for which we are fighting.... We are playing for very high stakes, but we have to do so with clean hands. The prize was the French Fleet and also the capitulation

Government. Once I thought this was Parliament, but in these days they appear to be separate things.

Colours. I had thought 'fashions' were a thing of the past, but colour names still alter. Newspaper today says we can have stockings in carib, Newmarket, vogue, pagan, praline, Mayfair, and to me these colour names convey exactly no meaning. Would 'pagan' be flesh-coloured or nigger-brown, I wonder. What is the difference in colour between Newmarket and Mayfair? What colour is the vogue? Pralines are sweets but I've no recollection of their hue, and carib – what is carib? Might it be a horse, or a sea?

Public Assistance Institution. Elderly man from institution came in today. At dinner another inmate had cheeked him and so he gave him a kick on the shin, seeing which the labour master had given the kicker a slap on the face. Man wanted to know if the labour master had any right to hit him. Gooch promised to see that he would receive no more corporal punishment.

Douglas. Am not expecting to visit Douglas but the Home Office are long-winded in supplying the permit I asked for weeks ago. It appears to be their policy. As a rule they will authorise visits but everything is made so very awkward that there can be extremely few visitors. I went in May, but had to risk getting accommodation in Fleetwood and Douglas and getting on the boat. No visits were allowed weekends, and not until I was talking to my internee did I know whether or not the authorities at the camp would allow me to see him. I both fear and hate the Home Office. To me Hitler appears like some distant unknown quantity which might perchance (though I hope not – fervently) materialise in a bomb on my furniture or (preserve me!) myself, but the Home Office is a much nearer huge wheel which could crush me as if I were an ant or a gun which could shoot me in the back. My internee fears Hitler very much more than he does the Home Office, but unlike him I do not know Hitler's regime and to me Hitler is almost a myth but the Home Office is a reality which can at any moment seize and destroy me. If a policeman called at my house in these days I think my heart would stop for fright!! I laugh as I write it, but it isn't quite a laughing matter, really. It seems to be a deadly reality. The Home Office has taken my internee even if it has not yet entirely destroyed him, and that may be the root of my fear for both of us. They warp my whole life, and annoy me no end, and sometimes my own helplessness against them brings me to the border of hysteria, and asking God to grind his mills quicker, and destroy the wicked in the Home Office, destroy them utterly....

---

of the French Armed Forces and the Government in North Africa. We landed, not the prize, but Darlan' (*Parliamentary Debates, House of Commons*, 5th series, vol. 385, col. 271). 'Quisling' was a synonym for traitor or collaborator with the enemy, after Vidkun Quisling, the pro-Nazi ruler of Norway during the war.

Thursday, 19 November

… Laval has been made Dictator of France.[28] Newspaper still a bit queer regarding Darlan. Talk of execution of Daladier among others – I imagined he was the so-called 'Strong Man' who destroyed France's 40-hour week and later turned Quisling, but apparently not if the Axis or Laval intends to execute him.[29] The life of a politician on the losing side isn't so pleasant. Horrible lot, to execute anybody. May all executioners be executed! This does not apply to me for I never go further than to ask *God* to destroy the wicked – I wouldn't do the dirty work myself! I would always prefer to wait for God, though he is slow. Possibly he finds the universe very complicated. …

Friday, 20 November

One of my typists recently gave a month's notice and the office-boy is being 'called up'. Yesterday Ruth, the other typist, had to go home and looks like being there weeks. Doctor suspects scarlet fever but I don't know. She comes daily from Stowmarket, is 21 and doesn't look after herself, and she does Control duties some nights,[30] has decidedly scrap meals, and says she hasn't menstruated since she gave blood for blood transfusions several months ago. She has had a very heavy cold and cough and was vomiting yesterday. Anyhow a rest won't do her any harm. If Gooch got called up now I think our public assistance department would close down! Fortunately he has flat feet! He is quick and can turn out as much work as three ordinary men such as my boss or the clerk. Sometimes I think he tackles too much, with the result that some things are forgotten or can't get done, but he certainly thinks and makes decisions quickly and dictates easily, in unusually good English. He was very blunt today, told the public assistance officer (just to rub it in) that Ruth didn't earn enough to go into lodgings in this town and, as she didn't like the British Restaurant, couldn't afford to buy a decent meal midday. He also, over the phone, told the Ministry of Health that the clerk and steward at Newmarket couldn't send in their returns because, owing to the short-sightedness of the county council, he was never allowed enough staff to cope with the work and some things were always in arrears.…

---

[28] Pierre Laval was perhaps the most prominent Vichy politician who espoused a policy of collaboration with the Germans. He had just been given the power to issue decrees and laws.

[29] Edouard Daladier, a socialist, had been prime minister of France on three occasions in the 1930s. He was arrested by the Vichy regime in August 1940, prosecuted for 'causing the defeat of France' (the trial had to be called off), and held in prison until the end of the war.

[30] Winifred is probably referring to the duties associated with Air Raid Precautions.

Sunday, 22 November

One feels more energetic after porridge, even if the milk is short. Milk in winter is one of my problems. It is true I have dried skimmed milk which makes cocoa all right, and lately all my 'points' have gone on condensed milk (unfortunately almost always unsweetened), but compared with liquid milk these things are awkward and troublesome, and in fact the condensed milk just goes up to the attic and remains there, along with the dried egg which I do use for cakes. The latter smells rather horrid but seems OK in the cakes.

All the week I look forward to Sunday, and when it comes it exasperates me. I stay in bed late and think and look at the dust on things (I'm doing it now). I feel I need a bath and haven't even water enough for a decent wash. If I change my underclothes those I take off will want washing. Hair and hairbrushes want washing. Water wants emptying and fetching and as I can do neither without going through other tenant's rooms I object to doing either, and think there is some virtue in the village pump to which all would have unrestricted access. Had I put my name down for a council flat two years ago I might perhaps have got one by now, but they were inconveniently situated for my job and I think pokey and had no bathrooms, so they did not appear to be worth having. This town is simply packed with people, natives and outsiders. The three cinemas do a roaring trade. There is a public lavatory in this town and I begin to feel that I shall have to get up to go and visit it. It might be as well. Once being up, I'd probably come back and clean up and cook some dinner. I have managed to get enough paraffin so have not yet this winter lit a fire – less from patriotism than from aversion to fetching coal from the cellar, laying the fires and clearing up the extra dirt they make. Besides, with these huge chimneys it is nearly as warm to keep the broken trap closed as to have a fire and open it and let the rain and gusts of cold air blow down.

Mrs Webb, committee member, told me Thursday her only rest was to come to meetings; that she had a huge house and could get no maid and the work seemed to get on top of her. I said I had two rooms and was in a similar plight. The trouble is that after a week at the office, I just don't want to do any work at all. Mrs Webb *looked* as if it was getting on top of her. She has a husband but no family I understand. I ought to cook some dinner today, because there are 6d. worth of Brussels sprouts lying on the floor simply dying to be cooked! One has duties these days even to Brussels sprouts. And I get very few green vegetables at the British Restaurant here during the week. I am not very fond of London in peacetime, but it had this virtue, that one could always get at a reasonable price an adequate meal without effort and at any time. That is not so here and now.

Weather cold and invigorating so I went for a walk, inspecting windows to see if any rooms looked unoccupied. None, except St Michael's College for Girls, which looked derelict, with attic windows broken (not by bombs).[31] There were two lights burning inside, however, so presumably *somebody* was there. Despite the invigorating air, wanted to weep for no particular reason. A few Observer Corps men riding cycles and little groups of Home Guard standing about, two or three civilians at borough offices and a girl typing in evacuation offices, and that was about all the life there was. Got home. Kettle in hearth overflowed and downstairs tenant wanted to know where water was coming from as there was damp patch on her newly whitewashed ceiling. Told me Mrs Jarrold had told her to stay indoors between 11 and 3 as there was an invasion exercise or something on and civilians outside would be taken prisoners until 3 p.m. Anyhow, nobody spoke to me. It is now 2.30 and outside a lot of little guns seem to be popping and exploding and making the dogs bark. After a skimpy breakfast 3 p.m. would not have suited me too well. Came home, reheated beef and tomatoes and cooked sprouts – no potatoes because I couldn't be bothered to carry them from the shop last week. No pudding because no spare liquid milk and the suet which the shop allowed me for the next three months I sent to the internment camp, under the impression that I could buy food (at a price) whereas the internee cannot. Now I hear he has no facilities for cooking, so I'm sorry about the suet. I'll have to continue to cook and live on cakes, plus less interesting savouries, plus the British Restaurant midday meals. Breakfast now [that] milk is cut down will be a nuisance as I'll either have to shop and get bacon and sausages and get up energetically and cook them, or I'll be ill. So far I've had less time off for illness (one day) than anybody in the department, but that, my experience suggests, is because I live alone and so catch fewer colds than I otherwise would. Bangs outside sound like a magnified Guy Fawkes Day.

I'd like something to break the monotony of life, if it were only a few squibs. I saw a notice this morning of university extension lectures 'next Monday, 19th October, 42', at [the] Angel Hotel. Did not know there had been any and it looks as if I ought to take the local newspaper, as I miss these lectures each year. There are only five lectures a session I think. That was a tiny notice in the window of a private house. There is a huge poster at the Corn Exchange (I'm getting tired of those deeper guns which make one want to vomit and also of the lighter pops) saying that the Marchioness (hope it's spelt right) of Cadogan is opening a free course of instruction in hay-box cookery, cooking on the hot-plate, and a few other items.[32] Should think any fool could use a hay-box if she had the mental energy to plan meals and had

---

[31] St Michael's Church of England College for Girls was at 18 Northgate Street in 1939 and closed soon thereafter.

[32] In the autumn of 1942 Cambridge University Extramural Department offered weekly lectures in the Angel Hotel on such topics as India, with discussion of its social structure and the prospects for independence, and Anglo-American relations (*Bury Free Press*, 5 December 1942, p.7).

the hay and the box and somewhere to put them. I should imagine that most people here can cook – the place is cold and breeds hearty appetites. Twice I went in a grubby eating-house here and each time they gave me meat, a lot of Yorkshire pudding, and five different vegetables, all of it beautifully cooked. Cabbages here are usually delicious, but my own experience says that it is the gardener rather than the cook who determines the amount of virtue in a cabbage. I did not continue at the eating-house because I do not appreciate grubby places and because I could not afford it. If only we could live in a country where we could reach up and pluck a banana and require nothing else! At Bexhill I had plenty of them – with cream. But housekeeping in Bexhill was a holiday compared with this present, and I had a very nice landlord, pleasant acquaintances, time to entertain and a telephone linking me up with my friends.

Bexhill was fun, though only about £30 then stood between me and destitution, and there was nothing to guarantee that I would ever again be able to earn a living. War, I knew, would bring me work, though I dreaded the idea of war if I happened – at Bexhill, where I never read a newspaper – to think of it. The internee – to whom war meant complete disaster, for he was not allowed to take a paid job – took *The Times* whether he could afford it or not, and didn't like my ostrich-like existence, as he called it. He worked for board and lodging only, in a shop, and spent his leisure hours working up a business in numismatics in my office, weekdays and Sundays. He was on his own in Bexhill and so was I. He worked liked hell, and I often helped him, not with the actual coins but with correspondence. I still have some of the catalogues he prepared and sent out to numismatists, and which I used to envelop and post for him. He had a permit to 'deal' though not to work for wages. All that 'au pair' business with foreigners seemed to me rotten. It provided people who treated English servants so badly they would not stay with wageless servants, prosperous boarding-schools with wageless teachers, and swelled our own unemployment problem accordingly. I often think that if we had not had war we should have drifted into revolution. In the few years before the war the labour exchanges were always packed with young, able-bodied men and women who were, presumably, with the aid of relations in regard to lodging and clothes, living on that pittance called 'the dole', and contributing nothing in work to the nation. I read somewhere, however, that they were necessary as, when war once started, they could immediately be drawn upon. Which merely makes me shrug my shoulders and (impolite as it sounds) snort. I was in the labour exchange too, not because I was young and untrained, but because I was nearly 40 and so too old to be given work, whatever my qualifications. That was why I went to Bexhill, knowing not a soul there, and opened an office in the hope that someone would bring me in some work, sooner or later. To pay 12s. 6d. a week for an office I could live in was no more expensive than paying a landlady. When I had no work I drew the dole and otherwise the eight months in that office cost me about

£25. Had I drawn the dole all the time and lived in lodgings I should probably have spent about the same, as I cannot live under £3 a week with clothes and extras or 30s. a week without clothes or extras. I should 'go under' on 30s. a week even in peacetime, for food and bed are not everything.

6 p.m. And the week's dust still on the floor. It is energy and interest which count much more than time in this life. To clean, these rooms take 2 hours; to think about, 12 hours, or longer.

Tuesday, 24 November

… *Typists*. We have not been able to borrow a typist from the clerk's department, perhaps because one of them has been off duty. Ruth, our own typist, has *not* scarlet fever, but from the symptoms more likely influenza. She was isolated with two pails of Izal disinfectant and 'a raw onion to draw off the germs'. The doctor allowed her up as soon as her temperature went down and has treated the temperature but not Ruth. She writes humorously about all of it.

I am feeling slightly more energetic today and *if* I had some port wine and biscuits (which I haven't) would feel normal. Unlike Ruth, who, at the age of 21, doesn't menstruate at all, I, aged 46, get enough for four persons every 3½ weeks and get sapped of energy until I make more blood a few days afterwards. Eggs in milk and a tin of sweetened condensed milk put new life into me one time recently, but that cannot be managed every 3½ weeks on rations. I do not know if a doctor could assist – I have not much faith, if any, in iron. Curious effect the sweetened Nestlé's condensed milk had; as if new life tingled into my fingers.

18B. Hurray! Some British Union man bringing an action against my arch enemies [Sir John] Anderson and Morrison. Don't suppose it will affect them, though I wish it would, but it will at least show up prison conditions, than which nothing could be better. I know nothing at all about Fascists, or whatever they are, and black shirts looked far too much like death to please *me*, but I'm glad when any stir is made against Regulation 18B and I abhor Anderson for creating the internment mess and Morrison for not clearing it up. They may be useful men in other directions – that I don't know. They have caused me personally so much worry, expense and annoyance that I have no room for them anywhere. I have no interest in politics but I object to the injustice and dictatorship of 18B, and that is the sort of thing for which such men appear to be responsible.

Sir Stafford Cripps. Had an idea, from conversation of a few people, that he was about the most popular man in the country and likely to be almost its salvation. These few people did not know each other, but I heard how nice it was to have a man on the radio who talked as a gentleman and did not blackguard other people, and the general opinion was that as well as being intelligent he was honest – a somewhat rare qualification in these days. I don't know enough about him to form an opinion and have not heard him speak. It seems queer that he has been turned out of the War Cabinet – or whatever it is – and put into a merely commercial job. Still, I suppose he may be useful in it, one never knows – anything.[33]

Casuals. Bury St Edmunds relief meeting this morning. Mrs Greene not present and very few present and so Mr Cragg (retired insurance agent) was very dominant and there was a good deal of wrangling. The public assistance officer held his own as I have never before known him and Cragg had to sit back. I am afraid there is a lot of unnecessary ill-health among our relief cases, because on our skinflint allowances anybody who falls ill has very little chance of regaining strength. Cragg takes the plate round and is a big noise at his chapel but he certainly 'grinds the faces of the poor'. Hunt (chairman) fought him a bit this morning, but it was a rather deplorable meeting. At the end 'casuals' was brought up. There was a letter from Mrs Corser, keeper of a common lodging house here to whom we have paid a retaining fee to take in any casuals who might arrive in Newmarket or Bury St Edmunds. The institutions do not take them in now and the police stations won't have them. They have been warned not to come to these parts but some drift in, and the relieving officer, Mr Mobbs, has been extremely glad of Mrs Corser for some time as he considers it his duty to find casuals a night's lodging. During the conversation I learned that St Michael's College for Girls (mentioned previously in this diary) accommodated Irish labourers working for beet sugar factory. Some Irish, however, had gone to Mrs Corser's, for she complained that she must give up her lodging house because she could not stand lice and rough Irishmen. As a rule she takes in 20 to 30 lodgers a night but (this sounds like Bury St Edmunds) the landlord would not put a bathroom in the place for her. The committee decided that the county council could disinfect her bedding and the borough the house, but it was pointed out that it was no use doing this when the next day would bring more lice. The public assistance officer decided to refer the matter to the chairman of the Joint Vagrancy Committee, a Mr Cecil Oakes. He will probably put up another notice warning casuals against coming this way. Canon Browne at

---

[33] Sir Stafford Cripps, whose popularity had soared through much of 1942, was seen by some as a serious rival to Churchill. Cripps, Leader of the House of Commons and a member of the War Cabinet, disagreed with Churchill on some fundamental matters but did not in fact strive to replace him as prime minister. Winifred is reacting to the news that Cripps had just been appointed minister of aircraft production, an actual and perceived demotion (though a job he was to handle effectively). As Cripps's biographer has observed, 'At the time, the bland official announcement of the government reconstruction left the public bemused. Cripps was replaced in the War Cabinet by Herbert Morrison and as Leader of the House by Eden, thus strengthening the grip of party hierarchy within the coalition. Cripps's move was big news, received with some bafflement by the public' (Peter Clarke, *The Cripps Version: The Life of Sir Stafford Cripps 1889–1952* (London, 2002), p.368).

Newmarket fixes a few up, as part of the work of his church, but nobody here does it at present. I suppose the Irish will have to crowd into St Michael's, or sleep in ditches. If Mrs Corser cannot cope with them, after her long experience of casuals, the townsfolk will hardly take them in. Moreover, there is no room in the town's houses. I do not blame her for objecting to lice – today's paper says that there is an epidemic of typhus in Eire. We are asking her to carry on for another week, but it would be disastrous to get typhus here through lice. It is bad enough that the London evacuees have filled the place with that hitherto unknown thing, scabies (the itch), which is still rampant, despite treatment and disinfection, because it is impossible to disinfect adequately. Mr Mobbs gave figures 5 to 6 casuals daily in summer, 15 to 20 in winter.[34]

I think there are some public baths here, but evidently not enough for the military, as they use our county institutions whenever they get the opportunity. A few townsfolk who have baths invite soldiers or airmen to Sunday tea and a bath. *When* they get their new Ascot heater installed in the moral welfare home I suppose there is just a chance I'd be allowed to bath there if I paid them. They have a staff bathroom but at present not enough hot water. There is a YWCA but I fancy it is for girls in the Forces.[35] Several canteens for the Forces. Some very common dances are sometimes held for both sexes, Forces and civilians, but otherwise I don't know any place here where they can meet, except on the street or in picture palaces. At night soldiers loiter on the town pavements watching for girls, and the girls here think it is just lovely. I suppose they had very dull lives before the war and any strange man gives them a thrill. Parents complain they have no control over the girls, and the moral welfare home cannot step in at their request until *after* the girls are pregnant, when in the parents' eyes the damage is done. Mrs Jarrold, manageress of the Playhouse bars, takes it as her duty to keep the *men* from harm, turning out all women who go there to loiter about for the soldiers, etc.[36]

---

[34] Two years later Winifred reported new details on casuals. 'We have unofficially reopened part of our casual ward in Bury. Mrs Corser, lodging-house keeper, refused to take casuals in any longer. They had been stealing her blankets and boots and she still could not stand the Irish' (10 December 1944). Mrs Corser's lodging house was at 59 Long Brackland. The lack of accommodation in Newmarket for 'casuals' had been recognized as a problem in the summer of 1942. At the Newmarket Area Guardians Committee meeting on 18 August 1942, 'The Relieving Officer reported that owing to the withdrawal by the Newmarket District Council of the Lodging House Licence held by Mrs Williams, The Dolphin, Drapery Row, Newmarket, she was no longer able to provide lodgings for casuals, and that during the past week it had been necessary to provide three casuals with the necessary rail fare to enable them to travel to Bury St Edmunds, in view of the fact that alternative accommodation was not available' (Suffolk Record Office, Ipswich, WS 125/11).

[35] The premises of the Young Women's Christian Association were at 1 Churchyard.

[36] The Playhouse cinema was in the Butter Market and its bars were a favourite gathering-place. In 2008 the ex-cinema was the Argos store.

Mice. I'll really have to do something about my mice. They used to arrive after I put the light out, but now they come before. I can hear them now and last night I watched two very big fat ones wandering all about this room. I cover all food up but expect they come from house to house all along the street, and it's not much use looking for holes when there's about an inch of space (two inches or three inches in the case of the front street door) under-neath each door to give them entrance.

Downstairs tenant was saying she thought it ought to be against the law pinching people's back ways to put up an ice cream factory, because it allowed only one exit in case of fire. I don't know if it is against the law, but it seems to be characteristic of this town for the houses to have no back entrances and for the dustbins to have to be brought through the house and deposited on the street pavement. I had never previously imagined a house without a back way. Perhaps I live in the slums, but with about £40 worth of furniture downstairs purchased from a tenant who felt it necessary to sell her home and go to work when her husband was 'called up' to the Forces, the landlord charges 31s. a week for this place and it is just an old agricultural town. For 18s. 11d. a week in Cambridge, which, after all, *is* a town and not a large village, my brother has a house with back and front garden, semi-detached, two lavatories and a bathroom, all in first-rate repair – as a house, worth quite six times as much as this one; a pleasant house in which anybody could live. A sunny house (not dark like this one) and a long private garden with lawn, flowers and fruit trees.

I have been relieved to see my mice – they made so much noise I feared they might be rats.

Wednesday, 25 November

Asked Mr Mobbs today if he thought his poor relief people better off since war began, and he said they were. Said committees just ran amok these days and assistance board and all the rest had an effect in bringing relief to higher level. I said 'Yet you have the meanest committee in the county.' 'Yes, I suppose so, but old Cragg doesn't realise what he is doing, he's a bit funny in the head.' As an example of the better conditions, Mobbs reported that one of his women recipients told him her family were getting on very nicely indeed, 'thank you, Mr Mobbs', since they went on relief. They were really very comfortable now and had been able to pay something off the bills they owed when they went on. If that is so, then I think the woman deserves a medal for good housewifery!

After all, we are offering to take some Great Yarmouth children into one children's home, Crofton House, Sudbury.[37] We are charging 28s. a week

---

[37] Crofton House was a children's home in Sudbury run by the public assistance committee of the West Suffolk County Council.

each and I said that seemed a lot considering that the matron had about £85 a year resident and the assistant matron (both very good people and better class than most) £55, the only additional help being a charwoman. The public assistance officer said the actual cost was 22s. but we charged 28s. to other counties. That seems nearer and I suppose it would cost the average parent an extra 22s. to bring up a child in the private family.

Heard this morning from my internee. He still seems to be in a queer mood. Suppose I'll have to answer carefully so as not to aggravate it. I think his hopes of release may have dropped nearly to zero by now. This accursed internment business. And when peace arrives both he and I look like having a hell of a time getting on our feet. If I were 20 instead of 46 I wouldn't mind at all. Or if I'd been born with an annuity! I used to think it would be terrible to be an elderly spinster, but now I know it is only lack of money which makes it unpleasant. It's a queer world, and yet rats and mice and men go on breeding as if it were worth while, which rather suggests that it may be. Thank God it is a decision I am spared, along with many other decisions I'd hate having to make. Apart from that, there is nothing in myself that I should want to hand on to the future – that, of course, may be the reason why nobody has ever shown the least inclination to want to marry me! Realising, I mean, that in me there is nothing worth handing on. One troubles to live, I think, mainly for the sake of a handful of friends and relations, or sometimes (in my case) out of sheer cussedness. I should not like to have to die. I cannot imagine that I ever wanted to be born, either, and yet, strange to relate, my mother wanted to have me. So here I am, and I'd better write to that internee and wash myself and wash up greasy dishes.

The public assistance officer told me today that if I didn't wear stockings tomorrow he'd send me home again for some. Actually I wear two pairs of ankle socks instead and I can't be bothered to repair stockings to make any wearable. At least two dozen pairs have waited since the spring to be mended. Tomorrow I ought to buy bread, sausages, potatoes, paraffin, matches, soap, chocolate, oats and exchange my points for provisions, and take bed linen etc. to the laundry. If I ask I can get a half hour off for shopping, but how far will that take me? One day, with a bicycle, I shopped from 9 a.m. to 5 p.m. and did hardly more than the above list. Yet in peacetime it would have been fairly easy, in fact a note dropped into a shop would have got them delivered at my door. My hair has needed a good brush for weeks! And my nails have needed a manicure for months!

Thursday, 26 November

British Restaurant. A diner there today told me the dearth of a second vegetable was because so many people did not like vegetables and that was why they asked me if I liked turnips before putting three small thin slices on my plate. Strange, in a town which has such a very large supply of vegetables and when other things are rationed. This British Restaurant is very clean and pleasant and useful, but I am not used to so little at my main meal; but there may be a lack of supplies, for no-one is allowed to buy a second helping of the sweet, which is about the size of half a normal helping. It may be an almost minute piece of suet pudding with jam or sauce, or two prunes in custard, or stewed apples with just a spot of custard; but whatever it is the average person could accommodate double.

My Diet Today. Three cups tea with liquid milk, porridge without milk. A jam tart somebody gave me at 11 a.m. in the office. Soup and bread, beef, beetroot and potatoes (all hot), apple and custard and a cup of tea. Another cup of tea at the office. Two cups tea, bread and butter and cheese and some hot pudding made of dried milk, dried egg and cornflour.

St Audry's Mental Hospital, Melton. Looking at November's county council minutes today I found a report on the food provided at this place. It was inadequate and ill-balanced and the inspector who made the report suggested they should start more allotments to provide vegetables. He had complained that although vegetables were easily obtainable they were conspicuous by their absence. On the day of his visit there was cold tinned meat and bread followed by rice pudding, but only on three days a week did they have a second course and on two of those three days the second course was bread and cheese. The war has not created this shortage of food and with right management any institution can feed its people quite well. It suggests to me that the management does not care or there is an incompetent and greatly depleted staff, so that there is no time to clean vegetables and cook meals. I think that the food in our own institutions is quite good at the moment. The committees are all generous on that point and those in charge have, within reason, a free hand in purchasing supplies. Kitchens are things in which our committees take a pride. They understand the meaning of a good meal even if the idea of using psychologists makes them scoff.[38] It used to be funny when the ministries sent round circulars explaining how to make stews, etc. I used to take the circulars for them to read, and hear 'Waste of paper! Waste of paper! As though we don't know how to make stews.' We haven't had that type of circular lately, so perhaps the shortage of paper is really now being taken into consideration....

Work. We are nearing a jam this weekend. My one typist has been on rest centre work all the week (we do that as an addition to our normal work and it entails a lot of typing etc.) and now the public assistance officer is getting in a funk because minutes of meetings *must* be drafted, checked, stencilled and sent out in time for the next meetings. Bury guardians meeting is tomorrow week so this weekend we must send out notices to call the meeting and at the

---

[38] The St Audry Hospital was in a former workhouse. Melton is in East Suffolk and the hospital was probably used by both counties to accommodate people with mental health problems.

same time send the minutes of the last guardians meeting, the relief meeting and the house and children's and a special house sub-committee. Ruth may have stencilled the last guardians (I haven't looked to see yet) but I have not started to dictate the others and in fact the house and children's meetings don't take place until tomorrow. We will get through but whenever there is a bit of a jam the public assistance officer hovers round and becomes more trouble than the work. Tonight he very kindly tried to help me, telling me how to do the job by just getting the relief books and case-papers and dictating, his theory being simplicity itself but somewhat useless in practice when I spend my time answering his bell and taking down his letters, answering the phone, accepting particulars of all sorts of things to come up at other meetings, giving information to architect and accountants, hunting up letters and documents from files, preparing for the next day's meeting, and so on. Then as I typed Sudbury minutes from my notes he stood over me and thought it would help if he fetched that relief book and hunted up a few case-papers. I'd got all the information in my notes but had too much to do to argue and as they are kept in the next room it got him out of my way. When he got there he couldn't find them and Elsie Foulger was called in to help him – so she got the job of entertaining him instead of me. He means well and by doing some meetings on his own *does* help me, but the trouble is that I am quite a good shorthand-typist. When men did my job they were not and so he had to dictate to whatever shorthand-typists were available, but now he will dictate to me even though he knows I shall have to re-dictate much of the stuff to someone else, and even though I have a load of other stuff to get through.

So far as promotion and earning decent wages are concerned, my liking for and ability to do shorthand and typewriting have been my complete undoing! Yet I'd be frightfully bored if I'd got to be a matron, a housekeeper, a hotel manageress, laundry manageress, or any such jobs in which one can earn good money, perhaps with much less brain. Taking him all round, the public assistance officer is pretty decent, and crowds of men are much worse. The clerk is also much better than many. The staff laughs about the public assistance officer but usually mimics the clerk's way of talking. All the 'permanent' staff feel secure in their jobs, rather different from the employees in private concerns in London. What shorthand-typist in peacetime London, for instance, could have any sense of security, when if she displeased her employer in any small way he could telephone the network of private employment exchanges and have 50 applicants to replace her on his doorstep in an hour or two? I don't think these Shire Hall people are ever sacked without adequate cause, even in peacetime.

Newspapers. Don't think there has been much in these lately. If there has, I have forgotten it as soon as read.

Adelphi Players. December 18, 19 and 20 are to do *Don Juan*, *Easter*, and a Nativity play. Their prices have increased from 1s. and 1s. 6d. to 2s. 6d. and 3s. 6d. A good many people are looking forward to their coming. The musical set in the town are interested in CEMA concerts.[39] I find them rather boring owing to their lack of variety, perhaps only one pianist, or a pianist and one singer, or just one quartette during the whole evening. I seem to need variety to 'warm me up' to appreciation. Even a lecture seems to gain a kind of life by being delivered quickly, the items following each other in such rapid succession that they stir one's brain to pleasurable activity. I heard a very good quartette here one evening but it perhaps just lacked 'genius', for despite its talent I certainly could not lose myself in its music and at half-time I came out because it was just a waste of my time to stay longer. The man at the door remarked to somebody else who also had come out that that sort of thing could be heard any time on the wireless. I think the musical set of the town thought the quartette wonderful.

Today I went into a little exhibition of pictures held by a Miss Mead, who had painted them. She is an elderly woman and I believe specialises in flower studies. Some of them were very nice – all in oils. I don't know anything about her but Jarman the photographer here always shows some of her work. The room was of course very colourful. She says it is difficult to get picture frames now. If I'd had a lot of money and no use for it I might have bought two pictures of tulips which I liked. I wonder if people like that can earn a living, or if they live on what their parents have left them. Pictures are so cheap for the work in them, the outlay and the skill. A pleasant life, though, probably, if one can afford it.[40]

Friday, 27 November

7.30 p.m. Diet, etc. Tea and cold pudding made last night. At noon a rock cake given me in an institution kitchen. Minced meat, carrot, potatoes and bread, suet pudding with golden syrup sauce, tea. *Tea*. Tea, bread and butter and cheese, jam, Virol,[41] one beef sausage and bread. Since which I have made a meat pie which is now cooking on one oilstove and on the other stove I am cooking parsnips, cabbage and potatoes. A marvellous big, very crisp cabbage tonight for 2½d. Went over [to] Bury St Edmunds Public Assistance Institution this morning. A lovely kitchen with lots of windows and the Aga cooker which is liked so much wherever installed and is always

---

[39] The Council for Education in Music and the Arts was set up in January 1940 with government support to assist serious cultural endeavours. Its functions sometimes overlapped with ENSA's, especially with regard to music. CEMA organized, among many other activities, art exhibitions and tours by the Old Vic Company and the Ballet Rambert.

[40] Rose Mead (1867–1946), daughter of a Bury builder and plumber, practised as a painter in the town for most of her adult life. She was educated locally and at Lincoln and Westminster Schools of Art and in Paris. Harry Isaac Jarman was a photographer at 16 Abbeygate Street; he was deputy mayor in 1944–45.

[41] Virol is the trade name of a vitamin preparation based on malt extract.

considered to be so economical in fuel. All men working in the kitchen, not women as at Sudbury and elsewhere in the county. Apparently, no St Audry's dietary here. About 50 men and women (probably more) were being served by the men with dinner. I don't know if they have a second course – a woman in the infirmary eating an orange soon after said she was doing so because she preferred fruit to pudding. I have not myself had an orange since war started and they are mainly reserved for children. I have seen no pork either except in the Isle of Man, where rationing started much later than here. Suppose I may get pork if I trouble to go and stay with farmers who keep pigs and are allowed to kill one for their own consumption now and again. They are killing two pigs at this institution for Xmas, and they will certainly be big fat ones. The first course being served to the inmates was meat, greens and potatoes, but it was on big dinner plates and each plate was very full, holding quite three times as much as the British Restaurant gives. I myself wouldn't have wanted more than half of it, but the matron said they would all be ready for their tea. They looked happy enough. The infirmaries were much more pathetic, colourless and bare and ugly and full of white counterpaned beds. TB cases there are in outside huts with a pleasant outlook of lawn and garden, and I should imagine would have a chance of recovery not provided for by London County Council hospitals. There is a TB ward in our Newmarket Emergency Hospital, also a few huts, and I hear there is some disturbance among the nurses because they do not want to nurse TB. They are mostly VADs [Voluntary Aid Detachment] or CNRs [Civilian Nursing Reserve] at Newmarket. One cannot blame them for not wanting to nurse such an infectious disease, but what are TB patients to do when sanatoria are lacking and in any case only tackle such people as could probably be put right by a good holiday? Institution nurses of course have to tackle *anything*. I really cannot understand why in peacetime we could not have put nursing and the treatment of TB on a reasonable basis. Things now are excused because there is a war on, but nursing was always done as if there were a war on, and as far as I could see had not progressed one jot since the time of Florence Nightingale, apart, perhaps, from the operating theatre. There is more bluff and pretence now, perhaps – quite a ritual to go through to give the patient the idea that things are done in a hygienic fashion; though the nurse herself is aware that it is only pretence, in almost everything except the washing of her hands. I do think there should be medical teaching in schools so that the medical profession cannot bluff the public to the extent they do. This morning's institution is having a good-sized new maternity ward built as they need it badly. It is getting on very well but they have only one bricklayer and one carpenter on the job, and I don't suppose they can get more....

Young woman in the British Restaurant with husband away in RAF was saying how she used to shop and cook in a job and that she wanted to go out again but her daughter aged 3½ kept her busy. I said I supposed there was no available nursery school and she said no, she didn't think people in this county troubled much about children, the place seemed to be all dogs, rich spinsters and motor-cars, and run for them only. She did not understand why there was no nursery school. I do. Nobody desired the trouble of running one. Plenty of children were available, and *if* the authorities had the necessary sense they could easily find suitable staff. Plenty of women would like such part-time work if they were allowed to do it as part-time work. It is by no means as easy to find part-time employment as the newspapers suggest.[42]

The matron this morning remarked that we were old-fashioned in expecting girls to get married nowadays before having babies. I said present-day novels took it for granted they would have them beforehand. She said the government approved of it and helped to that end, copying Germany she supposed. I myself imagined it was copying Russia. I said it was to increase the population, and thought but did not say, for the next war. I suppose the government's attitude to unmarried mothers and women living with other women's husbands was so very continental that it gave a big shock to most women of my age and older. We had not been brought up on the teaching that prostitution was a virtue, even though our personal experiences may have taught us that virginity brings no rewards, except freedom from venereal disease. Times change. One of these days I suppose women will be proud of bearing children for wars and not object cynically (as many did before this war) to giving babies just for 'cannon fodder'. Depends on the outlook. Strange to feel that soon I shan't be able to have babies even if I want them. Up to present I have not wanted them.

Our office boy has passed A.1 [medical fitness] for the Forces. He is tall and perhaps strong but is such a youngster I do not think (judging by the look in his eyes) he likes the idea of becoming a soldier – rather puzzled and afraid. I myself think 24 is a better age and that the older rather than the younger men should make up the numbers. If anyone is responsible for war, it is the older, not the younger, and it seems a shame to kill off children who have not yet had a chance to live their lives.

---

[42] A nursery had been opened in Sudbury. According to the *Suffolk and Essex Free Press*, Thursday, 13 November 1941, p.7, 'Under the auspices of the County Council, a war-time nursery was started on Monday, at the Baptist Schoolroom, Church Street. The primary object is to look after the children of mothers who are engaged in war work, but actually any mother is welcome to send her child along, including evacuees. A hot midday meal is supplied from the British Restaurant. This is fetched by boys from the Senior School in a very useful-looking truck. Similar nurseries have been started at Hadleigh, Haverhill and Lavenham and that at Sudbury should become very popular. Complete supervision is assured for every child, the ages of admission being 2 to 5 years.' Three weeks later (*ibid.*, 4 December, p.7) it was reported that twenty-six children were enrolled in Sudbury's nursery, with space for more.

Saturday, 28 November

An interesting item in newspaper today. I saw it on my way to office, then forgot it while I dictated and corrected draft minutes, then remembered as I looked at paper on my way home. Headline says: 'French blow up their fleet and forts at Toulon'. My first thought on the subject was that those boats would do no further damage and it was the best news I'd had for a long time. Reading, however, I began to wonder whether their loss was fortune or misfortune to us, and concluded it was a draw between us and Germany, and the only gain was that the belligerents had less weapons to fight with. Felt sorry for the men who had perished in the scuttling of the vessels. The whole situation was more dramatic than I had conceived possible.[43] Wondered (not for the first time) why there always seems romance and glory and even beauty about naval affairs whereas military are just dust or mud, or weary troops, or ammunition, pain, burning, blood and death, rape, starvation, disease, drunkenness, ugly khaki, discipline, saluting. Perhaps it is because I have never come into contact with the navy, whereas in a war soldiers are always kicking about, together with RAF. Or perhaps the sea itself gathers a glory because we spend our holidays beside it in normal times. Anyhow, the fact remains that, though I have no connection with the navy, naval exploits give me a thrill no military achievement ever does. RAF exploits also leave me cold – I want the RAF to get the job done but I don't want to hear details. I am not the only one who gets bored with the details and turns the wireless off before they arrive. I really should not like to belong to France these days – the populace cannot know where they stand or whom to trust. So many leaders prefer a winning side. France is in a mess and will be lucky if she escapes being crushed out of existence in the conflict. I suppose De Gaulle is her only hope. He at least knew how to go on one particular side and remain there, which would suggest to the French that he is trustworthy.

I think people here feel that events are now going in our favour and there is less likelihood of air raids over Britain.

Postal Parcels. One after another I sent five wooden (fairly thick) card-index boxes by post to Isle of Man, containing cake, etc. They are all broken in transit. Some weeks ago I enclosed small but valuable oil painting in centre of hearthrug many times folded and on arrival the canvas was torn into three pieces. It appears impossible to get a parcel through undamaged these days, so I have decided to send no more. I thought the railway terrible with their breakages but the Post Office is as bad. Presumably there is no redress with recipient in a camp.

Thank goodness I need not shop this afternoon so can (at long last) do some housework. I'd better get active right away.

---

[43] With the German takeover of Vichy France and subsequent occupation of the naval base at Toulon, the French scuttled their fleet.

Wednesday, 2 December

... *Beveridge Social* Services. I have not read this business thoroughly but from the few remarks I have heard it appears to have been received favourably.[44] Suppose if the war lasts long enough for this scheme to come into operation first, and if they take over public assistance and I have not left it, I *might* be offered a job after the war. I'd prefer to help the internee with numismatics, but it might be safer for me to be earning money until he got on his feet. One has to spend a lot on advertising before results begin to show in that business.

Saw a note from a committee member saying that after the war West Suffolk villagers were likely to be keenly interested in local government and who represented them. Long line of cars today outside my window – meeting of county councillors to discuss future of local government or something akin.[45] They were not only representative of public assistance of course, but it struck me that at some future date it may seem quaint for people to hear how the guardians of the poor used to ride round in their cars merely to attend to their poorer brethren – one set so rich and the other so destitute.

Alice Smith rang up today and asked Gooch if he would do her a favour. She is one of our adopted girls. Her mother neglected her and was uninterested until the girl was able to earn a living. Most of the parents become interested about then. Mother now lives with a man not her husband. Alice has a fairly good appearance and is 16. Is in domestic service. The favour was to ask the public assistance officer (her guardian) to let her go to a town some distance off because a military policeman she had met in Bury St Edmunds had asked her to visit him. Public assistance officer said 'no' so Gooch rang the girl's mistress (knowing that whatever he said Alice was quite capable of telling her mistress she had permission to go) and gave her the public assis-

---

[44] *Social Insurance and Allied Services* (HMSO, 1942), the report of a committee chaired by William Beveridge, proposed improvements to the existing social insurance provisions. Often informally called the Beveridge Report, it was published to great acclaim, coming at a time of intense public interest in the creation of a Britain better than it had been in the 1930s. Though not so revolutionary as sometimes suggested – for the unemployed and sick it recommended flat-rate benefits in return for flat-rate contributions – it became the basis for the Welfare State established by the Labour government from 1945.

[45] The County Councils Association had recommended that smaller district councils should be abolished. At this meeting of the West Suffolk County Council, their wholesale abolition was opposed, since they gave 'personal service'. An exception was made for the so-called Part III education authorities – municipal boroughs which, though lacking 'county' powers, had since 1902 run their own elementary schools. In West Suffolk, Bury St Edmunds was the only such borough. The county council thought these authorities were anomalous and ought to be abolished, despite the vehement objections of E.L.D. Lake, the mayor of Bury (*Bury Free Press*, 5 December 1942, p.2). Part III authorities were abolished by the 1944 Education Act.

tance officer's message. 'No, but if the mistress was prepared to ask the man into her house Alice could be allowed to see him.' Alice is simply crazy over men, but on the other hand, what interests can a girl in her position have, apart from the cinema?

It was arranged today that the Howe and Davison girls should be kept at Sudbury 'as in a place of safety'. Dorothy Davison is the more remarkable. Her mother is in a mental hospital (or was) and I think Dorothy is being certified as mentally deficient. I hear she does not look it and I know she can write an excellent letter – almost a literary style and grammatical. She appeared to be happy with a foster mother but the committee did not consider the home suitable – the foster mother still writes and would take her again if allowed to and the girl apparently would like it. I personally know nothing about the home. Anyhow, Dorothy went to a moral welfare home for two years but the person in charge let her take a domestic job after six months and another moral welfare home person said she needed the two years. Since then Dorothy has gone from job to institution and from institution to job, and been satisfactory nowhere. She now keeps imploring to be allowed to join the Forces. Dr [Alison] Rae [assistant county medical officer of health] here considers her unfit to look after herself morally in the Forces, and I think she and the Howe girl may go to the 'Helping Hand Home', Radlett. Perhaps it is a pity that Dorothy cannot write a book on her life – it would be interesting in many ways. A 'Helping Hand Home' could be interesting if described by an inmate, though I don't know this particular home. The girls there have to be certified first.[46]

Asked and got permission to have Saturday morning off with a view to meeting my brother and his wife in Cambridge. He is now in [the] Royal Artillery but is on leave. Says soldiering would be all right if they could take their homes with them but anyhow it is a rest cure after his civilian job on assistance board. It appears to be one course after another and the last one has been lectures from morning to night and some of the men get lectures in their sleep so he is becoming a good shot with a slipper in the dark. Don't suppose lectures worry him, though they would some. He could take all the prizes at school and yet worried so little about homework that you hardly realised he did any. I don't think he did much, anyhow. I did not think he would like soldiering because he has never roughed it – compared with me, he has always had a luxurious existence, but when he was a child (the sixth) my father was earning more than four times what he did when I (the first)

---

[46] This 'Helping Hand' Home was described as 'a small certified Institution where the girls go out to daily work after a period of training in the Home' (Suffolk Record Office, Ipswich, WS 123/11, West Suffolk Public Assistance Minute Books, meeting of 8 October 1942). The name 'Dorothy Davison' has been invented by the editors to protect the privacy of this individual.

was a child, and in addition three of us were self-supporting, and contributing something to the home. I think he thinks he knows what we are fighting for. I don't, but it struck me recently that we are better off in that respect than the French, for we do know what we are fighting against, and they can hardly know even that.

Home Office. Letter this morning – very courteous, and signed 'Your Obedient Servant'. I wish they were – I'd put them through it! Lot of tripe – 'I am directed by the Secretary of State'. Anyhow, they will not allow internees to be visited between 22nd to 26th December, and add 'If you would be kind enough to inform us on what other date you would like to make a visit the requisite permit will be forwarded to you'. Well, thank God I've made other arrangements for Xmas, but they are a lot of swine not informing the relations etc. of internees that they cannot visit at Xmas before the beginning of December. It doesn't matter to me, but where a husband or wife is interned it is damnable that visits are, in effect, only allowed to the leisured and wealthy classes. Swine! I had already told them that my only possible dates for visiting were that week and I'd like to reply (only they might take it out of the internee) 'Go to Hell', or 'I am a working woman and do not belong, as you have on more than one occasion suggested, to the idle rich'. There is no point, of course, in replying at all, so I shan't. I can keep all my fury to myself – it cannot hurt them. I wonder if any measure of justice will ever return in this country? Churchill's remarks about the duration of war depress me lately. Girl in shop suggested not enough money made out of it yet.[47]

Thursday, 3 December

Think I ought to amplify remark of the shop girl yesterday. She has a husband abroad in Forces and herself works behind counter 48 hours weekly in very busy grocery shop, doing her housework in her spare time. Something was said about the war and I said I wished it would end but Churchill didn't sound optimistic and surely he ought to know something about it. She suddenly drew back her shoulders and said defiantly: 'They haven't made enough money out of it yet'. I have been in the shop before but had not held a previous conversation with her. There has, of course, been a great deal of apathy about this war. I contrast her attitude with that of the clergyman's wife who had lost her only son, a naval officer, in the war. With the latter there was pride. She and

---

[47] In a radio broadcast on 29 November, Churchill, while acknowledging and celebrating recent advances ('The Bright Gleam of Victory') had declared that 'I know of nothing that has happened yet which justifies the hope that the war will not be long, or that bitter and bloody years do not lie ahead.... The dawn of 1943 will soon loom red before us, and we must brace ourselves to cope with the trials and problems of what must be a stern and terrible year' (Robert Rhodes James, ed., *Winston S. Churchill: His Complete Speeches 1897–1963*, 8 vols (New York, 1974), VI, pp.6714–15).

her sort *were* Britain and it had been a privilege for her son to take part in the defence of Britain, and she was immensely proud of him though sorry to lose him. He had died a noble death to preserve the things which made life worth living. The shop-girl is different. War to her is probably an ugly giant which has burst forth from Hell and is threatening the existence of everything which has made and could make her life worth while. If her husband is killed then nothing else is of importance – *she* is not part of a glorious Britain but merely a servant of the people who reside there. The position is, I think, very different, and largely accounts for the apathy.

I went into a medical missionary exhibition this evening and found people running it delighted with the Beveridge Report. I said to one that I didn't understand why foreign medical matters should have to be run by voluntary societies and I thought in places like India our government should have done the job. She said that nothing would come from the top until the people themselves showed their desire for it and vested interests were in the way of government action and though this country was called Christian it wasn't really.

Conversation with another of the helpers was a bit quaint. I had been looking at photos of blacks who looked like bronze statues and beautiful and when we got to two sitting down and wearing ungainly cotton frocks I instinctively remarked: 'What a pity to make them wear clothes'. The lady looked taken aback and asked if I didn't think it nicer and I said I preferred them without and thought it must be healthier. She said but surely I'd agree that just something round their middles should be worn. I began to feel she was being 'not quite nice' and just looked at her, so she asked if I would like to go about without any. I said I wouldn't because it wasn't fashionable and was much too cold, but in a hot country I thought it healthier and I liked the look of it better. She said that of course blacks who became Christians were taught to wear clothes and it taught them to be modest. I said that if by teaching them to wear clothes lessons of morality could be instilled at the same time, perhaps the clothes served a useful purpose, but I thought they looked nicer without and that it would be healthier in hot climates. Actually, I think life might even be worth living in a country hot enough for clothes to be discarded, and I'm certainly not sure that the lady's 'modesty' is a virtue – it may be a vice peculiar to ourselves. I've yet to learn that clothes produce chastity. We've got the habit of covering everything up in this country, just to pretend things are just as they ought to be, and much stripping might do us a world of good. The stripping of our own souls might even cure the world of its woes, though I doubt if many of us would survive the exposure!

Friday, 4 December

Seems a bit daft, but perhaps I ought to ring up Dr Rae about Ruth. Public assistance officer has already done so and she (Dr Rae) has seen Ruth in his presence and got Ruth's doctor to overhaul her – he says bronchial catarrh. Ruth would have told Dr Rae about herself but didn't like to in front of a man (public assistance officer). The other typist has got a job with McAlpine's contractors, at nearly twice her present salary, and goes shortly. Clerk's department advertised two weeks ago with no result and didn't trouble last week, and I should think Ruth could get a job any time at much more money. Our fools continue to risk losing her just for the pleasure of keeping her salary too low to allow her to be self-supporting. If Dr Rae would state that she ought to live in this town instead of getting up at an unearthly hour [in Stowmarket] and coming without breakfast on a workman's ticket, perhaps it would have *some* effect. NALGO got it allowed that juniors doing responsible work (as Ruth does, for she practically runs the boarded-out children on her own apart from understudying and helping me) should be paid accordingly, but when Ruth applied the clerk turned it down on the plea that she was not doing responsible work. He is just about like the majority of committee members and quite as short-sighted. Our public assistance staff is a very small one and there is enough rest centre work to keep two persons going, which leaves (apart from public assistance officer and relieving officers) five, of whom two are definitely leaving and one may be called up. This would leave two and if Ruth left one only to run public assistance for West Suffolk. By that time we'd either have to give up holding meetings or I'd give my notice in! …

Saturday, 5 December

Went to Cambridge. My brother was in mufti and looked not a scrap different for having been in the Army for five or six months. Says in the Army you hardly know there is a war on and you don't trouble to follow events as when a civilian. His wife is still alone in the house but must share it. Thinks she will offer accommodation to a school teacher who at present pays 30s. weekly and does her own work, and may be glad of a change. The British Restaurant is next door and they could both lunch there, as she does now. Says it is beautifully clean (as Bury is also) and there is plenty to eat, with liberal supplies of vegetables which Bury has not, except of haricot beans. Swedes to eat the other day at Bury so they were preparing some plates without and some with and asking all persons if they liked swedes. I do and so got about half a normal helping, but some people who came later got about a teaspoonful. Perhaps they haven't the necessary cooking utensils, or people to prepare vegetables. Shops are packed with vegetables, and they are cheap enough. A schoolmaster has asked my sister-in-law to take him and his wife and child in and provide firing and light for 23s. a week. She does not want to as she thinks she would feel a lodger in her own house and in view of the wear and tear of her things (which are nearly new and very good) she might be out of pocket. Yet if people are billeted I think the housewife gets about

5s. weekly, though that may be for only one person, plus, in some cases, the itch, impetigo, vermin or only dirt. I still think that in this war the housewife has had a very rough deal.

In the train a woman going to see her husband who has been in a nursing home for six months with nervous breakdown supposed to have occurred through working at his own job by day and as an unpaid warden at night. A lot of these wardens broke down – some with bad legs, some with TB, and so on. All right so long as few raids but men cannot work night and day. As they were unpaid there were not enough of them to make the duties light enough. On that account I was glad when my brother-in-law got in the Army.

I wonder if any of my letters to M-O have been censored yet. The very address 'Mass Observation' seems to suggest that they would be. In my disgruntled attitude, however, if they are they are, and to hell with the censors. If the swine desire to destroy me they will, whether I write or keep dumb. In my fear I loathe and hate them, as one mostly does when in fear. I suppose if they let the internee out I'd immediately forget them, but what chance is there? Having imprisoned him for nothing since June 1940 why should they now let him out? Nothing on this earth can make them and God is silent. I suppose there is a God but in these days the world seems to be wallowing in the deepest hell. Hell could not possibly be worse than this world is now, even though I personally have so far kept on the crust of it and have not fallen in.

Man in waiting room saw me reading newspaper and asked the news. Said he didn't think people in this country were all they should be. An old man and said in his youth if villagers met people from another village there was a fight, because villagers then were so ignorant, but as villagers became better educated that stopped, and he didn't see why, with the spread of education, this war should have come about. Said in his time a clergyman might earn as much as the whole of his village and often clergymen had to help decide amount of poor relief and were inhuman. Said he used to know a cripple who was allowed 1s. 6d. a week and a dirty old sack of black flour, and the flour used to be thrown in his doorway and he was such a bad cripple it would take him a quarter of an hour to fetch it in.

Hats. My sister-in-law saw a hat she liked – a brown felt with green suede band round crown. Went in shop and tried it on and said she'd have it and what was the price. 'Four guineas, madam [i.e., £4 4s.].' 'Then I won't have it. I would have gone up to two but I don't think it would be right for me to pay you four guineas for a hat.' In a lukewarm fashion the assistant agreed with her. I still keep wearing scarves round my head.

Monday, 7 December

… the chief interests of the day have centred around food. Breakfasted on oats and tea. Gooch gave me a small pastry at 11 a.m. left over from a party the

ARP Control people had the previous evening – they have to cater for themselves on Control work and the men take turns with the girls in preparing meals. The Shire Hall possesses a gas stove for cooking in a very small kitchen. Took from 12.30 to 1 p.m. off as my sheets, etc. had been waiting for two weeks to go to the laundry, which is shut when I am free, except on Saturday afternoon, and of course this Saturday I went to Cambridge. Having gone to the laundry I decided to lunch at home, so reheated mutton, parsnips, turnips and potatoes. It was a profusion of vegetables but I don't suppose I'll get many the rest of the week as it will be Bury British Restaurant except Friday and on Friday it will be sandwiches in committee. One gets very hungry here, which in a way is fortunate because one can eat rougher food. At Bexhill-on-Sea I walked around my first three weeks there before I could get enough appetite to eat any meat and I never got hungry but only a bit faint. Here I started by getting so hungry I felt hollow inside. After the mutton etc. I reheated porridge I didn't finish at breakfast and drank tea. It was time to return. Tonight I went to fetch paraffin so bought ¼lb (1s.) egg powder. The milkman had left me no milk so I thought I'd better make an egg custard with powder milk for tomorrow's breakfast, for I don't expect to be energetic enough to cook the remainder of last week's bacon. When I had unlimited milk I ate corn flakes, but these now being rationed I eat oats, with milk if possible. This egg powder smells fresher than the tinned egg powder we are allowed on our ration books and at the moment the shops have lots of it for sale to anybody. So I mixed two ounces egg with milk powder and sugar and water and it cooked while I finished up my weekly meat ration, toasted scone and margarine, almond cake and jam and cocoa made of cocoa, sugar and powdered milk and boiling water. Since then, though I wanted it for breakfast, I have eaten more than two-thirds of the custard – *could* have eaten the lot, but remembered breakfast. The newspaper says among other things we should eat a pound of potatoes a day and says eight ounces [of] cheese a week. If that were all, how simple life would be – provided they were all clean potatoes. If I ate that lot I'd want no more, but think the diet would bring results not to be desired. The cheese could be managed if I ate a good ounce every teatime, or, as I fear I couldn't manage an ounce at one sitting, a quarter ounce at breakfast, dinner, tea and supper. I prefer potatoes to cheese, but to eat a pound a day would mean two ounces at British Restaurant and fourteen ounces here at night, and as it takes me three hours to bake them I reckon I'd sit from 9 to 10 p.m. each evening stuffing myself with fourteen ounces of potatoes! Still, I'd rather do that than eat eight ounces [of] cheese weekly.

There still seem to be other things on the market, however. Saturday evening I bought fish and chips and was surprised to find the fish still being sold cooked at 4d. a piece. It was excellent fish, too. Not like the fish we had in a London County Council hospital. There we had lots and lots of Roman Catholics and so RCs and Protestants had an abnormal amount of fried fish and chips, but the fish wasn't firm and cheerful like fish-shop fried fish, it was always limp and tired. I had it for three years. Speaking generally, that diet in hospital was the coarsest I personally have ever had, but to my surprise (for I always imagined nurses were half-starved) we had plenty to eat. It gave me piles, but nothing worse. Despite rushed meals and coarse food, I think I never met a nurse who suffered from indigestion – they seemed altogether more prone to rheumatism. A few (usually Irish) got TB, but almost certainly they caught that nursing TB cases in closed wards and under unhygienic conditions, I daresay they still do.

I can write no more – even about food!

Ruth. Public assistance officer said, as if he had accomplished something worth while, 'Miss Romaine is going to be X-rayed at Newmarket Thursday'. I said, 'Well, I've never had any idea that her chest is weak (she has bronchial catarrh at the moment) but I think she doesn't take enough care of herself and comes here from Stowmarket without breakfast. What I'm afraid of is that one of these days she'll decide to work in Stowmarket. I wish they'd pay her enough here to make it worth her while to stay.' He said 'They won't do that', to which I answered 'They will find themselves in the soup if she goes'. And there the matter rests and meanwhile she will be X-rayed. She probably had influenza and the doctor allowed her out too quickly. She says the only decent doctors in Stowmarket have either died or gone on war-work.

Built-in Wardrobe. My chief recompense for living at 62, Guildhall Street, has been the temporary possession of a really good wardrobe for clothes and bed-linen, etc. Lately I wondered why my black fur coat was wet when I took it out, but I dried it for a couple of evenings before the fire and put it back. Tonight I find the woodwork at the back of the wardrobe is all wet. Lucky I've escaped rheumatism, for I'm always wearing things out of that wardrobe without airing them first. Suppose it is on the outside wall or my neighbour's roof is leaking once again. Her house also belongs to my landlord, but the rent is only 15s. a week, so she must expect a few more inconveniences! Her house is always leaking through here somewhere, though previously it has been in the downstairs part of the house. I've nowhere else to put my clothes, for the other cupboard is open to the elements where plaster has come away from laths, and anything I put in there goes mouldy. If the wardrobe is no good, I think I really had better look for other rooms – there are none, that's the trouble. Besides, half the houses in this town are probably about the same. *If* somebody were building estate houses I'd buy one and risk letting part of it, but nobody builds in wartime, unfortunately. So here in this decrepit old place I'll have to stay, and thank God each morning that the ceiling hasn't collapsed on me or the floor beneath given way! After the mice had kept me awake an hour or so last night planes sounded low and quick and angry. I hoped and presumed they were our own and hoped in any case they would not fall on our decrepit old town.

Once war ends and people are housed, anybody who likes can use gunpowder and blow up these habitations. Even though, of course, they are quaint to look at and have become almost a living entity in their antiquity and unlikeness to each other. You never know with these houses where to look for windows or doors, and even doorsteps may be round the corner instead of in front of the door. And at sunset time they acquire charm and you feel you are living in a somewhat grotesque fairy tale and not in an ordinary town. They are alive in a way a modern place never is. But unfortunately the owners have neglected them shamefully throughout the ages. But for this neglect, the place might almost have rivalled Stratford-on-Avon, which of course is well-kept, speaking generally. It was nice to spend a day in Cambridge in a house where the windows aren't broken, where the ceiling is white instead of grey, and where the wallpaper is good, tasteful and clean. I really felt better and more alive for that day out. Suppose if I disposed of this furniture I might get a job in Cambridge and live there, but I don't want to get rid of the furniture until after the internee has been released. Occasionally I hear of quite decent lodgings here, but no one has rooms for the furniture in addition to me. Also, I like space enough to dump my possessions, even if the wardrobe *is* wet! One cannot have everything. I'd better see if I can rinse the soap out of the washing I did Sunday. They have to be rinsed in a hand-bowl (as I've no bath or sink) and most of the soap gets left in. I can't help living like a slum woman in this house, when I haven't even a sink. My landlord says – well, my landlord says the utmost, but as far as I know, never acts. I have no room for my landlord, nor, for that matter, for his wife. She is, at any rate, as scrooge-like as her master. Besides, my last landlord was a gentleman!! He painted a partition for me and gave me all his unwanted tea chests! And he'd got a sense of humour and wasn't a scrooge. In short, he was a gentleman and this one is not. He went away in the Merchant Service, and then the war began. This one won't ever go away – he's doing something with 'Man Power' now, I believe.

Tuesday, 8 December

… *Casuals.* Public assistance officer was talking today about something making excellent casual wards after the war, and I said, laughingly, 'But we shan't have any casuals after the war'. 'Don't you believe it,' he answered, 'we always do after a war. Look at last time, ex-soldiers selling matches in the street.' 'Yes,' I agreed, 'with their medals on'.…

General Election. Possibly through newspaper mentioning this in relation to ration cards, I heard it said today that probably we would have an election and some members of the Cabinet would find themselves outside the Cabinet. If we do, I'm wondering who I'll have to vote for. I looked it up the other week and found that a Captain Heilgers is MP for here. I take it he is a Conservative, this being a Conservative place, but I've never seen or heard anything about him. In districts such as these it is no good attending election meetings with a view to knowing your candidates, because the Conservative meetings consist entirely of 'He's a jolly good fellow' and at the opposition meetings you would probably get a stone in your eye.[48]

Bacon. On Mondays and Tuesdays and until after 2 p.m. on Wednesdays my shop reserves bacon for country customers. On Saturdays they are sold out so for other people it leaves Thursdays and Fridays. I shall be at Newmarket Friday so it leaves Thursday; but as bacon doesn't interest me much three times out of four I don't trouble to get it. There are lots of beef sausages about at 8d. a lb so I substitute those if necessary, i.e., if milk is short.

Wednesday, 9 December

Beef sausages all day. Got them ready for breakfast but as my watch had lost an hour missed breakfast. British Restaurant 1 p.m. Had 1½ beef sausages. Came home this evening and ate my breakfast. I also had a tiny fragment of suet pudding and golden syrup at the British Restaurant, four little slices of carrot and a few potatoes, and I helped myself to a slice of bread to fill up. I think they *must* have cooking difficulties at the British Restaurant, or they would not offer bread when Lord Woolton keeps appealing to people to eat potatoes. Funnily, the wall is decorated with many posters saying carrots will enable us to see in the dark and we must eat more vegetables and salads, so we look at pictures of cabbages in gardens, etc., etc., and eat our own very meagre supply, while the shops outside are full of them.

Potatoes. Big space in today's newspaper saying it is patriotic to eat potatoes. Better than the last war, when they were scarce and we had to eat rice instead. The newspaper also gives recipes for serving potatoes at breakfast, lunch and supper. These fiddling recipes are all right for people with unlimited time at their disposal and a kitchen which is always ready for the cook, but the average housewife would prefer to fry her potatoes at breakfast, boil them at lunch, and bake them in the evenings. In this part of the world, too, the housewife has done enough cooking when she has cooked breakfast and lunch, and she hopes for a cold supper which won't make much washing-up. She may be forced to cook for supper now, but she doesn't like it. I think in Whitechapel they used to sell hot baked potatoes in the streets – a pity we can't start Baked Potato Snack Bars. I'm sure we would eat baked potatoes at 11 a.m. in the Shire Hall *if* we had time to cook and eat them and a room in which we could eat them. I asked today why Miss Penly Cooper [former Chief Health Visitor] got her OBE and was told for starting CNR nurses in West Suffolk, so I said I'd get one for starting a canteen for the Shire Hall! ...

---

[48] Major Frank Frederick Alexander Heilgers (b.1892) was the Conservative MP for the Bury St Edmunds division of Suffolk. He had been first elected in 1931 and returned unopposed in 1935. His residence was Wyken Hall, Bardwell. He was to be killed in a railway accident in January 1944.

M.P. Looking at a list of our county councillors today I saw the name 'Major Heilgers' so asked if he had any connection with Captain Ditto our Member of Parliament. Was told one and the same but had risen to Major. Asked what he was like and was told 'Nothing out of the ordinary, but pleasant, dapper, and liked by the ladies'.

Our county councillors are mainly my Public Assistance Committee people but there is also a Sir William Brunegate (whoever he may be)[49] and a few others and some from the borough including my landlord, Robert Ollé. You say the name sounding every syllable and in the best 'county' bawl, for (though I'm not Irish) ''Tis a very important person it is.' No, he is not 'county'. Most people hereabouts are, but he only mixes with it. The 'county' business tickled me when I got here as I hadn't been used to it, but in Bury St Edmunds you either are 'county' or you are not. Robert, like myself, is not. He is not, I should say, any better for that. My God! Fancy my landlord being a member of the high body the *county council*!

Booze. Paper says 850,000 acres of land now used for brewers. Mr C. Roberts of Cumberland wanted this reduced but Lieutenant Colonel G.H. Long of Bury St Edmunds opposed as it would affect public morale. He said that shortage of beer in this district had caused more dissatisfaction than anything he knew of during the war. I asked Joan at the office (whose father works at the brewery here) if she knew Long and she said she had heard of him but didn't know if he were a brewery shareholder. What a country! Strikes me if the morale of the public is dependent on the supply of beer, then we are all a lot of moraleless wallowing swine, whether we get the beer or not. To think I was born in the county of West Suffolk!! Where the intellect rises to the heights attained by Lieutenant Colonel Long.[50]

Actually, I do not know anything about drink here. The public assistance officer manages to get a bottle here and a bottle there. Real port seems unobtainable but I think anybody can get a limited supply of spirits and other things. People say beer in these days isn't worth drinking, anyhow. Joan talks of poverty in the Hill 60 district because the men won't forego their beer and other luxuries – that is one of the slum areas, mainly council houses. A Birmingham girl was amazed at the terribleness of our slums here but I don't go into houses. If one looks in the windows of the better-class tumble-down

---

[49] Sir William Brunegate (1867–1943), who had held positions with the British government for many years in Egypt, lived in Boxford and had served on the West Suffolk County Council.

[50] Lieutenant-Colonel Gerald Hanslip Long, OBE, farmed in Fornham St Martin. The demand for beer increased significantly during the war, not least among members of the Forces, of whom there were many in West Suffolk, and efforts to meet these demands were thought to be important to morale, especially men's. Winifred clearly thought differently.

houses there is nearly always lovely and expensive antique furniture, though the shops only sell the most shoddy furniture procurable and at exorbitant prices. The smaller places I do glimpse are usually clean and tidy.[51] I don't know if there is a lot of drinking here amongst civilians, or even whether there are any civilians to speak of to drink. The Suffolk Hotel and some others I fancy cater very largely for officers, who of course usually do drink a lot. The Playhouse Bars seem to specialise in NCOs, though I think if any of them want to make beasts of themselves, Mrs Jarrold quickly has them sent out. A rowdy lot of privates sometimes turn out of a snack bar in this part of the town and there's a certain percentage of drunken soldiers who roll by this house – it used to be every Saturday night in particular but I haven't lived in the front of the house lately and it may not be so now. The Irish (many are on aerodrome or sugar beet work) drink and sing in pubs or outside. About the morale of the civilians I know nothing, but I would venture to suggest that the morale of the troops might be considerably *raised* by some interest or occupation other than guzzling or sexual intercourse with any girl they can pick up at the Corn Exchange dances (1s. or 1s. 6d. hops but about the only form of recreation provided where they can meet women) or on the streets. Bury St Edmunds does what it can in the way of canteens, but the Forces have a lot of time on their hands and nothing to do with it, and they get demoralised....[52]

Petrol. I suppose shortage of petrol makes people instinctively want to go for car rides. Some of our committee members have become amazingly regular in attendance since they could get petrol for attending meetings.[53]

Wangford – I believe that's the name and it is somewhere in Suffolk. I heard today that its population averaged eight persons to a square mile. Should think, if that is so, they can get plenty of fresh air. As we still have no signposts on our country roads I will not take out my old bicycle to explore it.[54]

---

[51] Hill 60, an important and contested site on the British sector of the Western Front in the First World War, was the name given to the Priors local authority housing estate in western Bury, which was built between the wars. The name arose from the rough character of this estate – 'our slum district', Winifred wrote on 28 September 1943. An outsider who visited Bury in early 1944 considered the town's housing to be poor (M-O Archive, FR 2035, pp.2–4).

[52] Apart from the Corn Exchange in Abbeygate Street, there were few rooms in Bury large enough for dances, which were much in demand, especially from members of the Forces. After £900 was spent on blacking-out the windows of the Corn Exchange, dances were often held there (*Bury Free Press*, 16 January 1943, p.1).

[53] No petrol was available for private motoring as of the beginning of July 1942.

[54] Wangford is six miles north of Mildenhall. See Map 2, p.xvi.

Thursday, 10 December

'God bless the Squire and his relations /And keep us in our proper stations.'

Elderly gentleman said in his youth they used to sing that. I think the atmosphere of it must have stretched to 40 years ago, for I attended a church elementary school and my parents belonging to the Church of England (Non-Conformists were excused) I was compelled to learn by heart the whole of the church catechism, and the part which made me really in the blackest mood in school was the bit 'that state of life unto which it hath (or shall – in these days I don't possess a prayer-book) pleased (or please) God to call me.' I was under seven years then and don't remember anyone ever explaining the phrase, but I know it used to put me in a state of revolt against religion. And although I never remember my parents taking the attitude, at a very early age and until I left Newmarket I used to burn with resentment at what I considered the patronage of such people as church district visitors. I am not so sure that this 'atmosphere' I am talking about has not lasted in Bury St Edmunds until this day. Of course even the remainder of that hated catechism was one of the horrors of my existence. It amazes me even now that my young nephews and niece *like* to go to church! ...

British Restaurant. Surely there must be a shortage of cooking utensils or something. The manageress always overlooks the serving of vegetables as she dishes out meat and at 1.05 p.m. today she said to me 'Do you like turnips?' and looked annoyed when I said 'Yes, I do'. The other woman picked up a fragment of turnip with a spoon and was going to pick up another bit, when the manageress took the plate away and remarked that they were nearly at the end of the turnips. By 1.07 p.m. no turnips were left. There are tons of turnips in the shops at 2d. a pound retail.

Nursery Schools. I see they have these in such small places as Lavenham, Hadleigh and Haverhill. Bury St Edmunds, with a population probably exceeding the population of all three together, has not. One is wanted here but nobody wants to trouble about running it.[55] They were late in starting the British Restaurant in a little old-fashioned disused school, but the mayor (and brewer) had hired the place for recreation for his employees and so was able to offer it and perhaps, as the brewery is near and has no canteen, he is glad of the British Restaurant to serve his staff too. There are one or two very nice women who help there – the one who serves tea has a Brigadier-General husband (I hear) and on 11th November '42 she was relieved to hear that he had been taken a prisoner-of-war and had not been killed at Singapore.

---

[55] There had been talk in late 1941/early 1942 of setting up a nursery school for the children of women engaged on work of national importance, but apparently nothing came of it (*Bury Free Press*, 3 January 1942, p.4). 'Because there's no nursery school,' Winifred wrote on 29 October 1943, 'mothers keep trying to put their babies in public institutions so they themselves can go out to work. Another case today.'

I lunch there with various people, including my late boss the Wool Control chief executive officer and his brother, the public health milk officer (very Scotch, like his boss the county medical officer), Shire Hall staff, usually female, once with several members of the Adelphi Players, and lately with a youth whose father is a Suffolk rector but who works I think in gas or electricity showrooms and who is studying for his LRAM [Licentiate of the Royal Academy of Music]. He originated in Yorkshire I think and at first I wondered why he was so interested in books on music. Today he offered to lend me plays of Chekhov (*Seagull, Cherry Orchard*, and another) but I read them a few years ago. He says they were recently on the wireless.

Downstairs tenant has put up new net and cretonne curtains at her front window downstairs. Just fresh and ordinary and cost her £4 4s. They would be no good for blacking-out, but there are some green velvet ones behind them. She started work today.

I was interested to get a note of some M-O activities from Mr Willcock today. It is interesting to know what is going on. I wonder if the authorities will allow it to continue or if, being creative, it will get blotted out.[56]

Jews. Papers continue to say that Hitler has decreed the massacre of the Jewish race. It seems unbelievable. I wonder if it is our propaganda, or if it really is happening. I quite believe many are getting massacred, but I can't understand *any* government deliberately ordering it. It makes the killing of the First-Born in the hope of killing the baby Jesus appear quite a trivial pastime. I still wonder what we shall do with all our foreign residents after the war. The young ones, like my internee, who is Swedish-Dutch-German but not Jewish, can quite easily blend with us, but the Jews on the whole are a race apart, and even before the war they seemed to control most of our trade – cinemas, hats, clothing, food, etc., etc., so that round Whitechapel and Stepney way it seemed that the wealthy were Jewish and the thin, tuberculous, poverty-stricken ones were the Gentiles. Londoners are extremely kind to Jews, but will there arise trouble if after the war we British get hungry? Still, the English (not Scotch, Irish and Welsh) are extremely docile.

Tuesday, 15 December

Diary neglected lately. My 'lack of energy' period is on again and Xmas is looming near and I've been busy regarding NALGO. I *ought* to be writing Xmas letters and packing up books for my small relations and looking out clothes for the holiday and doing the last three or four weeks washing and house-cleaning, instead of which I'll just ram something into a case Xmas week and with luck get the postal affairs done, and leave all the mess until

---

[56] H.D. (Bob) Willcock was at this time a director of Mass-Observation and a central figure in its day-to-day work. He was author of the about-to-be-published article 'Mass-Observation', *American Journal of Sociology*, vol. 68, no. 4, January 1943.

I return. There is one bright spot on the horizon – the Adelphi Players are doing *Don Juan* and *Easter* and a Nativity play this weekend. Thank God for that.

An invalid (late policeman) friend of mine wrote me recently. He has a chair he can get to an office in and the office have made him a special desk and he likes the job and his wife has a massage business and they live in a pleasant place in the south of England and he is always optimistic and now says the war news is such that unlike last year people can this year have a Happy Xmas in the hope of victory. Sounds O.K. but two girls today with husbands in the Forces out East were not looking forward to it and one said she'd prefer to be at work. I am too much 'in the dumps' to look forward to anything though am lucky in that my soldier relations are still in England. I shall have as much creature comfort as usual. And if not turkey to eat at least chicken and pheasant and if I get as far as Staines [Middlesex] and St Albans that will be a bit like old times. Yet I feel encompassed in gloom. I haven't heard from the internee for weeks and though he tells me nothing, or next to nothing when he writes, I get afraid the strain of being shut up has resulted in the almost inevitable nervous breakdown, or some other horror has occurred. He is not the only one in that camp, either, who is in danger of a breakdown. I want to curse and call upon God to hasten his vengeance upon rogues and brutes – all because I hate being in this fuming, completely helpless and fearful state. My temper ordinarily is a placid one but it now centres itself entirely in one place – if this is Bunyan's 'Valley of Despair' (or whatever he called it) I don't like it, and am in the way of climbing to the top and throwing myself to destruction. And anybody feeling like that is, I should say, in a *very* bad temper, a devilish bad temper. I'd better eat the meal I've cooked or it will be cold again. What a horrible life this is.

The siren went today at 1.30 p.m. and seemed a ghastly howl. It has been howling all the wartime and today I wondered if it could possibly howl for nothing for the entire wartime. In the office we spend countless hours preparing for raids and invasion and yet I feel sure most of us would get the surprise of our lives if we were invaded. A Scot of my acquaintance – by birth in a particularly high position – tells me, I think in all sincerity, that St Edmund will look after his realm in these parts. I suppose he has a Celtic touch, for I, a Suffolker, expect as much from a dead saint as from a dead worm. This last war, however, has suggested to me that this world of humans does represent the struggle between good and evil – I wonder which will win, or whether, if evil should triumph, it will destroy even itself in the extinction of the human race. I was feeling sorry the other day that Noah ever built an ark! No, I haven't even any belief about that ark, though it used to be one of my favourite toys.

Now for the diary proper. I went to Newmarket Emergency Hospital meeting on the 11th instant and going along in my boss's car a retired former committee member remarked that there was an old saying 'It's a poor man who can't eat a partridge for his breakfast'. We talk a lot about food these days. At the afternoon meeting (or rather during the tea – with nice cakes – which followed it) a man who used to be governor of a colony or something said he had four sprats served to him at breakfast and the clerk laughed and said he thought in peacetime if he had sprats he had forty, not four. Mrs Stafford Allen said fishing yarns were now being replaced by stories about feeding chickens, and everybody seemed to be going about asking 'What do *you* feed your chickens on?' …

At the hostel meeting it was agreed to pay a young domestic £40 a year all found, and to my great surprise the clerk said it made the county scale for a clerk with school-leaving certificate, £45 a year and nothing found, seem very low. At the hospital meeting Mrs Allen had ticked him off a bit when he said that although persons in billets needed ration money when on holiday, those who went home on holiday did not because their parents would keep them. I suppose he thinks that all parents are like himself (I'm sure he is generous enough to his youngsters) but he forgets parents don't all earn his £1500 a year. Despite all my remarks, he isn't really a bad sort. I've met thousands very much worse – that may sound exaggerated but I believe I've taken dictation from about 300 in the course of my 25 or 26 jobs, so I probably have *known* thousands. Being a shorthand-typist and so without exciting prospects, I used to change jobs when I began to get bored. I did not want to change my work of shorthand and typewriting, etc. but I wanted to use it as a means for getting about the world and meeting people, and it was nice to change, say, from engineering to hats, and building society to, perhaps, horticulture. But after I became a trained nurse and was 37 and in London I found nobody wanted typists of that age, whatever their qualifications. In fact, the market was so bad that the private agencies had no jobs to offer to anybody who, being as old as 30, desired to earn more than pocket-money. That was London, about 1938 [in fact, she turned 42 that year], and by then I'd only 30 pounds left in the world, so I went to Bexhill thinking if I had to starve I might as well starve in pleasant surroundings as on London's grey streets. In London I had begun to visualise the prospect of selling matches at street corners, and the idea didn't appeal to me. It was good that I went to Bexhill, but life wouldn't stand still and so here I am now, moaning my life away. The policeman suggests that if my job is temporary I should get a permanent one, but what is permanency, and where should I get it? I could get a dozen tomorrow, but they would all be 'for duration'.…

Wednesday, 16 December

Ruth the typist has to go to hospital for a fortnight after Xmas and Dorothy the typist leaves us tomorrow. I suggested postponing my last summer's holiday until after Ruth's return but Gooch said to the public assistance officer very pointedly that *he* would borrow a typist from the clerk's department and the public assistance officer said he would do the meetings, and I must go. The bigger meetings do not fall the week I am away. Today I have been playing with the idea of writing to the county council to ask for increased wages – can't see it would do any harm, even if they won't agree. (A plane has just gone over – very noisy and I fancy the lowest that has ever passed over this house during my occupation. Only one plane, I think. We had an air-raid warning at 2 a.m. today but I slept through it, as I usually do the early part of the night, fortunately. I suppose these warnings are useful for people who have to go on duty, but so far as I know they have been very little help to the general public, bombs being as likely to fall before or after as between the alert and all clear. I should have been a wreck by now if I had got up for them – or even dead if I'd spent too much time sheltering in a cellar, or an Anderson shelter supposing we had one. I do not know, however, if these shelters have been supplied here. A few people have built their own under-ground shelters but lots of these old houses have cellars with thick walls and thick arches overhead. If we had prolonged bombing I should descend to this one, because it is a congested area and the cellar would probably prevent surrounding houses from striking one if they fell. A field with an open trench might be safer but the field is not available about here.)...

I am not often nervous and this old house gets all sorts of bumps and bangs and shakings when traffic passes or the wind blows or one walks across the floor or somebody shuts a door downstairs or in the street, but during the last few minutes (it is now 10.20 p.m.) two very big shocks rattled the door of this room. Probably it is a rough night – there are lesser noises too – but that door shook much as one did at Staines when bombs were dropped ten minutes' walk distant, and also much as it did when a land mine was dropped ten miles or so away in a field. The siren has not gone – a plane is droning overhead – I'll find out tomorrow if anything did fall anywhere. So far as bombs are concerned I do feel much safer these days: when I go out I expect to find the house still standing on my return, and that didn't seem very certain a year or so ago. I was at Sudbury the day our only bombs ('touch wood'!) were dropped, but the tenant downstairs said she stood in her doorway and the whole of Guildhall Street seemed to sway to and fro. I think it might and in that way such houses might remain standing when the more modern ones, unable to sway, would break off.

Children get used to war. My young niece felt perfectly safe in an Anderson shelter because she had an idea they were bomb-proof! Each time a warning came she first bid goodbye to her nearby rabbits, thinking they were left out in the danger zone. In the shelter she usually cut out dolls' frocks in cardboard. In the house one day she was playing with a model village and I asked her why she had arranged it so that a lamp-post and a few other things were lying on the ground; she answered that the village had had an air-raid, of course. She was about six years old then. One game then with her older boy cousin was for him to be a soldier and get shot and she was the nurse and somehow managed to drag him on to a settee and bandage him up. Both her father and mother attended first aid classes and the child knew as much about bandaging as they did through watching or helping them. She was very keen to be a nurse until she concluded she did not want to get married because there would be such a lot of homework to do, and then she remarked that she'd be a shorthand-typist like myself because that would be easier! A small friend told her, triumphantly, that anyhow she'd *have* to get married when her mother died....

Miss Eleanor Rathbone wrote an excellent article in today's paper, calling it 'Let the Hunted Come In'. Apparently she does not consider the story of the wholesale massacre and the threatened extermination of European Jewry propaganda, for she speaks of it as a fact. She thinks that we ought not to shut our doors to genuine refugees so that they perish, at least when we have every evidence that they are genuine. She quotes a bit of Chaucer I like: 'Christ's law and that of His Apostles Twelve He taught, but first he followed it Himself'. She goes on about the internment question, which of course concerns me. 'It should not be regarded as the principal concern of a Home Secretary, over-burdened with other departmental duties and now a member of the War Cabinet, who apparently regards dealing with refugees as a tiresome extension of his previous duties concerning casual wards, prisons and other places of deterrent treatment for undesirables who must be kept from being a nuisance and got rid of as soon as possible. The refugee question is too big for that. It deserves the undivided attention of an internationally minded minister who could view the question as a whole, deal with its present developments in co-operation with the other relevant ministers and plan for its future. If that had been done several years ago it might have prevented incalculable suffering and saved tens of thousands of lives.' We ought to thank God on our knees that we have women such as Miss Rathbone who dare speak the truth despite the fact that the Home Secretary could by a word throw her into prison for speaking against him. Perhaps at last something will begin to be done about our heedless destruction of friendly refugees. I wrote her tonight and thanked her, telling her my own hands are tied in this connection owing to the fact that any action of mine is supposed to have an adverse effect on my internee's prospects of release.[57]

Heard tonight that my brother-in-law has had his embarkation leave. I was not expecting it yet and cannot say that the shock was a pleasant one. I only hope if he goes abroad that he will return to my sister and niece safely.

---

[57] This article was published in the *News Chronicle*, Thursday, 17 December 1942, p.2. Eleanor Rathbone (b.1872), feminist and social reformer, was Independent MP for the Combined English Universities. She had a longstanding commitment to addressing the plight of refugees. The fact that this item was published the day after the date of this diary entry is not surprising, given that Winifred did not write for M-O every day and occasionally erred in her dating. Such chronological confusions are common in diaries.

There is just a loophole that may prevent him from going yet. Some months ago a lorry went over his foot and apparently recovery is not yet entirely complete. So I *may* see him after Xmas. Lots of youngsters are being called up before Xmas and don't like it – they wish it had been left until *after* Xmas. But war, of course, can't be expected to suit our convenience. A girl told me the other day that her soldier husband had been on the water 10 days before she knew there was any question of his going abroad, and that certainly was very bad luck....

Rugs. The downstairs tenant couldn't buy a rug so went to Smith's the furnishing people here. I think it was £3 15s. they asked for one but as it was a second-hand and worn piece of stair runner about two yards long she refused to buy it and says the shop assistant was very offhand and said he could sell it easily elsewhere, there was no need for her to have it. Their things have been terribly expensive for years now.[58]

At lunchtime today I went into a Sudbury second-hand shop and bought two pictures. They are in apparently new gilt frames 24 inches × 16 inches outside. I got them because frames are difficult to obtain but I see the views are pleasant. They are water-colours, I understand (and they look like it), and behind glass, and one is a view of near and far mountains (I imagine Welsh) and the other is a harvest field with mountains in the background and also, I imagine, Welsh. I take it they are modern. They are signed 'F. Robson'. Now if I had bought a cardboard copy of one of them, with a calendar hanging below it, and no glass or frame, I should have had to pay from 5s. to 7s. 6d. Being what they are, however, I got them, and the man tied them up for me and dusted them for me, and charged me two shillings and sixpence each. Who would choose to live on the salary of an artist!! Five shillings for those two pictures and £3 15s. for a bit of carpet which in peacetime would have been put in a jumble sale – truly the days of the material, not the spiritual, are here.

R.H. Ward of the Adelphi Players has courage, I realised tonight as I watched *Don Juan* (by James Elroy Flecker). We all need courage these days, courage to be individuals and if necessary to give up life as a soldier gives it up. I am not a soldier's wife but I realised tonight in that room at the County School where the play was acted, that there is no reason why I should escape the horrors of the times, even if hitherto my life has been humdrum and without highlights. I went to the Moral Welfare Home to tea and a young woman had arrived with her baby. It seemed she had lost her home and was following her soldier husband round and finding it difficult to get accommodation with little money and a baby. She had some bad teeth too which were aching but was a fine-looking young woman, a bit in the tragic mode. She had been plodding around looking for a shelter in the

---

[58] Smith's Furnishing Company was at 37 and 38 Cornhill.

rain and then the police suggested St Elizabeth's. A big baby of nineteen months, big enough for three years, and it seemed friendly enough. She says its clothes are frightfully expensive to buy and I'm sure of that. *Don Juan* was very good.[59]

Miss Jarman, daughter of the photographer who photographed myself and my internee's belongings, came in to see *Don Juan* and in passing my chair told me the authorities had returned the photo to her despite her permit to send them. Oh, I'm scared of those people and scared because I've received no letter for weeks. It is like they used to remark about the war 'a war of nerves'. That is what it is for me. I was worried just before last Xmas because, though he was on his way from Australia, the authorities told me he was not and that the cable he had sent me was a mistake. The weather was bitterly cold too and I did not know if he was on the sea or would have to remain in Australia for duration. I was worried then. I am glad he has got as far as the Isle of Man, but again I'm scared. Last year I thought the authorities stupid and I was mad with them, but this year I am terrified of what they may be doing to him and what they will do next to either of us or both. This is my portion of the war and I may need courage even as so many in the world need it. One needs cleverness too as well as courage and I may not possess the former. This devilish inhumanity which is now dominant in the world is apt to make its victims quiver. Sometimes I feel that I am important as an individual and that my actions in the world count. Perhaps one is conscious just at those moments that one has that apparently highly dangerous thing, a soul. It is all the inanimate soulless stuff in the universe which tends to destroy one's body. The soul may win but if one has no belief in a future world, if one is dead and all one cares about is dead too, then all is tragedy. One is just crushed out of existence, that is all. Many of us, one way or another, may be in fear of that now. Surely if there were a God the agony of the world at present would bring some definite response? It is man's wickedness, not God's, which has made this war, but surely God made man – or was it the Devil who made most of them? One might say I ought to trust my fellow men, but does one trust a human brute who is beating a baby with a stick?

---

59 The Adelphi Players were founded in 1941 by Richard Heron Ward (b.1910). They were a travelling company, committed to progressive and democratic values and 'an ethical theatre of service and integrity' (Peter Gillingham, in his Introduction to Cecil Davies, *The Adelphi Players: The Theatre of Persons* (London and New York, 2002), p.xvii). At this time all the male actors in the company, including Ward, were conscientious objectors. Cecil Davies, who was a member of the Players, recalled 'a conversation in a commercial hotel in Bury St Edmunds. At table, the landlady began, in the manner of one who thinks she is about to uncover some unsavoury secret, to remark that what puzzled her was how it came about that so many men, young and apparently fit for military service, were permitted to remain in the Company and do this work' (*ibid.*, p.52).

I'd better go to bed – I've work to do tomorrow morning. Don't know yet if I'll go and see *Don Juan* again in the afternoon. Meantime and all the time, whether I get letters or not, there is this long-drawn-out torture of fear and uncertainty. The hideous, callous brutes. Perhaps I write these things in the hope that they will reach somebody and something will be done, but it is *most* unlikely. Babies are not given what they cry for and God never answers specific prayers. At least, I suppose he might answer a prayer for courage, but it is useless appealing to have a horror averted, so far as I know. Whatever one is doomed to go through must be braved – there is no escape.

What cynicism – a Happy Xmas! To think that a world like this dare celebrate the birth of an innocent child. I would not be a mother for anything I can see; there could be no crime so great as to bring a helpless baby into this world of fiends.

Monday, 21 December

Well, I went to see *Don Juan* again. Very few people there but not many like using their brains or having their souls questioned. Mentality in all classes of West Suffolk life is very dark, though other people also in all classes are enlightened. Heredity probably accounts for a lot. Sunday afternoon I went to the nativity play *Holy Family* by the Adelphi Players (written by one of them – R.H. Ward). A good number there and the play was given in the Congregational chapel. A smaller but similar chorus to that in T.S. Eliot's *Murder in the Cathedral*. They are excellent actors. The play was by the chorus who also acted individually taking several parts, in some cases, each, as well as returning to join the chorus in between the parts. I daresay most of the audience got more than they bargained for. We had gone for the scenic effect of a pretty religious play suitable for children. We got drama and poetry and realism and elocution, and probably to most an unheard-of idea. Into the nativity play was the background of war, crucifixion, and Easter, and *we* were the people who refused room to Mary and crucified her son, and we'd got to realise that God's light was *in* us, not shining *on* us, and every baby was holy and had to live his life even if, in saving men's souls, he brought crucifixion on him. Actually, this play was the nearest answer I've ever got in regard to my remarks on page 56 [of manuscript diary: the last paragraph for 16 December] to the effect that giving life is the biggest sin. It isn't a thing anyone could answer. We have to take it that Mary felt God was with her and therefore she had courage to let her son live his life and to bear the pain of it. Perhaps to greater or lesser degree all pregnant women feel like that. I don't know and have never courted pain. I know that many girls in St Elizabeth's Moral Welfare Home are enraptured with their illegitimate children after arrival and there is nothing too good for the children, but there are others with brains no more receptive than those of animals who will probably neglect the children and 'fall' again with other men. It is a *great* story, anyhow, this one told by R.H. Ward and dedicated to Phoebe Waterfield who acts with him.[60]

I think one reason I broke away from the church was its unreality. Christ was someone who took all our burdens on himself by getting crucified and he was divine and we were ordinary and human and born in sin (presumably all born in lust) and I didn't like the idea of having to suffer death and didn't see the sense in the crucifixion when we also were doomed to die and it was all black and gloomy and lifeless. Then I realised that the pagan poets found or promised something worth while in this life and I was glad to proclaim myself an atheist. I'd have had no light or life at all if I hadn't, and even now I haven't learnt the way to face annihilation except, perhaps, by becoming so fed-up with life that one doesn't care. I hate death, though of course the story of the play gives it that out of death springs life. Maybe! Perhaps if one lived one wouldn't mind death rounding it off – not so much, anyway. I should probably fight it tooth and nail! I suppose in life there is always the feeling that in the future something may make life worth living, and so one carries on. My life is not satisfactory now. I don't know what is happening with the internee – perhaps he dare not write me again or they are intercepting our correspondence. That is my dark background. But there is also my listlessness and antipathy to physical exertion, and the work at which I earn a temporary living is varied and fairly interesting, but I never get finished in the office or at home and there are always duties to perform and I never feel I've any leisure or pleasure, apart, perhaps, from the visits of the Adelphi Players, when I shut the door on my housework and go to listen. I wrote R.H. Ward last night asking if his publisher would send a copy of *Holy Family* to the internee. As I am not allowed to keep the latter in touch with outside life I thought this play might do so for me. And I told R.H. Ward I'd probably tell Mass-Observation that they were like a lighted torch in the thick blackness of this district.

I am going to Newmarket for Xmas and then on to Staines and St Albans, leaving the undone things in office and home behind me, and knowing they will 'get me down' on my return. I'll be glad to see relations. And, oh God, there's a pile of washing-up awaiting me, and it's bedtime, and somehow I've got to get round to catch a train Thursday at 5.40 p.m. There's a bowl of washing been soaking for a week – fresh water daily – and really I ought

---

[60] *Holy Family* was first performed in the parish church of Stoke-by-Nayland on 16 November 1941 and elsewhere during that Christmas season (preface to the 1950 edition of the text published by the SPCK, p.vi). The *Bury Free Press*, 26 December 1942, p.8, reviewed the Adelphi Players' performances enthusiastically: 'They are all professionals, keen on the welfare of the drama, especially in war time, and, with the barest minimum of scenic and lighting effects, rely on their acting and presentation rather than theatrical effects – and the way they succeed many in Bury St Edmunds now appreciate to the full.'

to wash the things and hang them in the cupboard to dry. It would take ten minutes and I think of it for hours and the exertion of thinking about it tires me nearly to death! If I'd got a sink and a tap it would, of course, be easier. The landlord called tonight and I paid him £7 for 14 weeks' rent.

Gooch said Sir William Brunegate of the county council did his best to keep the WVS [Women's Voluntary Services] out of West Suffolk and the mayor even now 'will have no truck with them', but when Lady Reading [head of the WVS] came here to talk on WVS these two were there in full glory

1943

During the thirteen days between 22 December and 3 January, Winifred produced no entries in her diary. She was travelling and visiting relatives for part of this time. Upon returning to Bury St Edmunds early in the New Year, she resumed her writing.

Monday, 4 January

Fuel Economy. If I could spend about £300 I could turn these rooms of mine into a habitable flat. I have had my Xmas and last summer holiday together and went back to modern life in Staines, Richmond and St Albans, where there are electricity, baths, hot water, clean ceilings and walls, things such as clothing and crockery (especially in Richmond) for sale in the shops at reasonable prices. Richmond had even got a breakfast service for sale in one shop. The Zeeta Café gave us an excellent lunch for 2s. a head, and Richmond even retains a theatre. Now I am back. The tenant downstairs took some milk in readiness for me and invited me to take anything I lacked on arrival from her larder (or, to be correct, her food cupboard, which has no window). Her children had gone to Dovercourt for a holiday and were not back again. I am now shivering over a large fire though my legs are scorching. This might be obviated if I could afford to buy heavy curtains to hang over the doors. I suppose it is my glassless window in the attic bedroom which had caused the mildew on my trunk etc. there. I tumbled them downstairs in the midday daylight and into my front sitting room and the contents are now drying before my evening fire. I also lit a lamp and an oilstove in the other room to dry out the built-in wardrobe in my absence from the room. There were no mice in the houses of my recent hostesses, which was rather pleasant. It was necessary tonight to have a fire here which would warm things grouped round it even if it had no effect on the distant corners of the room. I think a large-sized pail I fetched coalite and coal up in holds about a third of a hundredweight. I emptied the whole of this on my fire plus a large, square log and I have since added three more very large logs. The same amount of firing in a modern grate would have lasted four times as long and given at least twice the heat. I am about two feet away with a thick frock and four-ply knitted jacket, stockings, ankle socks and fur-lined boots, and my back would certainly appreciate another coat.

I ought to start this diary from where the last bit left off and there is a lot to write, but it is 10.15 p.m. and I want to go to bed early. For the moment, therefore, I will report that Professor H[arold] Laski is talking in our Guild-hall, I believe on Saturday evening, about the Beveridge Report. I thought he would be very busy over the Jewish Refugee situation and it seems amazing Bury St Edmunds should receive the honour of his visit. I have heard him talk at Toynbee Hall and though I prefer Bernard Shaw shall be pleased to hear him again.[61] On Thursday there is another NALGO meeting regarding cost-of-living bonus etc.

Upon enquiry today I find that after the first three years at the Shire Hall employees do not pay unemployment insurance though they pay health insurance.

Tonight I have packed some grey wool (my sister being unable to procure any in Staines just now and I having some I bought months ago) for ankle socks for my niece aged 10. For the same reason – though the shoes I bought years ago – I have sent her two pairs of my rubber-soled shoes. She takes the same size as I do and about 1½ sizes larger than her mother. She had spectacles recently, the doctor saying that she had grown quicker than her eyesight but this would right itself in due course. He also said that menstruation at her age is not uncommon and women are now starting earlier and ending later, most women not finishing until after 50 in these days. He thought it was Nature getting her own back because women were limiting their families....

Today I collected the photo returned from the Isle of Man. I think the internee returned it himself so my annoyance was unrequired. I don't know why he returned it unopened but it might be because he had asked me not to send it and I had done so. There usually is a conflict of wills between us. Well, it can go in with my junk. I had a letter from him just before Xmas which was a first-rate effort and let me know that he would make the best of his Xmas and that the study of painting broke the monotony of his life. He also said that he had not yet given up hope of one day finding himself released. I don't know if I liked that entirely because this continual raising of hopes followed by continual crashing of them is perhaps more nerve-racking than to be without any particular hope. (I flew out of this room just now, for a series of bangs outside my window made me think I might be getting machine-gunned and that it would be better to get out of direct line with my window. It sounded like aeroplanes but may have been a car having a few explosions.) It is curious the effect a letter can have, for after receiving that

---

[61] Harold Joseph Laski (1893–1950) was professor of political science at the London School of Economics. He was a prominent writer and activist in the Labour Party, and a brilliant orator.

one I felt content about him and able to forget him and enjoy my own Xmas. This does not mean that as a rule he moans but I was worried because I had not heard and did not know what was happening.

Miss Rathbone passed my letter to the Parliamentary Committee for Refugees and they have written me saying that they already have a *brief outline* of his case and will make further enquiries and that in their opinion also it will be better if I do nothing. Anybody might imagine that I had become a suspect instead of being an indignant English citizen. Still, life is like that, people are rarely killed for their sins but mostly crucified for their virtues, and whether I like it or not I'm in the world and will have to put up with it. It is for that reason that one fights against the idea of Christianity, which probably gets hold of us in one way or another, sooner or later. I wonder why it is that a woman like Miss Rathbone can print what she likes whilst I am not supposed to say a word?

A boat containing refugee writers and painters was sunk recently as they were returning from Australia. Had it been 12 months previously the internee I write to would have been needlessly killed and I would never have forgotten it. It is one thing to fight of one's own free will and to get killed and another just to be wantonly destroyed by muddle: the former might cause me sorrow but the latter chagrin and bitterness. Perhaps I am averse to realising that in this world the law of the jungle operates. If I were a typical jungle woman I shouldn't care what happened to a refugee, I should just take any man who came along and get some sort of physical satisfaction out of all of them and care nothing about any of them – *then* I should be considered a most attractive woman! I, like life itself, am queer.

But I ought to be in bed. I ought, for the sake of my health, to regulate my life. How I keep up to working pitch and how my brain retains public assistance items as it does often mystifies me. The work lies outside my personal life and interest and yet I accomplish it, if with some strain, at least very well. It has turned midnight and it is stupid to go to bed so late when one has to get up early. I wonder if other people are as miserable as I am and why as a human being I am such a complete failure and without hope of being anything else. Tomorrow is merely a duty to be got through, in order to provide bread and butter, and I eat to be fit for the duty. I don't think people *ought* to be as miserable as I am.

Tuesday, 5 January

In the train, lights very dim. Left my boss at the hospital with his wife as they are attending a dance given by the medical officers tonight. I am not jealous as I dislike dances and the Shire Hall pays my railway fare – we went by car and they require the car to get back to Bury St Edmunds after the close at 2 p.m. [presumably a.m.] There is usually a good amount of drink at these dances so the boss had taken a dose of olive oil which he says enables people to carry liquor. He will have to keep sober as he is driving and the clerk of the council is to accompany them back.

After the meeting today I visited my typist who is there for X-ray of lungs and washing out of nose. She does not look really fit. She is in one of the old wards which is drab in workhouse style. The other patients there are girls from the Forces so she is satisfied with her company. They were talking of one nurse saying she was callous but efficient. The sister comes from Addenbrooke's Hospital, Cambridge, and my typist says if she is representative she would not like to go to Addenbrooke's. I was rather tickled while I sat there because the matron walked round. Several of the girls were up and sitting with Ruth (the typist) and myself round a stove in the centre of the room. We continued our conversation and the matron went out. I had a feeling that the correct procedure in the matron's presence was to get on our feet but saw no reason why we should. The sister returned and asked if on future occasions there could be silence when the matron walked round. Later Ruth said she did not like the matron and she was only a matron anyhow and was there to give service – that was all. Mrs Osgood, the clerk and steward's head clerk, had been to see Ruth and invited her out last weekend but the sister could not authorise the visit so Ruth did not go. She seems to like Mrs Osgood and would like a clerical job at the hospital but concluded our boss would stop her from getting it. Ruth also likes her present job apart from its salary. She does mostly boarded-out children.

Newmarket station tonight was dark, the weather is frosty and the station had no fire in the waiting room. Fortunately the train was not very late.

Twice this Xmas I have offered money and had it refused. The first time it was pounds but the second only 6d. The second was to a man who carried my bag and Corona typewriter from the station on Sunday. He was to start work in a factory the next day but meantime wanted a ticket from the relieving officer for a night at the common lodging house, and I offered the 6d. for carrying the luggage. He 'thanked me all the same' and did not know the amount, but would not take anything. I learnt he had once been on a trawler at Lowestoft but liked changes. The relieving officer later told me he was not a bad sort but that some of those Irishmen who go to the common lodging house are awful and like animals rather than human beings. The offer of the pounds was to some people who I know are very hard up but used to be wealthy.

I am now home and bought fish and chips (very palatable stuff) on my way from [the] station. I had a mixture of cheese and rice at the British Restaurant today as there was no meat and I thought the fish might make up for it. War seems to have caused no deterioration in fish and chips and the only difference is that the fish is dearer. I wonder if the British Restaurant profits go to pay their staff, because there must be a profit. The main dish is 6d. and very often cannot cost more than 3d. Soup and sweet would cost about what is charged and tea at 1d. a cup would bring in some margin of profit. After my holiday it is rather a come-down to get back to this food! My sister in Staines kept the standard up by using several tins of condensed milk and tins of American sausage and we were able to buy lots of cakes there and in Richmond. She was able to buy some pork, too, which is more than I can here. She also gets liver. I heard in St Albans that rabbits when obtainable are 6s. each and apples were very scarce. I had big meals in St Albans, Yorkshire pudding included and good Xmas pudding and cake and mince pies and wine. At St Albans I had my first wartime orange, due to the fact that the son of the house is under 18. I do not feel that I robbed the young man, who looks very fit and is now tall and comparatively broad. His mother is an excellent cook.

The Forces girls in the hospital today said food in their camps varied but was sometimes marvellously cooked and plentiful. They (three of them I spoke to) agreed that the hospital food was good and plentiful but spoilt in the cooking and serving, and Ruth said something must be done about it and suggested telling the clerk and steward. I pointed out that only one cook came under his jurisdiction, the several others coming on the medical side. She said they must be very bad cooks without any idea of balancing meals or imagination to vary them. I pointed out that most of them had been trained in domestic science, were highly paid and considered first-rate. It may be that Ruth's food is coming from the old workhouse kitchen where there is a lack of suitable cooking apparatus. She is in that part of the hospital. If so, nothing can be done. She also says that the crockery is 'thrown at one' which rather surprises me because these nurses are not probationers but CNR and mostly from wealthy houses.

I talked to a CNR nurse at Staines. She had had about ten years' nursing experience previously but ignored this and during the war has worked as a CNR auxiliary nurse. I think they get about £55 a year plus a guinea a week for their board. She has a house of her own and a private income but says she knows [that] some of the auxiliaries who live out are hungry because naturally they can't get enough to eat at that price and can't afford to spend much for food out of their £55 a year. She says there is some sort of trade union but it won't have anything to do with CNRs as they are a government concern. She said also that recently they had engaged a chef and now the nurses' food was excellent but though she always told possible patients that the patients' food was excellent she could tell me, as a nurse myself, that it was insufficient, badly cooked and badly served. It is an emergency hospital but unlike the Newmarket one seems to be staffed with county council, not voluntary hospital medical staff. She likes the matron. Says the place is a training school and probationers are treated as senior to auxiliaries. Says nine probationers sat recently for the Preliminary State exam and only two passed and they were Germans! Says despite being an auxiliary she has to run a ward at night with help only for half an hour in the mornings and 36 patients. Says the nurses don't like looking after TB cases and the doctor

7. *Evacuees arriving at Bury St Edmunds railway station, early September 1939.*
© *Suffolk Record Office, Bury St Edmunds, 2027/2/3, a photograph probably intended for The Bury Free Press*

won't allow nurses to sit all night in their wards (as we used to, though as a rule there was little time to sit). Said she really had to tell off a probationer who was in charge for the girl had received schoolroom instruction but had had little practice and there was a poor man going blue in the face and at his last gasp and the probationer was standing over him trying to force him to swallow a mug of milk.

Middlesex County Council are still, after several months, advertising for staff for their nursery schools. Edith [her sister] tells me that months ago when they interviewed her they interviewed several others, some of them nurses who thought the job might be easier than nursing, some who wanted to keep out of the Forces, and some who liked children. She herself is most suitable for that work in every way but could not get the interviewers to adjust the job to suit her. They wanted mobile staff and she wanted to 'stay put' in one school. She wanted her daily hours off to be from 7 to 8 a.m. and 6 to 7 p.m. but they wanted her to have them in the middle of the day. She has a home to run which in ordinary times takes all her time and her soldier husband comes home for supper, bed and breakfast and her daughter goes to school at 8 a.m. and returns [at] 4.30 p.m. for tea. They suggested she should let the daughter stay at school as a boarder and she replied that from the £2 odd they would pay her for the job the Army would deduct a pound and on the remainder of the wage she could not afford to pay boarding-school fees.

They told her there was a war on and she said she knew that. So she did not take the job though she would have liked it had it been a part-time job.

[My nephew John] … is apprenticed at De Havilland's aeroplane works and has frightful journeys by train and cycle there and back each day. My sister-in-law, who lives nearer, had taken him in with her own boy and an evacuated boy (all 17) but after some months has been ordered a rest, so John had to return home. For John she received 15s. a week and for the evacuee 13s. but says she was out of pocket owing to wear and tear of bedlinen, breakage of crockery, and so on. She thought it would have been better not to board out evacuees in private houses but to take over larger houses and turn them into boarding-schools where the girls could learn domestic science and the boys do the garden (I think both sexes should do both) and allow house-wives like herself to give voluntary services if their help were required. Her evacuees recently have been quite nice youngsters from Hastings grammar school but she thinks it will be a comparative rest if she takes a half-day job and merely has her husband and one boy and the house to look after.

Sunday, 10 January

I've been working (housework) the last 12 hours and as it is now 10 p.m. will only give headlines of what I have to write about.

NALGO meeting – other counties.
Professor Laski – medical – venom in Guildhall.
Accountant – me the scapegoat, apparently.
Jam and food. Curtains and blankets.
Hours.
R. and TB patient, nose and X-ray – anaesthetic – catarrhal jaundice.
People going round to find out how others live – Edith.
Likeness between Lake and Ollé and Lindsey the billeting officer.

Sunday, 17 January

… *Beveridge Report.* It has taken me 2½ years in this town to learn that it has a Fabian Society – even now I don't know what a Fabian Society is, though I hear it is socialist. It happened that on the 9th instant Professor Harold Laski was supposed to lecture on his friend's (Beveridge) report at the Guildhall here, a long narrow room with oil paintings of dead and gone celebrities (just as well, from the look of some of them, though others look better) and crystal candelabras (with electric candles) down the centre. The paintings, of course, on the walls. The place was packed and people standing at the back. Miss Penly Cooper, OBE, well to the front, probably to ask questions. The county medical officer much further behind, but he was probably late. A good-looking man with a monocle next to me and the [welfare] worker of the Moral Welfare Home sat making notes on his report. Many Army officers were there. Also people from the borough and from the Shire Hall NALGO. I was, I think, the sole representative of the public assistance department, and I am only a 'temporary'. I saw Lindsey the billeting officer for the first time and concluded he had a similar expression to that of Lake the mayor and my landlord Ollé ex-mayor – Gooch says it must be something to do with the borough. I was not interested in him but the welfare worker has a soft spot for him, perhaps because he is supposed to be delicate. She is the only person I have ever heard say a good word for him [the billeting officer], though I have never heard anything really bad though only that he is not liked and is officious and rude – but of course the unpopularity of his job may account for that. Not many people take evacuees who can squeeze out of it.[62] The bulk of the people, however, looked well-dressed and well-fed and intelligent: where they came from I don't know but I have never *seen* people like that in this town. The people the Beveridge Report really concern, however, were not there. The little shop-keepers and cottagers from this street, for instance, were not there, though some were from the bigger houses (for well-to-do and poor live here higgledy-piggledy). Mrs Pelly the rector's wife says that anything at all intellectual here is always attended by people who have come here from away, and not by the people who are native stock. The chairman at the Fabian meeting is reputed to have been a schoolmaster in London. The musical clique here were not present, but on the whole they are natives. I am a native too but didn't run true to breed, or something. I remember when I was about 12 at Newmarket I attended an absolutely marvellous elocutionary recital – and there were about 11 other people in the audience! I actually didn't meet an educated person there until I was 17, and he was a Londoner. However, to get back to the Beveridge Report and Laski, I do not know why the average person here was uninterested. It may by dullness, it may be cynicism, it may be that the life of a healthy, happy animal is to them the sanest, best of lives.

Laski did not turn up and I have heard since that a diary entry was incorrect. He is due to arrive *next* Saturday at the same time....

Ruth the typist is due back at the office tomorrow. I hope she has written me a diary of her stay in hospital. They have X-rayed her lungs a few times and washed out her nose a few times. The latter they did without a local anaesthetic (I rather fancy they are getting scarce these days) but one other girl fainted before hers was done and after that Ruth got gas for the job. Personally I think this nasal washing out is stupid and just provides a bit of practice for surgeons. On top of that they put a patient in the next bed who was in the last stages of tuberculosis. Just like hospitals!

The London County Council is suggesting to other local authorities that they all combine in keeping down the wages paid to nurses from co-ops to a stated figure.

---

[62] Later (27 June 1944) she remarked that 'only the poor or uninfluential would have evacuees billeted on them'.

My niece Shirley has catarrhal jaundice. I hope it won't affect her chances of getting a school scholarship, which would cover her £7 7s. a term school fees and a few other expenses. One is so near the pauper line when one's father becomes a soldier and doesn't get his money made up by his employers. To think of Shirley, poor child, being supported on the Army allowance of 6s. (I think it is) a week is ludicrous. She costs more than that for clothes, for she grows rapidly out of everything and has always had very nice clothes. I don't think, however, that she has yet realised there is less money in the home. But the rent does not get paid. Doctors' bills get paid out of capital her grandfather left her mother. There is about £10 owing for a costume for her. Her mother made her a party frock this Xmas out of a sister-in-law's old dance frock. The piano wants £17 spent on it but won't get it. The home still looks precisely as it used, and her mother is as well-dressed though she has less changes. Any inspector of any kind going into that home to see how soldiers' families lived would conclude that they managed admirably. Shirley still has her music lessons (I presume out of capital), and she lives in a spot-less, up-to-date little house, with her own bedroom and childish treasures and a host of story and other books. They still have good china and silver and cut glass and baths and dressing-gowns. It is true the dining-room now merely contains an indoor air-raid shelter, but it only meant removing the dining-room table into the front room, which is a larger room in which they always lived, anyhow, for the dining-room was only used for meals.

I got more to eat today but last Sunday, because I had failed to shop and cook, I was short. To fill up, I ate a month's jam ration with a spoon, though it was quite good greengage jam I had made myself with sugar and golden syrup.

Monday, 18 January

I worked overtime all last week but not tonight. At long last I touched the fringe of my sewing, darned some two-year-old woollen stockings of a fawn shade, and sewed the sleeves in a dressing-gown and altered the buttons and added a belt. It may not be much but it is something accomplished. I also cleaned my front room window (nasty job as the sash cord has been broken about two years) and washed some underclothes in a hand-bowl, hanging them in my cupboard near the fireplace – things get fresh-air breezes from the outer world in there through the plasterless laths. Recently I have also washed two bath towels (I had to fetch and take down a lot of water for those) and put up a curtain over the cupboard door and the internee's orange Australian blanket over the door near the fireplace in the front room. I burned an oilstove in the wardrobe all day yesterday but it is still wet inside. If we get housing reform after the war, what will they do with all these old houses in Bury St Edmunds? A few weeks ago Mr Bostock had the scullery here whitewashed and distempered for his secretary [the tenant below], but the

water comes through the roof and today the middle of the ceiling in consequence fell on the floor – making her a beautiful mess. The landlord is used
to falling ceilings and I presume won't leave it to the tenant to put a new
one up. He has known about the roof for years but I expect is content for
the place to fall down so long as he can collect rent for a few years before
it does. Still, if it falls on anybody's head, I hope it will be on his. (Later, he
repaired it and the roof.)

I have felt lots more energetic since my Xmas break, but today felt
'Mondayish'. It may have been because the newspaper this a.m. said London
had had an air-raid and I just wondered how my relations [in] Staines way got
on. I have not been afraid but they now have tremendous guns practically on
their doorstep and the shrapnel isn't pleasant and is quite capable of cutting
its way through the roof, as it does sometimes. The guns are frightfully noisy,
too, and the bigger ones belch in a way that makes me want to vomit. We go
about these days feeling as if *our* share in bombing is over, and then we get
a slight reminder that it isn't.

The master at Sudbury institution keeps ringing up and dilating at length
on the obstreperousness of his staff – so far as I can see, he can't run a
rabbit, much less human beings. He is comparatively young and looks as if
he could be very nice, but something is wrong with him. It *might* do him a
world of good if they called him up for the Army and so took responsibility
from his shoulders. If he goes on as he does he won't have any staff left and
won't deserve to, but it is rough luck on his staff, who have no redress. Yet
he has a nice house, plenty of food, service and money, and a wife and two
children – one would think he ought to be all right. Nobody to boss him
either, for the public assistance officer and committee pander to his every
whim so as not to upset him. His wife is an efficient matron, or considered
so, and he has no definite vices, apparently. His chief clerk may be sacked
next meeting, though he may give his notice in beforehand. That will leave as
clerical staff only one small and new boy to run the institution, and the master
himself apparently has no idea of clerical work. The chief clerk is accused
of insubordination and if there is another it will be the fourth chief clerk (of
the previous two clerks, making six, one was called up and the other escaped
being sacked by a transfer to Kedington) in about six months. To the best of
my knowledge, all the lot have been perfectly good clerks. At the moment,
too, the master would like to sack a perfectly good stoker. I suppose they
object when he 'goes off the deep end at them' and then he gets offended and
wants to get rid of them – I don't think in his case it is merely or at all a liking
for fresh faces. They tried a female clerk but she resigned after two days.

Had a visitor tonight, so no sewing done and the washing-up etc. still
await my attention. Am still wondering how the internee is getting on, though
I did have a letter recently offering to sell me a flowerpiece painting for
whatever I liked to send him. I can keep him in pocket-money by selling all
his belongings, or buying them, but only if the war doesn't last more than

another year or so. Captain Wilson recently tried (but failed) to get £5000 from Sir John Anderson; I reckon the latter owes me and the internee a few hundreds, but like Wilson I'd be unlucky. Anderson would need to be a multi-multi-multi-millionaire if he had to meet all the claims which could be made upon him in circumstances such as my own. And in any case, though he started the trouble, he cannot be blamed for prolonging it. When I think of the messes that men get themselves into it seems time that women had a go at running the world – and yet, where are the suitable women? Most of us even now have the mentality of concubines rather than free women and our only aims in life are to trick men and sell our wombs at the highest prices obtainable. Wombs are the only commodity for which men as a rule will pay lavish prices to women, but of course that comes in with their self-indulgence and not with their 'duty to their neighbours'. Men are so irresponsible and if you find a decent one he almost certainly has a good mother or a good wife in the background who works through him, or did at one time; by himself he seems a most helpless creature and usually depraved, and entirely selfish.

I believe the Russians are making good headway against the Germans. I never follow details of the war as I find details gory and unpleasant and I've not the least idea of the towns the Russians have recaptured, but I like to know the broad outline of what is happening. If we had captured Rome, for instance, or started to fight Spain, I'd like to know it, but *how* it was done wouldn't interest me in the slightest. I don't know one aeroplane from another and I've no idea at all how to distinguish a lieutenant from any other officer. If a uniform looks strange I conclude the wearer is an American, but he might equally well be a Czech, or an Austrian, or anybody else of the white races. I presume Germans still wear grey, so I'd distinguish them from the colour, but I hope they'll remain on the Continent. I've seen a lot of niggers lately driving lorries – presumably they hail from USA. We heard from our late typist today and she says they have a terrible lot of Irishmen working on an aerodrome who fight with beer bottles and break each others' ribs, etc., and that quite recently one has been killed but they have not yet traced the murderer.

Wednesday, 20 January

So the name of the assassin of Darlan was Bonnier de la Chapelle. Rather a good-sounding name. I wonder what the historians will make of him? I suppose an act like his touches the romantic side of one, or perhaps appeals as tragedy. It stood out as the one great item of news at Xmas, 1942, and I, at least, was sorry they executed him, though perhaps such a swift execution was merciful. I have not yet heard an expression of sympathy for Darlan from anybody. I take it we have judged Darlan from newspapers and perhaps this shows the power of the press. The idea of people I have met here is that it was a good way out for the Allies, and that it would simplify matters and was a stroke of good luck. It was thought that the assassin would be imprisoned and his execution was a surprise. A few days later a big American talked of it as a cowardly act, with which I disagreed. It may have been unwise, fanatical, hot-headed, irreligious, unbalanced; but not cowardly. No one person who dares to shoot another *knowing he will have to pay with his own life* is a coward. To my mind it requires intense courage. His repeated remark at his court-martial that he 'had no accomplices' and 'no accomplices were needed to do justice' confirms his courage, as does the testimony of the priest regarding his death 'that he never flinched'.[63]

I am still of opinion that it is better to wait for God's Mills than to commit murder, but then I somehow have a secret feeling that all these callous, bloody brutes only *appear* to be callous, bloody brutes and are in reality only stupid and unfeeling because they were born and brought up so. It is too big a problem for me to solve. Anyhow, there's a damned lot of murder going on these days, so it doesn't look as if my sentiment in this respect is general, but rather as if I am old-fashioned. Or, unlike a good many, I have never got the lust for blood. Perhaps men all through the ages who have made wars and sacrificed masses of human life only realise that this world is a jungle in which to kill or be killed, and perhaps that is why, despite their ghastly crimes, they still can laugh as if free of all care. I suppose such an existence gives them excitement and that is all they understand. I don't know that Darlan was such a one but I have gathered – rightly or wrongly – that like the bulk of us he chose, regardless of right or wrong, to be on the winning side and save his own skin. He could not have had a kinder death, being unaware of its approach.

The Assizes was at the Shire Hall today, with Judge Asquith in full glory of crimson and wig. Several people, including fire service girls, were peering for a look at him. I understand he attended church beforehand. His car came slowly up one of our churchyard's elm avenues, with one bobby walking in front and others at the side, and Joan thought it would be funny if the one in front tripped up, fell over, staying the procession. I don't know why he is surrounded by police, unless for show. The trumpeters don't usher him in now, as they did in peacetime. From the look of the Shire Hall front steps, it might have been a good idea to clean them in his honour, for they are so dirty now they make me feel sick when I look at them. Our Shire Hall, thank God, isn't a show place like the LCC county hall, which appears to have aimed at outshining the Houses of Parliament. Still, the LCC has a nice room for teas, whereas all we've got is a gas-stove in a tiny old kitchen such as one would find in almost any old small house, and the ability to buy a tea on occasions would be a delight. I don't think we've even one carpet in the Shire Hall.

---

[63] Admiral Darlan had been assassinated on Christmas Eve by a young French royalist, who was executed two days later.

The clerk's desk is always entirely tidy but most desks are simply littered with papers. My own, with letters, case papers and the boxes I take them in to meetings, plus sometimes large relief books and files, frequently overflows to steps and chairs and sometimes even the floor. The typewriter also is on it, and a telephone. But then, of course, I have to do my own filing, and the clerk doesn't.

Friday, 22 January

Nurse from Liverpool went to hairdresser here to have hair done for her wedding and the hairdresser phoned the matron of the institution to say the nurse was verminous – which she was.

Councillor Ollé my landlord sent workmen to patch the roof and ceiling in the spot where ceiling had fallen, but workmen said he had given them instructions to do nothing to the rest of the roof and ceiling. Mrs Nudds the tenant pointed out the damp places which are left, but those parts of the ceiling it appears must fall first. But for the mess I'd have to clear up, it would be a joke to prod my own ceiling where the plaster hangs in flakes ready to drop, but there is no guarantee that he would repair it if I did make a good hole – he cannot behave to Bostock quite as he would to me. Joan this morning said he made a very good mayor [in] Coronation year [1937] and had plenty of energy: I agreed he would have because in his own estimation he was a person of very great importance. I also said that as I understood the town had kept industry away, I could not understand them allowing him to take the backs away from a row of houses for his ice cream factory, leaving the houses with no back exit in case of fire, and Joan answered: 'Well, he was the mayor'.

I see from the 'local rag' that one of our very rich townsmen is a fuel over-seer, whatever that may mean.[64] I don't know him but from what I have come across in business I think he must be a bit cracked. Paid his staff disgustingly low wages and as mean as can be, but has lately been paying court to a young woman, nearly falling over himself to do it. I think he imagines that she is loose morally, but I don't think she is. Anyhow, he has provided her with a Xmas chicken and various other gifts and I suggested to her she should take all she could get. Then he wanted a kiss, which she refused, so perhaps the gifts will stop now! Just as well for the money of some of these old idiots to do some good.

Mrs Newman, an old tenant here, called the other evening with her young-ster. She left here when her husband was called up so that a sister-in-law could look after her child aged about three or four. Says she got a job as a cook at £3 10s. a week and liked it but after six months the sister-in-law had

---

[64] A notice from the Ministry of Fuel and Power listed B. Freeman as 'Local Fuel Overseer'. Bernard Freeman lived at 95 Westley Road.

had enough so she went south to join her husband. At the end of a week he was moved to the Orkneys and the south coast town was so depressing she returned to her mother, who would not accommodate her husband when on leave, so she got rooms elsewhere and will join him when she can. She is only about 22 or 23 and thinks she could have 'the time of her life' if she had no child – she would like to join the Forces. But says she can do nothing with a child. There is no nursery school here, either.

The other evening at the Moral Welfare Home here a couple of girls in the Forces came who had missed a train. The scanty accommodation at the YWCA was full and there was nowhere else for them. Newmarket has no accommodation (not even a common lodging house) for casuals, no moral welfare home, no YMCA or YWCA. Bury has all the latter, such as they are. I think the Moral Welfare Home should be more like a YWCA. It certainly is a 'shelter' but apart from domestic work there is nothing except knitting for the girls to do. The library *might* fetch three shillings in a sale and there isn't a table big enough even for table tennis. The staff usually play cards with them in the evening or play the piano for the girls to sing. Once or twice a week there is a little church service in the small chapel upstairs. They now have an Ascot heater to provide hot water from the taps in the scullery where the girls do their washing for themselves and babies, so it will no longer be necessary for them to draw water in buckets from the kitchen tap and heat it in a copper.

Royal Observer Corps. This matter [was] raised because apparently [a] school in which children were killed in a raid recently got no warning. It was in the beginning of the war rather a shock to find that bombs preceded a warning or fell after the 'all clear', but it seems pretty general everywhere. Now after a warning I listen for a minute or two and then forget it, and I do the same after an 'all clear'. It is now suggested that the substitution of young girls for men over 50 in the Observer Corps may account for the recent absence of an alarm. It may or may not. Locally I have heard that girls cannot stand the work. For one thing it is intricate and requires training and a flair for it, and also – which seems to me even more important – the room in which observers work is gas-proof and therefore almost airless, and if the people do not faint or go to sleep their brains do not act as efficiently as they would under normal conditions....

Now the papers keep harping on the U-boat menace, and say the public ought to know our losses. Well, the public know they are heavy and lists of figures, which may be correct or incorrect, won't help. What is it desired that the public shall do about this? It is no good changing heads of departments, because every change delays matters and probably one head is as good as another, for none of them are there long enough to grasp the working of their departments. If the public is desired to produce more labour, well, openings for part-time employment will have to be made. It has apparently been decided that the Shire Hall will engage nobody for the vacancy caused by Mrs Brown's leaving. Fortunately correspondence has fallen off lately, though Gooch says he has never seen case-papers in such a mess as they are in now. That, however, is not my concern or funeral. By the time the Beveridge Report comes into action and our Public Assistance Committee gets taken over, we shall have so cut out the work that there won't be anything for them to take over merely by neglecting to do it! Quite a number of relief cases, too, have lately found work. The number of persons in Bury St Edmunds public assistance now is 303 against 300 the same period last year, so that is not very different. On the other hand, the new hostel has been opened, creating a new monthly meeting at Newmarket. Rest centres are having a quiet spell. I went earlier to British Restaurant today and was amazed at different kinds of school uniform there. Even elementary schools these days have their uniform and there were also children from the County and Grammar schools.

I have been altogether more energetic since my holidays at Xmas. May be partly due to egg powder being put on the market – I think the lack of eggs did have some effect and lately around menstruation periods I have indulged in egg powder, milk and sugar.

Cakes. I can get buns or something in the cake line each fortnight in Sudbury, but in Bury I cannot. My nearest bakers are named Berry so I usually get bread there, but they reserve all their cakestuff for their prewar friends, and have done since the war. They are not alone in this, and that is why shopping for a stranger like myself is difficult. The real natives can get anything they want. I don't mean I go hungry – I could get all kinds of vegetables anywhere here by the bushel or cwt. – but just things which are a bit short are kept back by the shopkeepers for their friends and so scarcity of certain commodities is more apparent than real. We still have plenty of apples here, too. I should imagine that if shopkeepers and shoppers had all been honest people, we should have been able to run this war so far without any rationing at all!! I live by myself and yet have been able to give away sugar, golden syrup, fruit, soap, flour, oatmeal, fats, milk, soup, meat, cocoa and coffee and Ovaltine and Horlicks and jam and marmalade and eggs and chocolate and sweets and fish since the war started. If I substitute egg powder for eggs, I could still give all those things away without myself going hungry. Tea is perhaps the one thing I get short of. I don't draw a quarter of my cheese and bacon rations, and yet I don't starve, and in this town one gets very hungry. I should have found it more difficult to manage on my rations in Bexhill, because there I could not get hungry and so had to buy bananas and cream and easy things to eat so as not to starve – here one can tackle beefsteak pudding and coarser foods, which is better in wartime, as they are obtainable, as well as cheaper. Hunger here makes me cook but at Bexhill I could sit on the beach from 10 a.m. to 5 p.m. and then not feel hungry; though by 8 p.m. I'd feel a bit faint instead. Nevertheless, I liked Bexhill, and the people in it.

Saturday, 23 January

Laski came to the Guildhall here this evening. The audience was almost as large, but it was not the same audience. Less Army officers, for one thing, but this may have been because this time the meeting was announced by letter to persons who had left their address and was not in the 'local rag'. I think the *Bury Free Press* this week consisted of 12 pages – in a paper shortage.[65]

Laski is dark, rather small, uses his hands noticeably, chiefly by putting the left in his pocket or thereabouts, and the right moving between his watch on the table and clutching the revers of his coat. I prefer the absolute stillness of an immaculate Bernard Shaw, who seems to move nothing but his eyes, but Laski's movements are part of himself. Bernard is probably more of an actor.

Laski has an unusual grasp of English and one realised it is a deep-seated knowledge. He understands the meaning of words in a way the average person, rich or poor, does not. It allows him to say things in a different and satisfying way. His brain, of course, is alert. He is decidedly humorous and humane, even when describing his five-story drop on to a hotel bed in a big raid and his rescue by a man who scaled 60 feet of wall to the ground with Laski over his shoulder. (The 60 wants confirming, but it was a lot, anyway.) He dealt adequately with the history of the Beveridge Report and its importance. Said how marvellous it was to watch for half an hour in the BBC [building] Beveridge and the chairman of the Prudential looking at each other. Said he did not think Bury St Edmunds was exactly a Socialist strong-hold. Placed the report outside party politics. Was as scathing to medical profession as to insurance corporations. I was surprised to hear a sudden, thunderous burst of applause when Laski said hospitals should be national, not voluntary.

Questions were very few. Any opposition kept silent, knowing itself no match for the speaker. A few men, probably soldiers in the last war, stayed behind, perhaps to speak to him. One or two of them had raised points in the meeting. In one case I wondered if the men would understand Laski's academic language. Another said at question time that in the last war the

---

[65] The *Bury Free Press*, 30 January 1943, p.3, gave extensive coverage to Laski's 'brilliant speech', which was presented under the auspices of the Bury Fabian Society in a packed Guildhall to 'a gathering representative of all shades of political opinion and of social standing'. Laski spoke about the Beveridge Report for 70 minutes without notes. Acknowledging that Bury was 'not a fortress of socialism', he portrayed the report as a natural and necessary development of welfare provisions already in being. 'You cannot in one generation', he said, 'send the youth of this country to die for a dream without making some effort to make that dream come true' (Applause). The goal was to achieve basic freedom – freedom from want. He also, 'amid further applause, hoped that soon there would be nationalized medical service'. At the end of the meeting a lady in the audience 'suggested that the meeting should send an invitation to Major Heilgers to discuss the Report with his constituents, and a resolution to this effect was carried'.

returning soldiers had been promised a land fit for heroes to live in and they didn't get it and he was a bit doubtful that they would get anything this time. Laski hit him straight from the shoulder, saying it was up to him and the general public to put in Parliament the right people and let their MPs know what they wanted, and that if Churchill knew the public wanted the Beveridge Report the public would get it. In Bury St Edmunds, of course, the ordinary public have always been in the habit of leaving government to their 'betters' and not thinking themselves, and I concluded this man was like that. As Mr Ward of the Adelphi Players puts it in his *Holy Family* (not exactly in these words, though), they expected the light to shine *on* them, not *in* them. A girl at the back proposed that the MP for the district should be asked to attend a meeting and talk on the Beveridge Report, and this will be done. I asked Miss Westell his name but she had never heard it, and then I remembered it was Heilgers, once captain, now something higher. The trouble is, who will be able to question him?

Newspaper today said Tripoli had been taken and there was a retreat, and I had to read on to find out whether the Germans or ourselves had taken it and who had retreated. I found it was the Germans who had retreated and we who had taken. How great in regard to military importance Tripoli is I don't know, but when Miss Osgathorpe remarked tonight how wonderful it was, I agreed. There was also a very tiny paragraph saying that the Germans said they had sunk several of our ships. That seems to be the way we announce our losses, and it looks rather as if we are losing a lot of shipping just now. The paper had a big bit about Tripoli, though that is no guarantee that news is important but rather that they are dealing with something which is favourable.

I wish it had been possible to buy French newspapers after war started, so as to get news from the Continent. Those now printed in French are just English newspapers in French, so they don't help. I was interested years ago when our own papers were packed with Japanese atrocities in China to find that in a French newspaper the Chinese–Japanese war was dismissed in about four lines, and their newspaper was packed for about three days with some triviality ours didn't even mention! Was it that France had no vested interests in China?

I think I'll have to keep in touch with this Fabian movement. I am usually cynical and think money and force rule the world and political parties are no good owing to the selfishness and rapacity of the human head; that Labour leaders sell themselves to the people who possess gold and power; that most if not all movements are a ramp, despite the ideals with which they are founded; that all ideals are utilised by cunning men to achieve purposes never intended by the people who perhaps died to establish them, and so it is stupid to work for any ideal. Yet I do realise the complete helplessness of an individual and that any society, however small, has a chance of getting something accomplished.

The medical fraternity said not one word at the Laski meeting, at which

Miss Westell laughed and said they must have thought that in this case 'silence was golden'. They would have done their cause more harm than good if they had raised any point. It was laughable, after their conviction that to join a trade union was lowering to the nursing profession, to hear Laski call the medical profession the 'second largest trade union in Great Britain'.

Laski gave me the most favourable picture of Churchill I have ever had, but deprecated, as I do, his habit of promoting the failures in his government. This, however, may be a Civil Service rule which he follows, for it has been said that if a man is incapable of managing a Ministry of Labour employment exchange he gets promoted and given another job, because you must have efficiency at the bottom. I was talking to a typist the other day and she was saying that until you work for people in big positions you don't realise how inefficient they are. Most typists would endorse that. She mentioned in particular a man in charge of the defences of one very important town who was much more ignorant of his job than she was but who now (oh, miracle!) has been sacked – or, perhaps, promoted.

I am often surprised at the almost revolutionary way in which women talk these days. A hotel proprietor is one and she has had a good deal of contact with the Forces, naval officers and pressmen. The tenant below stairs here wants the Beveridge Report adopted and education made free so that the brain-power of the country can be developed, wherever it may be, and unless I am much mistaken her husband was a Conservative agent.

Laski said this country had been conquered twice, once by William the Norman and a second time by Montague Norman (Bank of England) and the second defeat was a bigger disaster than the first.

Sometimes I – and I am positive many other people too – have thought the Beveridge Report was merely a government sop to the population to keep up its morale, but whether that is so or not, the opposition to the insurance societies, and the medical arrangements, are most definitely to the good.

Wednesday, 27 January

Churchill and Roosevelt have been talking together in Morocco. I saw it in my newspaper today. Gooch listened to the 10.45 or 11 p.m. news last night which said that an important announcement would be made to various countries at 3 a.m. Owing to the queer time for a broadcast, he and his wife were worried, thinking it must be something momentous, and if it was invasion of the Continent there would be a terrific loss of life. However, they went to bed. Patterson heard the 3 a.m. news because he had to fetch dill-water at that hour for his howling infant. It was a notification of the talk between Churchill and Roosevelt, an interesting tit-bit for the morning wireless or paper, but an anti-climax for 3 a.m. This kind of thing hasn't happened lately, but it did several times a year or two ago. One Sunday afternoon in a college I recollect we all gathered at 3 p.m. (not a.m. that time) to hear an 'important announcement', and when it came it was a mere detail and we all laughed. There were other times too, until some people didn't trouble to listen at the stated times.

On the 24th instant I had a letter from Bloomsbury House to say that my internee is now permitted by the Home Office to submit himself for a vacancy to the Ministry of Labour on the Isle of Man, which means that if he can get fixed up in work of national importance he can, I presume, be released. Some internees work on the island and sleep in the internment camp, but I have concluded that the Home Office means he can return to civilian life so long as he does war-work. I shall get further particulars from him later, no doubt.

West Suffolk was in the news recently, to the effect that its women all want kitchens, not kitchenettes. They want a kitchen big enough to have a meal in, also a living-room where meals can be served, and another room where they are not served. Apparently they want what they have been accustomed to! I should agree with them in liking three sizeable rooms downstairs, but I like space. On the other hand, I hate meals in kitchens, and to my mind it is more essential to have a very convenient and easily-kept-clean kitchen than to have a large one. A good idea to have an Ascot heater in it so that it is kept warm, for one can shiver in an unheated kitchenette or kitchen when washing up. The most essential things in a house is a good supply of hot water, and the Ascot would provide that. Electricity is cleanest but as things are now the 'Regulo' gas cooker is better than an electric cooker. It is a pity that the Ascot does not contain an oven, because it seems superfluous to have an Ascot and a Regulo both in one room. If the Ascot could be made more attractive to look at, it could go in the dining-room, and the kitchen could be warmed by a central-heating gadget which could be turned off at will. There are doubtless all sorts of central-heating schemes on the market and all sorts of water-heating ones too. I certainly should choose a house for light and sunshine, with furniture which could be dusted in the least possible time, with no ledges on doors, etc., or skirting-board ledges to collect dust, with carpets (for comfort) covering the whole of the floor and leaving no surround to be polished.[66]

Looking round my own room, *everything* is wrong, except the divan-bed, which, thank God, has no head-piece! The walnut desk, though its corners are rounded, has rims everywhere to collect dust. The oval oak table has legs which some man (who never had to dust) carved into a design, and there are four bars to dust at the bottom. The oak chest, in addition to a multitude of

---

[66] Some 182 condemned houses were still being occupied in the Thingoe Rural District, surrounding Bury St Edmunds, and this news prompted the *Bury Free Press* to welcome the announcement by the Ministry of Agriculture that 3,000 new houses were to be built in rural areas, and that the 'wives of farm servants' had been consulted on their design. Most of these houses were to have three bedrooms and two reception rooms, which, it was said, would please Women's Institutes (30 January 1943, p.1 and 13 February 1943, p.9).

little rims everywhere, has sharp corners just the right height for a baby to run its eyes into if it stumbled. The Chippendale stool has four bars near the floor. The oak stool is about like the oval oak table. The dresser has ridges round the foot of it. The legs of the occasional table curve so that the dust can collect on them. Even the picture frames are all ridges. Men, having lots of time in which to do nothing, have spent their energy carving shapes so that women can keep busy by dusting them, day after day, week after week, etc., etc. Those who make pretty-pretties should be compelled to dust them. One could have beauty without all this finicky design.

Actually, I have not noticed that the so-called labour-saving houses save much labour. I think what happens is, that with the same amount of work they are much cleaner and more comfortable than the old ones. A woman with a vacuum cleaner puts it over her living-room carpet every day, but a woman who hasn't one sweeps the carpet less often, or, if she does it every day, she spends very little time on it. The carpet is not so clean but I doubt if she spends longer on it. Electric light and heating do, of course, save time.

Central-heating. Many advantages and it makes life much more comfortable, particularly when getting up, going to bed, and having a bath. Yet whenever I have had much central-heating, I've never been free from colds. Here, in this draughty old place and coal fires, I have (touch wood!) been amazingly free from them. Perhaps changes of temperature harden one, or the dead level of a centrally-heated temperature does something to the breathing apparatus, or there is something lacking in the way of ventilation.

My small nephew is in a Cambridge nursing home with ear trouble. His home is Newmarket, 14 miles away, but Newmarket has no hospital for ordinary civilians, but only a small one for stablemen and a large one for troops and evacuees. The specialist at Addenbrooke's Hospital I believe recommended the nursing home. I am not entirely clear as to what has happened, but it seems they did something to the child's ear from the inside to obviate the necessity of an incision from outside, and he was sent home before it finished discharging pus. On getting home the discharge stopped and the trouble started all over again, so back he went to the nursing home and it is thought he will later have the operation from the outside. Perhaps the child gets in draughts at school or in their badly ventilated sitting-room – his ear, nose and throat apparatus has been much trouble. Or it may have resulted through sleeping in a cellar when raids were thick. He has been a somewhat 'spoilt' child, by which I mean that his mother has given way to his desires when firmness and regularity in bedtimes would have been to his well-being. As a result, there is not the affection between them that firmness would have brought about, and he does much in defiance as a result. He probably gets irritable, too, because he does not get enough sleep. I am sorry for the youngster, though his parents think the world of him, and are proud of his brain.

I stooped to get a cake out of the oven, there was a quick flood and I had to rush for a diaper – or, rather, two. The second time since the New Year and a fortnight since I finished the last lot. Suppose I'll have to go easy and eat egg powder for the next ten days! Just as well I've the cake to eat. Certainly the Almighty arranged most things to make us work, even menstruation, though why he has very rarely allowed me to wait a full four weeks for it and only once in my life to wait as long as two days over the four weeks, I don't know. Can't say it has ever caused me any pain, but it is nevertheless a nuisance. Being sexless would have great advantages, and in my particular case it would have no disadvantages, so far as I can see, so long as I hadn't swung sufficiently to the male side to grow a moustache. I have always bemoaned the fact that I was a woman, except in wartime, when men get the worst of it, even in these days. In peace every advantage is theirs, but I don't think I'd like to have to do the killing in wartime. Still, some women have had a successful career, and got married (so maybe sex hasn't worried them, or even frustrated them), whereas I've achieved neither. That was a pity, but one cannot order one's fate, and compared with some lives mine so far has been pleasant and free from care and pain. I cannot say I envy anybody I know in Bury St Edmunds, man or woman, though as far as I know nobody here has achieved anything, anyway. Kathleen Long, the BBC pianist, belongs here, but then, no achievement in the musical world would ever have given me the least satisfaction, so I do not envy her.[67] However, here I am, menstruating, and I've to report a meeting in Sudbury tomorrow, and I'd better get to bed. A noisy plane throbs outside and the kettle is boiling inside. I am very glad the internee is going to be freed. The end of that bit and the beginning of something else, I suppose.

Thursday, 28 January

Tommy (the public assistance officer and named [Frederick] Thompson) had said he would be late so we'd start immediately on his arrival. His wife has been ill. She smokes about 40 cigarettes a day normally and it has upset her throat and she may have a bad cold. Tommy always takes care that office people wait on him hand and foot, and his wife is perhaps the only person who reverses the procedure. She looks about like him and he seems to think the world of her, so all night long lately he has been in and out of bed, making her tea, giving her friar's balsam inhalations, and all the rest of it. I keep expecting him to be ill, too. He usually has a month or two a year during which he sheds a skin and he seems to need a healthier life. They live in a flat above her restaurant, in a main street, with no garden, and he doesn't walk much. When we got in the car we went for some petrol and then to her restaurant.[68] He said he'd be two minutes and I concluded he'd swallow a cup

---

[67] Kathleen Long (1896–1968) lived in Whiting Street, Bury St Edmunds.
[68] The café run by Mrs Thompson – Katie Thompson – was at 7 Butter Market.

of coffee and come out, but the minutes went by. A little youngish woman came out of the restaurant, picked up their dustbin (like me, they have no back entrance) and took it through the restaurant. Then a big fat woman – either cook or manageress, but in a white coat so I'd guess the cook – went in. She looked 'gone to pieces a bit' whereas on a previous occasion she had looked very cheerful. People were inside for coffee and tarts. Nothing in one window and buckets, stirrup pump, etc. in the other. It was turned 10 a.m. and the meeting at Sudbury to start 10.30. He came out, in neither a good nor bad temper. Said his wife had fancied for breakfast a thin slice of grilled ham on a thin slice of fried bread, and he had instructed the staff accordingly. They had taken her fried ham on thick fried bread and lukewarm coffee, so she had refused anything, and he had been cutting her thin bread spread with farm-house butter and made her some hot coffee. Then for lunch she had wanted flat fish and the fat woman had brought back 3½lbs of codfish. The fat one sometimes turned giddy and fell and said she felt like it that morning and he had told her not to fall there. I asked what was wrong with her and he said he supposed 'change of life' and it was a nuisance. I made no comment. I had heard his wife say the staff were a nuisance and she'd pay some of them back when peace returned. Still, she makes about £1000 a year profit out of the business, and can't expect to earn that without trouble – I couldn't earn it if I killed myself with work.

At Sudbury he went into the master's office while I got books etc. from the car and carted them to the board room and got ready for the meeting. Nothing very unusual at the meeting. Miss Todd, a trained nurse and matron of the Children's Home, had attained the age of 65 and completed 25 years' service and I've to minute it and puff her up. They all think they have had a wonderful servant in Miss Todd and so do I. Recently they gave her what Tommy called a 'substantial increase', making her money from £70 a year all found to £90 rising by £10 a year to £110. I don't know what she started at, but she cannot previously have had *very* large increments! £5 a year in 25 years would have made £125, even had she started with nothing. Still, she has now had a lot of thanks and I'll have to find up something nice about her for the minutes. After lunch Tommy went into the town and the senior clerk came through. The master had been very quiet in his complaints to the committee and Father Moir reported that the senior clerk was a Communist. They would probably have sacked him but for the difficulty in replacing. I daresay the senior clerk will leave if he can find something suitable. He told me the whole staff were seething with unrest and he had told the master what somebody ought to have told him about himself years ago. Said the office boy aged 15 was working over 60 hours a week and if he reported it to the Ministry of Labour there would be trouble. They are now engaging a woman clerk for part-time clerical work, paying her 1s. an hour plus dinner. Char-women get 11d., but if the clerk proves satisfactory she will probably get 35s. a week instead of 30s. for 30 hours. They also engaged a new matron's maid at 30s. a week plus all her meals. The maid is 19, the clerk 40. Anybody meeting the master today would have thought how nice he was. The Bury St Edmunds one isn't bad but a shopkeeper told me he wasn't sober for a week at Xmas....

... I sent a cheque for 5s. to join the Fabian Society here, and had managed in Sudbury to buy three small blue and white plates at 1s. 1½d. each to put under three blue and white beakers I bought (as I couldn't get breakfast cups) at 2s. 3d. each.

Sunday, 31 January

Doing housework in these two rooms is like running round in circles. By the time the kettles are filled the oilstoves and lamps want oil, and by that time it is washing-up and the emptying of bowls into pails and the cleaning and putting away of the bowls and other paraphernalia, and then it is time to get ready for a meal, etc. etc. Everything has to go in and out. One can, for instance, if one has a kitchen, leave things in it, but it looks terrible to have wiping-up cloths and so on in the drawing-room! My food I stow in a chest of drawers as the mice can't get in it, though for some reason I haven't heard a mouse since Xmas. I've a nice white patch on the ceiling now. I thought the plaster was falling so got a tin tray and a poker to help it down, but it was only two layers of ceiling paper dropping off. The last paper put on is grey, the previous one whitish, and the ceiling itself a glaring white and apparently quite firm. This would be a marvellously light room if it had a white ceiling. If it were my own place I'd whitewash it, but it isn't and I might be quitting any week. It is a pity because both rooms are a nice size and could, with the furniture I have, look lovely. I'd like to be back in my Bexhill place for the summer – the only trouble there was that I spent much more than I earned, because I earned next to nothing. I wouldn't have minded whitewashing that place, because I'd got a very nice landlord, and a helpful one.

The tenant downstairs says I ought to see the picture *Gone with the Wind*. Says Bostock won't pay the price to have it here because with 'tripe' he can have three houses a night and with that only two, and as many go to see the tripe as would go to see anything else. The 'tripe' pictures are very cheap. She thinks some of the pictures very bad for children. Her own boy has gone three weeks at a stretch now without wetting a bed and she is hoping it will last. Says she keeps him quieter than his last home did and she thinks his nerves are steadier. He tells her too that when he was away he found he got out of a lot of trouble by telling lies and she is busy teaching him, by degrees, that 'truth is the best policy'. I wonder what effect all this break-up of homes will have on our future citizens?

Another thing the tenant below stairs says, is that the usherettes in the cinema live in a world of their own, a world of jitter-bug dancing, and are more like savages than what she and I used to expect English people to be.

Like myself she gets an impression of slithering black naked bodies when the BBC plays its 'rhythm', and she is revolted whereas the usherettes glory in it. Queer, but there is this difference between the present-day youth and the 40 year-olds and over, and it doesn't only show itself in usherettes.

Something to do with North Africa – De Gaulle said unless a radical change were made there would be a bloody revolution after the war in France and then the French people would never forgive the American government. I should have imagined that when we invade France there will be a bloody revolution, so I can't see why they should have it *after* the war. Some other Frenchman also with a very pleasant name is now being tried for complicity in the Darlan murder, and it looks as if a Nazi fiend is going to try him. Queer business. Darlan was supposed to have 'quisled' over to us, but it looks as if the Axis must have been in power the whole time, and still are. A pity when that chap killed Darlan he didn't kill a few dozen like him as well! I prefer Germans to pro-Nazi Frenchmen, anyhow. I suppose one of these days we'll get an explanation of this Darlan business – a correct one, I mean. I don't really think the USA can have gone pro-Nazi! …

Thought I was 'free' [from national service] because over 45, but I now see by newspaper that persons (women) up to sixty are put on work of national importance if they leave their job, so apparently I can't change mine to suit myself exactly.

I hear my nephew likes his school of architecture. Lucky for him he was an 'only child' or he wouldn't be there. Considering the possible need for architects later, it seems a crying shame that *every* child has not the opportunity, supposing he had a bent that way. I do hope all education will be free after the war – not much sign of it at present, and I hear that scholarships are now few and far between. Why does filthy lucre run this world! No wonder we are a lot of rogues. My nephew at De Havilland's had always been interested in engineering: this other one who wanted architecture was taken all over the Vauxhall Works to see if he would like to start there, but he wasn't the least bit interested; so it had to be architecture. Again, it was lucky his parents had no other children, because they could not have afforded his architecture if they had had another child to keep, and he would probably have been forced into engineering to bring some money home instead of taking more out. No wonder the birth-rate is low!

Query now whether we pay for school lunches as well as school milk for our children boarded out at 12s. a week plus 40s. a quarter for clothes plus about £8 occasionally for a complete outfit. I know the foster-mothers don't get anything out of it, but it seems a shame that children who have parents and perhaps are good stock (our boarded-out ones are usually of low mentality if not feeble-minded or vicious) have to be brought up on about a quarter of that and be badly fed and badly clothed in comparison.

Whole batch of men in Sudbury British Restaurant, dirty clothes, Wellington boots, old caps and mufflers, some with a week or two's growth of beard.

Probably Irishmen working on aerodrome.[69] Somebody said 75 per cent of them are ex-convicts and certainly some looked it. Others were young, with some pretension to good looks. Others looked 'mad as march hares' and wild. Some drink-sodden. A terrible lot of creatures, taken all together. Gave me a shiver inside to think I had pre-war been unaware almost such people inhabited the earth. Behaved themselves all right. Like myself, temporary workers, only I live among Persian carpets and oil paintings and earn nearly £4 a week and they earn about double that and probably live on earth floors and have no pictures. Some of the young ones looked as if laughter could bubble up out of them, the old ones had no laughter but just looked like convicts with an almost vacant stare.

Town and Country Planning. Notices of a meeting at Ipswich sent to all our Shire Hall 'big bugs'. Don't suppose they will go as they would have to pay fare and expenses plus 2s. 6d. entrance fee. Wonder why town and county planning wanted them to attend. Should have thought it better to have a meeting for whole of Ipswich and another for whole of this town. Expect our big bugs quite satisfied with Bury St Edmunds and wouldn't like it changed. People like myself might like to put it in a museum and start afresh!

---

[69] This was probably the aerodrome under construction to the north-east of Sudbury. Winifred often mentions hearing or seeing low-flying aeroplanes, which might have been based at any of the several airfields in West Suffolk, all of which are described in Graham Smith, *Suffolk Airfields in the Second World War* (Newbury, 1995). Further details on these airfields are provided in Michael J.F. Bowyer, *Action Stations, 1: Wartime military fields of East Anglia 1939–1945* (Cambridge, 1979). The base nearest to Bury was at Rougham, which opened in August 1942. The presence of the US Army Air Force in the county was growing dramatically through 1942–43, and the construction and expansion of airfields required tens of thousands of workers and a massive investment of resources (Smith, pp.38–9 and 279–80). The presence and impact of American air power in Suffolk and other parts of East Anglia are described in R. Douglas Brown, *East Anglia 1943* (Lavenham, 1990), chapter 1.

PART TWO

February to June 1943

Winifred continued with her diary throughout 1943 and often produced volu-
minous daily entries, mixing together observations of others, self-examination
and musings about the human condition. Her writing, though, became more
intermittent – on most days she wrote nothing at all, in contrast to the early
weeks of her diary. While she produced diary entries on thirty-two of the
sixty-one days in November–December 1942, in April–May 1943 she wrote
on only fifteen of these sixty-one days – though often at extraordinary length
(several thousand words at a time), and not just about the events of the day
on which she was writing. The character of her diary, too, gradually altered,
for she tended over time to devote more space to opinionated digressions and
personal rumination, and less space to descriptions of the social world she
inhabited (aside from office politics). Consequently, the following extracts,
for the period between February and late June 1943, represent a smaller
proportion of the Winifred's full diary than those in Part One. As much as
possible, these selections have been chosen to shed light on her everyday life
and experiences in, and observations about, West Suffolk in wartime.

Sunday, 7 February 1943

Sunday evening again, and still water to heat and a bath to have, and I ought
but shan't darn some stockings. Life is a good fight against dirt. In a week
this place gets as dusty as a country lane, so again this weekend, as last, I
have spent hours sweeping. A good job I am not religious, for there would
be no time to go to church, anyhow. I rubbed up the windows and wanted
to throw the front one into the street because for two years at least the sash
cord has been broken and it is difficult to push it up and down. One of the
back windows has a bit out of it and a split down it, so that it is difficult to
clean, but it is the front one which makes me curse the landlord. If the second
sash cords breaks at any time I shan't be able to clean the outside of the
window at all, and then I shall look like 'Dirty Dick's'. I took some brown
casement cloth curtains down from the back window and put up clean green
ones. Owing to the shortage of paper the laundry has asked for their things to
be wrapped in material, so with luck I can use a brown curtain as wrapping
each time, and they then wash it free instead of charging 9d. They are only
little curtains which fit inside the bigger black ones. I have also filled lamps
and oilstoves and washed out two slop-pails, after which I emptied coffee

grounds in one and sprayed it with brown streaks! It is impossible to keep the dirt down in the time at my disposal. I *never* clean the attic, but at the moment three cupboards are looking a disgrace, two mainly because the plaster comes away from the ceiling laths and makes a mess. I also swept the stairs....

I saw a young woman in the British Restaurant the other day, with her young child. If an aristocrat she would have been considered a beauty, but she appears to be the wife of a private soldier, and dresses like it, in a coat about six years old. I met her quite six weeks or two months ago and she was then looking for rooms and her teeth were aching. Things are still the same, and she and the child sleep at the YWCA and walk about all day. Her teeth ought to come out, being badly decayed. She is not an employed person but perhaps the Army would stand the cost of it if she knew to what Association to apply, but that I do not know. I should have thought she could have got a domestic job and taken the child with her, but perhaps she does not like the idea and prefers to wander about and see her husband when she can. He is in camp a few miles away.

In his car, I asked the county medical officer if he heard Laski on the Beveridge Report, and he said he was there but went in late. He was disappointed at the absence of questions. I said: 'I thought *your* people were going to ask questions' and he said 'So did I. There were lots of doctors there, but nobody said a word.' He rather surprised me by saying that wherever you get public administration you get persons making money out of it fraudulently, even in West Suffolk. We had been talking about borough councils but I do not know if his remark concerned borough councils....

I heard from the internee about Thursday this week. He had just heard (when he wrote on the 28 January) that he was allowed to look for a job, and he advised me not to write to his friends as it would be premature and he could do it after his release.[1] He was not well but the news brightened the future and gave him hope. He expected to be out in a few months. I replied hoping it would be at the longest weeks, not months. I therefore still have no details at all. He had just received 20 letters I wrote him to Australia after he left there; he got back to the Isle of Man a year ago, so they must, at the rate of about one a week, have been floating about 16 months or so. Most of them were rather queer, because he had cabled he was returning; the Home Office, when I tackled them, said he wasn't, and when I exploded said, several weeks later, and about three or four weeks before he arrived, that they had just authorised his return. He cabled he was being sent back to take a job on a poultry farm and they informed me he was coming to join the Pioneers. So I really didn't know how things stood. Still, on the trip out to Australia he had been welcomed as a parachutist, and I don't suppose he had ever seen a para-

---

[1]   Getting a job was for some internees a precondition of their release. During 1941–43 there was a steady trickle of released internees from the Isle of Man.

chute! If the authorities re-examined this last batch of returned letters I shall soar no higher in their esteem, for I certainly put the word of the internee before theirs, though I did not know whether or not he had got on the water until I heard he was back – by a letter he sent me on arrival.

I had, of course, already written to a few of his friends about his being allowed to work. Some of them are anxious to get news of him. I may be wrong, but I think he is unduly frightened about communications. It would hardly in this case be because he is a trifle jealous that I write freely to some to them. As I am double his age he often fears I may 'boss' him, which he would resent. Some of his friends stand very high socially and I think some of this extreme reticence in him is fostered by them. They are British and perhaps accustomed to keep their own counsel, to order and not explain. They have been very good to the internee and are much more to him than I am, but I think the woman (mother of his boy friend) would like to dispense with me. She understands domestics and her own class, but I am neither and she is at a loss. She is quite a nice woman, as women go, but there is perhaps class antipathy between her and me. You see, I used to help the internee with his typing and therefore am a 'mere typist'. Had she wanted, she could doubtless have explained more to me herself, for she has kept in touch with Bloomsbury House even if they have recently cold-shouldered me. But she has not done so and I certainly shall not write and ask her anything, for I have quite as much pride if of a difficult sort. Perhaps I shall come to an understanding *when* I see the internee, and perhaps I shan't. If it came to choosing between us he would certainly choose them, not me. They are hardly likely to accept me as well. Why should they? He is young, ornamental, attractive, cultivated, and with a future, whereas none of these charms refer to me. He may require me – as occasional bread-and-butter when he tires of jam and cream and beauty etc. etc. Actually, I think he will. He wants something in his background, if it's me. I know his faults as well as his virtues and sometimes even that, I daresay, is a relief.

Wednesday, 10 February

Lit oilstove without getting out of bed, about 6.45 a.m. Made tea and cooked porridge on the oilstove. Milkman had forgotten to leave me milk the day before so I mixed powdered skimmed milk with sugar and oatmeal, added water, and cooked that for the porridge. Got up and did a few odd jobs and emptied a pail of dirty water downstairs and brought back the pail and two jugs of clean water to last until the following morning. Saw the newspaper man in the street on my way to the office so got my paper from him and read it as I walked along. As a rule it is the only reading I do in the day. For a change, and perhaps because I have to write a full account of this day, there was a most unusual quantity of news in the paper. The previous day the air raid warning had gone and it was so long before the 'all clear' sounded that people kept asking if it had gone, not because of any nervousness but because they had forgotten the warning was on and whether or not they had had the 'all clear'. We are all in danger these days in this town of forgetting if a warning is on or not. Today I saw in the newspaper that quite a number of bombs were dropped yesterday and machine-gunning took place, doing damage and causing deaths and casualties in southern England and East Anglia, where I live, so I suppose that accounted for the long warning. The paper does not say what places were bombed. It seemed strange that we have to find out these things next day from the newspaper and can be so oblivious of what is going on a few miles away.

Rang up the milk people to say I had only half a pint of milk in three days. Milk is more or less rationed and my ration is two pints a week but milk is plentiful here and they allow me 3½ pints a week. The girl on the phone asked me how much I wanted so I, feeling much astonished at such an unusual question in these war times, said a pint. She said she would send it up and see I had my half pint regularly thereafter. I think the trouble arose this time because where several milkmen were delivering in one district it has been arranged that one only should take over all the customers in that district, and the milkman had got confused with having additional customers. Also, there being a tenant downstairs, if he decided to shorten her supply at any time she and I wouldn't know whether the full quantity delivered belonged to her only or not. We shan't now, but I expect the dry season for cows will soon be over and then we can get more or less what we like. When I went home after lunching at the British Restaurant I found that either the milkman or somebody else had delivered a half pint [of] milk, so the girl's pint never materialised.

I received three letters during the day, one being from Mass-Observation, the second from Staines, and the third by hand from the Bury St Edmunds branch of the Fabian Society, which read as follows: 'In view of the interest in the Beveridge Report, we have decided to establish a forum for fortnightly study and discussion of the more important sections. The first meeting will be held at St Mary's Institute, Crown Street, on Saturday, 13 February at 7.30 p.m., for preliminary discussion and arrangement of programme. We shall be very pleased to have your advice and help. (signed) The Executive Committee, F.S.'

An isolated thought. I have often wondered at the French cruelty which made the guillotine a fact. Now I know that in days like these, when speech is forbidden and writing could endanger one's life, that 'it might happen here'. It is highly dangerous to write for Mass-Observation in these days. Yet I do not like the dumb, driven cattle overmuch. Sometimes I wonder if this is my deserved experience of hell or if the war is a nightmare of horror from which I shall awake. Compared with this world now, Dante's hell was heaven.

Other thing of interest in the newspaper was De Gaulle's suggestion to start a democratic regime in Africa by burning 15,000 prison dossiers. I endorse this heartily. Many of those prisoners are Spaniards who fought for the Republic in their civil war and I should think if they are not soon freed there will be neither body nor soul to set free. God knows why we are so scared of Mussolini's brother Franco, but in the world of yesterday and today almost nothing is done except by way of self-interest. I am probably as bad as the rest because I certainly would not have sacrificed an Englishman to help the Spanish Republicans at the time, though sometimes now it seems as if it had been better if we had started our war with them at our side. Still, of course right to the last moment I hoped there would be no war and was greatly surprised when we declared it, getting a feeling that we had taken our biggest step in the dark. Even now it seems a fluke that we are likely to win this war, for we seem to have done next to nothing but luck has been on our side. The Russians took the brunt of it from us, and now our money and American money seem to be getting into full swing so that by force of arms we appear to have Germany nearly on her knees. I suppose we have an army, but it always in my imagination seems infinitesimal in comparison with the enemy's. I think too that some of our people must have brains – the people in the background, scientists and inventors and so on. One rarely meets a brainy person and one hardly notices them, they are so rare among politicians, but we must have got them in the country hidden away somewhere. When I say 'brains' I mean creative brains – I know we have a good share of cunning amongst us, mainly in our dominant classes. But as soon as we get a war the results of our creative brain-power blossom and the creators are encouraged and helped, so that things happen in a short time which might normally take centuries. Owing to that result, wars are not all dead loss....

In these days I am all output and no input. It is bad but I cannot concentrate on taking anything in – one reason I write so much is because of this craze to put out and not to absorb or recreate.

Newspaper still worrying about German 'U' Boats. I don't imagine such boats worry many of us; they seem alien from our world. Perhaps the newspapers are making a fuss because the government wants to spend millions more on counteracting them. Well, why not? So long as the millions are going to be spent, why worry what they are spent on? We, who before the war were so poor we kept our old age pensioners half starved and half frozen, have all the money always that we want for war. We were not so poor, though, that we could not afford to increase the salaries of Members of Parliament about the same time.

Still more in the papers about potatoes. A pity they don't grow ready cooked, though. A lot of our precious paper being used to advertise potatoes – suppose Lord Woolton miscalculated and got too many acres of potatoes and not enough corn. Still, better this way than the potato shortage of the last war.[2]

---

2   The Ministry of Food was actively promoting potatoes for human consumption, mainly

As to cheese, I am amazed at the large amount eaten in the British Restaurant, most of the men eating bread and cheese instead of pudding, despite the fact that they must get lots of cheese at home if they like it. Potatoes would go bad if not eaten, but it would be easy enough to stop the manufacture of cheese if we have too much. As the only kind I really like is Gruyère, all this propaganda about the chunky, coarse, strong cheese we get these days makes me feel like vomiting. It was the same in the last war when a landlady gave us nothing but porridge for breakfast for three months – I felt half sick every morning on the stairs to the breakfast room. Mainly imagination, I suppose.

Another newspaper heading is 'The *Wall Street Journal* objects to British Planners'. They are afraid in Britain we are going to plan a 'managed economy' after the war. Well, let them object, and let them object until they are in a screaming panic because they can't alter it. I should imagine that if the Devil wandered round the earth looking for arch villains, he would find an especially high percentage in Wall Street....

I had walked from the British Restaurant practically to my rooms with a youth who was now reading Alexander Dumas. Said he had only been to London five times but would like to live there so he could get all the music he wanted. Said that whatever music there was in Bury St Edmunds the newspapers always called it perfect, or the equivalent, and he wished they would criticize properly and not just flatter. I said I had lived in London several years and though it might be all right if you had enough money to go about, it was pretty awful just to live in one spot and work for a living, and even though there were parks it was such an awful way out of the country even in a motor-car....

Thursday, 11 February

... Went with Tommy to Sudbury today in his car, 10 h.p. Sunbeam. Should have called at Long Melford to inspect emergency cookers but had not time

as an alternative to imported food and crops that produced fewer calories per acre. 'Eat More Potatoes and Less Bread' was one of the ministry's slogans, and the virtues of potatoes were promoted in various ways (R.J. Hammond, *Food, vol. II: Studies in Administration and Control* (HMSO, 1956), pp.144–7). This campaign on behalf of the potato 'combined an attempt to interest seller as well as buyer. The caterer was urged to give bread only when it was demanded, and to increase the size of his helpings of potatoes; ... and with the external help of the Potato Publicity Bureau the retailer was encouraged to increase his sales with some apparent success' (p.145). A couple of months later – and this was standard news – it was reported that 'Caterers, domestic science teachers, British Restaurant managers and other experts whose job it is to feed the people were invited to a special Ministry of Food demonstration and tasting display of potato dishes in the Gas Company showrooms, Carr Street, Ipswich'. Potatoes, it was said, could 'be used to save imported flour in the making of puddings and cakes, and samples of sweet dishes were one of the features of the show' (*Suffolk and Essex Free Press*, 22 April 1943, p.6).

enough. The meeting, like all or most of the Sudbury Area Guardians meetings, was for me a perfect rush. Tommy saunters round talking to people, drinking coffee, picking flowers from the master's garden, and so on – he does not keep a dog (that's me) and bark[s] himself. Nice people at that meeting. The chairman was at her snippiest but likes Tommy – they get on very amicably. Tommy ticked off one of the relieving officers. We dealt with Hadleigh, Lavenham and Sudbury districts and therefore three relieving officers. Lots of people going into the institution and having to contribute 9s. out of their 10s. old age pension for the privilege, and for some unfathomable reason I have to minute all such cases as well as the amounts we claim from their liable relatives. It all seems a bit daft. If people bring you into the world and you are a boy you have to contribute to their maintenance, though it wasn't your fault they brought you in, but if it is your sister instead of a parent you don't have to contribute, though I would have thought the moral obligation was as great in one case as in another. If, on the other hand, you are a daughter, and you marry a man with £10,000 a year, who has sworn to bestow on you all his worldly possessions, you contribute nothing, though if you have married a beggar and earn a few pounds charring you have to contribute, as you do if you are a spinster earning money.

In addition to taking notes of what the relieving officer says in each case, I have to enter up the blasted case-papers, confirming admissions and writing in longhand the decisions of the committee, while the chairman writes ditto in the relieving officer's book, and Tommy writes ditto in our book. As I have to open the said blasted case-papers I am supposed to do about three times the work in the same time as the other two. Right in the middle of the rush period Tommy wanted to know where a certain case-paper was. I had put it in its correct position before him but he never does anything himself if he can help it, so of course he asked me to hunt. He is probably nervy, wants everything at once and gets in a fluster in case things aren't there. Then a member came in very late so Tommy told me to give him my chair and get another for myself from the master's office. Inwardly cursing, I gave him the chair, but instead of going to get another stood at the desk trying to get the hang of the aforesaid blasted case-papers and being by this time about four behind the narrator. It is true I can get the skeleton entries from the books later, but it is I who am supposed to be able to relate the whole story. Tommy repeated the instruction about getting the chair and then a couple of members went out so to shut him up I went to get one of their chairs, telling him as I went that the minutes would be in a mess. At 4 p.m. he was in a hurry to get home (he never can wait a minute and he had probably just finished tea with the master) so I have still some sorting out of entries to do though I have finished checking over with the relieving officers. So tomorrow morning I will keep the case-paper clerk waiting until they are done – Tommy, thank God, will be out all day....

On our way home Tommy called in the house of one of our foster mothers.

It was a thatched, rather long country cottage with small windows and an unkempt garden and it provided beds and breakfasts and teas. Tommy went in and came out to tell me the place was simply filthy and smelt and that unknown to him the woman had taken in four men from the aerodrome, probably Irishmen. To the woman's chagrin the children are to be removed tomorrow. On the whole, the tone of our foster parents is not in any way high, although some of them are good. The county medical officer favours foster parents rather than homes, but I don't know if I do. These unwanted and usually mentally dull children are a problem. The only solution I can see is sterilisation. As a rule they are not merely dull but are our potential if not actual criminals, or some of them. Certainly all children need perfect parents! That is another reason why I'm glad I have none – one needs a philosophy of life, faith in God, or something of the sort, to be able to guide children aright. I should have nothing to give them and no light to lead them by.

Saturday, 13 February

I went to the Fabian Society meeting, which was pleasant. About 30 were there and we paid 2d. each for hire of the room – St Mary's Church Institute, which cost 5s. 6d. Emil Davies, I think something to do with the London County Council, may come down to talk – I think on medical arrangements in Russia. The chairman, who is a schoolmaster evacuated from London, by name Arkwright, is playing Beethoven symphony gramophone records in his school on Thursday and I hope to go. The ordinary Fabian meeting is Saturday and the following Saturday we discuss the first 16 pages of the Beveridge Report which we are to read meantime. Very amicable meeting, though audience mixed. A feeling that the scheme may be sabotaged and that if it isn't pushed through now it will drop, as everything else will drop, when the war is over. Idea that it is a chance of a century if it can be got through. Fabian Societies seem to be springing up all over the country and this one has been in existence six months. Only person I knew at all was the church deaconess, and she didn't recognise me! A pleasure to hear people talk, and a change.

The Heilgers Conservative M.P. – Tommy says he's a bachelor, about 50, and *charming*. Doesn't appear to be ready to talk about Beveridge, but the other day he flattered Tommy's wife by going into her restaurant and asking her views on the Catering Bill! Tommy thought it was so nice of him, and quite an honour. I said 'I don't know what the Bill's about' and Tommy answered 'Nor do I!'[3] ...

---

3   The Catering Wages Act, 6 & 7 Geo. 6, chap. 24, became law on 10 June 1943. Its full title was 'An Act to make provision for regulating the remuneration and conditions of employment of catering and other workers and, in connection therewith, for their health and welfare and the general improvement and development of the industries in

My typist (who also looks after boarded-out children and types generally for Tommy and Gooch) is now de-reserved. So is the county assistant solicitor's typist – he does the legal work for the county, the solicitor being the clerk of the council. Ruth (my typist) definitely does not want to go – there is more patriotism generally among youths, who, though conscripted, seem to suffer from a sense of shame if they are not in the Forces. They are sensitive about it, girls not. Elsie is not de-reserved yet and says she will go if she is called up, but not a day before. She is very cynical, though young, and most cynical perhaps about Jews, for some of whom she used to work in London before the war, in solicitors' offices. Joan has expressed a desire to join the Forces, but not if it means losing her present job after the war. She is a girl who has never left home or seen anything of the world, and the adventure probably attracts her in consequence. A very nice girl of the 'good girl' type. I have never seen her cross. The notice about Ruth and the other girl came from the man power board, not the labour exchange. They are more likely to be called up because officially we are not working 48 hours a week, though lately I have had to work some overtime because we lost our other typist some weeks, or months, ago.

I got my income tax credit for last year recently – over £9. If the war lasts another year I'll be quite rich! About £19 war credits plus about £30 superannuation, which will mean say £50 earned by myself to start on 'the dole' with! ...

Monday, 15 February

Elsie Foulger says I'm always grumbling about my landlord, but so might she if it took her a solid hour to get her fire going and at the end of the hour everything was covered in smoke and she couldn't stand in front of the fireplace owing to the down-draught. As I was writing the shutter and the bricks which keep it in place fell into the fire, so it took another quarter hour to get those back, with tongs and poker. I would pay a £50 deposit if I could get a new estate house, and risk letting part of it, but there are no estate houses.

Being at a loose end tonight, I got out the gramophone from the sitting-room, finding it covered inside and out with mildew, despite recent fires. Doesn't say much for my dusting, but it was in a dark corner and I presume I dusted too lightly. I had been hungry but had to wait while I reheated some stew for the third time, no, sorry, the fourth, for I've had it twice today. I was afraid, it being Monday, that the British Restaurant would provide boiled rice slightly flavoured with cheese, and I wanted a good meal. I prepared and cooked it Saturday evening and have eaten it Sunday and today (Monday).

which they are employed'. The bill, which enlarged the state's regulatory powers, had been the subject of extensive parliamentary debate in February–April 1943.

There was in it 1s. 1d. worth [of] mutton, a few haricot beans, a 3d. cabbage and one pound of potatoes, and tonight, as the mutton had vanished, I added some cooked bacon and cooked beef sausage. My butcher never has sausage other than beef and I've never seen any pork in his shop, except once some pig's trotters, which I don't like, anyhow. I think it was a silly idea to turn all the pork into bacon, and a farmer tells me that making it into bacon causes a lot of wastage. As it is, I go from any kind of mutton to beefsteak and back again.

Well, while the stew re-heated (and if this fire doesn't soon warm up I'll have to light an oilstove, for though my knees are burning my chest and back are shivering in the breezes) I sat on the hearthrug and started to play the gramophone. The third record was Beethoven's Menuett, and after that I pushed it away. I have an idea that if I could follow the works of classical composers I'd like the music and Beethoven in particular. As a rule I do not like musical people and shun musical gatherings, but I think if I listen to music on my own I might get as interested in it as I am in literature and painting and even sculpture and architecture. But something within me these days thrusts music outside my life. I could not stand emotional music, for one thing. It may be that I put my own emotions into the music instead of getting something from it. It might even make me weep, and I'd hate to weep. Besides, music is not for such as I. The Menuett told me tonight it might well be possible, by means of music, to escape into another world. But what good does it do to escape into another world? It is akin to getting drunk. This world is ugly and sordid but it is the world in which I have to live, so really it would be more sensible to wash up the day's dirty dishes, with their ugly and sordid saucepans and milk bottles, which at the moment grace the floor near my feet. Put aside all such things which might create emotion and be *hard*. The world is bloody and ruthless, so be steel to meet it.

Not everybody is like myself. The internee, for instance, is highly culti-vated generally and crazy on music. Nearly crazed me a year ago when he got back to Douglas, to send his gramophone, 'feeling in moral need of it'.

Suppose I'm sitting here in abject misery, with the washing-up waiting, and nothing to live for and less to die for and wanting nothing and nothing to read or get interested in and another day tomorrow as stupid and profitless as today. Sounds as if I'm nearly an idiot.

I ought to ask the Fabian schoolmaster if in his opinion proper food and environment do improve states of mental deficiency. Children at his school were given different kinds of food and he said the result was amazing, physi-cally and mentally. A Miss Bates of 'Roseacre', Alpheton, Suffolk, has just adopted one of our babies into a lovely house and hopes when she grows up she will want to be a doctor. I am sorry the child can't grow up in a few months, because the result might be of interest with regard to heredity. The child's mother keeps open house for men and her children have many fathers between them. In addition the children have been neglected and dirty and half-starved and probably would have been burned to death had there not been neighbours. The Bates baby is supposed to be bright and charming and has spent most of its life in the ordinary nursery which happens to be attached to our mental deficiency place at Kedington, Suffolk, where it doubtless received the best of attention and where we put it when we took her away from the mother....

Not much fuel being burned here tonight. The fire just keeps alight, fanned by the wind down the chimney, and that's all. Nothing has happened in my life all day today – just a void between waking and sleeping. No letters. Nothing in the newspaper. Nothing in the office, apart from ordinary routine. There may or may not be letters in the morning – probably not. Which reminds me that I'd better give the office boy some money to see if he, by going early, can buy a cake for office distribution – I attain the stupid age of 47 on the 17th.

There goes the air-raid warning: it is nearly 8.45 p.m. So apparently *something* has happened today, if only that! Well, I'd better start, via the washing-up, to get to bed. This room shook and my chair with it, but it was only the downstairs tenant shutting a door. The only way of recognizing bombs in the house will be by seeing them – though I hope it won't come to that. Now the wind is rumbling like guns. I wonder what the internee is going to do about this furniture if and when he comes out of internment. I don't know if he will hope to set up in another flat after the war and want the stuff. Even if I sold mine with his I've too many personal belongings to cart them round and pack them into the very limited space usually allotted to a lodger. There goes the 'all clear' – 9.12 p.m. Besides, with all its inconveniences, I prefer to be on my own. I think that last noise was a mouse scrapping in the wainscot. They have been strangely silent and quite invisible since Xmas. The adjoining houses, perhaps, have been poisoning them off. A cupboard downstairs smelt like it for a time. I suppose even the Lysol-soaked cotton wool I pushed in holes may not have agreed with them. I am wondering, of course, what is happening about the internee. I'd be most relieved to hear he was on English soil again and able to write letters at will, but of course it may take years to fix him up in a job even if he is now allowed to accept one, and my only role is to keep quiet and wait for news. Wait and wait and wait, and still again, wait. 'Wait and murmur not', as I believe the Scripture says! I've been in such a vile temper these last few years that I'm sure my face must look like it.

A clever move, I think, to start a Co-operative Party here. Anything to do with socialism would probably frighten the natives, who, despite their Non-Conformity, are Conservatives. They do, however, many of them, know their Co-operative Society, and may in many cases uphold that rather than their employers' Conservatism.[4] Looks as if preparations are now starting with a

---

4   The Bury St Edmunds Co-operative Party had been established in November 1942 (*Bury Free Press*, 23 January 1943, p.6).

view to an ending of the war in not many years from now. Supposing Labour got in, it would find it rough going just after the war and, if not exceptionally careful, could easily soon find itself out again. I am not very interested in Labour politics, but I suppose I think that improved social welfare would come from them and not from *Conservatives* and so I'd support them in preference. Wonder if it would be better if all parliamentary candidates put up as men of no party and one just voted for the best man and the best views. As it is, anything can crawl in under a party banner.

I'd like to know why many Co-op Societies refuse to make up pay of their employees on war service. I think it must be selfishness and greed, particularly as Labour wanted war or pretended they did, and Communists are probably pleased we are helping Russia. Ideals in Co-operatives are excellent but practice is often deplorable. I asked an employee why the Co-op Union he belonged to didn't press for pay to be made up, and he told me that the president of the society was the chairman of their branch of the union! How these people, in Co-ops as well as out, keep hold of the reins, while underlings let them. One of my brothers tells me that the chief aim of the Co-op Societies is not to be better employers than the private traders, to which I retort that if they are not out to be model employers then, for all the good they are, they may as well close down. Particularly, of course, where they act merely as agents to the big monopolies. I do understand, of course, that they are the only opposition the big combines encounter and in that to a small degree they prevent the world being run entirely by Woolworth heiresses and the like they serve a useful, if at present not very powerful, purpose. Perhaps it they became much more powerful Parliament would force them to close down, Parliament, of course, being mainly run by the Woolworth heiress class.

In a way I'm not sorry if the House of Lords now has more power, for where it is composed of the old aristocracy I think they are better than the blood-suckers who made fortunes in the last war and rose to our top positions or near them, and probably have seats in the Commons or are served by their friends there. It is a pity the last war killed off most of our best men and left these others. Still, it's all a problem too big for me. Once a man sells his soul for power, the Devil seems to help him get up to a very high seat before, perchance, he topples. Perhaps the scheme of things, I suppose. It may be entertaining for the Lord God Almighty, if not for us who have to endure it.

Tuesday, 16 February

I am feeling more cheerful tonight, probably because I received a parcel from my sister containing something I really needed. I have lit the two small oilstoves so as not to bother with the fire. Owing to difficulty in getting suitable wicks, the stoves don't burn properly, but at least they burn and warm the room, aided by the paraffin lamp. The tenant downstairs asked me to mention three things if the landlord calls tonight. She thought he might as the manager of the Playhouse Cinema rang him up and asked him to call. I owe him £4 for rent, so he may call, but he may not. She wants me to tell him the fireplace in her sitting-room wants a new back to it, the ceiling repairs (where the plaster fell down) have never been finished and whitewashed and the rain still comes through where the men put the slates on the roof; the furniture is all worn through at the edges and unless he provides some covers now the settee and armchairs will get worn so that they cannot be repaired after the war. If I have to tell him that lot, the situation will be ironical, because he must know that things are worse in my rooms than in hers....

At the [Public Assistance] Committee meeting a case came up of a girl who is due to go into the Forces. Her mother has such a houseful now that she cannot accommodate the girl's illegitimate child, and the girl has asked if she can pay her Forces allowance to the council and let the institution bring up the baby. Tommy, in a lordly manner, informed the committee that that should be referred to the Moral Welfare Home worker – it was a job for her, not for them, and if she would not deal with the baby the girl could take it with her into the Forces. So the case was left like that. I think after all I'd better go and see the moral welfare worker, for the relieving officer may be tackling her about it tomorrow and she may, just to oblige the committee, stretch a point and deal with it. Actually, she knows far less foster mothers than we do and her job is to get the mothers before the children are born and put them into the right paths, which she says is impossible to do after the children are here. She can hardly have any influence over an unknown girl in the Forces.

Back again. Things OK about the baby. She had said she would do the writing part and though she thinks with me that the Public Assistance Department could have done that she does not mind and it may be as well. Nelson, the relieving officer (a nice young man who, with a small district, has time at his disposal) rang her up this afternoon and as he had a car and she hadn't offered to visit the mother. She told him she had no available foster mothers so after ringing Gooch up he offered her our own foster mother Mrs Bridges, who used to have the little professional beggar Gerald Pearce and who really wants to have another foster child, though Tommy, for some unknown reason, has said she shan't have another. The health visitor reports it as a very good home and when the woman came to the office she made a good impression, and Tommy's decision may have been mere annoyance because she gave up Gerald Pearce....

We gave 35s. a week for parents and four children today, which is 5s. a head. Usually it runs out at 6s. Experts might say they could be adequately fed on 8s., but even on that, what an existence! I don't see how anybody's tummy can be in any degree satisfied under 2s. a day and I often spend 3s. myself, and yet food is only one item in life and usually the cheapest. Nelson was talking about an aged couple on relief today, how they went to bed at 6 o'clock each night so as to keep warm. Probably, too, they get less hungry if they do that. I have only been hungry twice, once when I had no money and once when I was residential secretary to a specialist in diets, for which reason I abandoned the job as I was losing a lot of weight after two months. The first time I got ill and had to go to bed until more food arrived. The second time I only lost my normal fighting spirit and had to go and get a good meal to provide courage to give a month's notice! I was at both times getting about the same type and quantity of food that poor relief cases would get. The second time I was sleeping in a building where there were sick patients, and I used to wake up hungry at night and remember feeling a mad impulse to make a clatter and wake people up and tell them I was hungry, or to get out of the window by means of knotted sheets and walk to the nearest town for food. Probably only the fact that I was amongst the sick prevented me from doing so. I am no advocate for meagre meals, though I find our present rations, plus unrationed goods, more than sufficient for my needs. The only hungry people during this war have been the people without sufficient money. Want is here amongst us, even while the war is on, and in days when old age pensioners are sometimes visited and asked if they want new blankets or pants, and so on. Pensioners are comparatively well off now, and I suppose the main sufferers are the sick and their dependants or widows who have so many children they cannot go out to work. Mobbs was talking today of a man he considered a very nice man but he had just died in terrible squalor and Mobbs reading through his papers found he was 'mentioned in despatches' in the last war.

Some fellow who was intended for our mental deficiency place was given a test recently and it was decided not to send him there. On hearing the decision, he asked: 'Does that mean I am liable for military service?' …

Monday, 22 February

I did a bit of housework Saturday afternoon but did not break the back of it. Read in the evening until midnight. Sunday was a lazy day. I still had a cold so stayed in bed purposely. Had the nearest approach to a bath which was possible and, as it was too late to cook sprouts for lunch, chopped them up and ate them raw with cold meat and cold cooked potato. Had also stewed gooseberries (bottled two years ago) and custard, the gooseberries being already stewed. Put on a wine-coloured chiffon-velvet frock and just managed to call on the borough health visitor about 3 p.m. as promised. She had some bulbs in a black pot and also a pot of white freesias and her place is very clean and cheerful. It is an old cottage for which she pays 11s. 6d. a week and as she has been there years she has had a bath and other conveniences put in. There are four rooms plus attic, cellar and a little back garden. Rather a doll's house, but comfortable. Says she will be able to take her superannuation in September so has told borough she will then retire. She is worried at the amount of work she has to leave undone because she has no health visitor or office boy or anybody to help, and owing to an accident some years ago she cannot cycle and so has to walk round to all her cases on the town and on its outskirts.... She will get not much more than £1 a week superannuation as, though she has worked 40 years or so, she has only been paying superannuation about 20. She will certainly have to reduce her present standard of living on retirement. She cooks better than I do and better than British Restaurants do, and I had the nicest meals I've had since Christmas. I think she is a Conservative but said she'd done nothing but work and sleep since Xmas and she'd like to come to some Fabian Society affairs, because the existence was telling on her. Wants me to book up for the picture *Gone with the Wind*. Hope I don't get another cold if I go! ...

We overlooked the big celebration at the Albert Hall (on wireless) regarding Russia, and it may have been a pity for there were some very good actors and actresses in it, including John Gielgud and Dame Sybil Thorndyke. We heard an interesting religious service from Student Movement House, London, and also a very good talk about getting our convoys through to Russia. We were both a little amused when the BBC gave out name after name of our government people who had been praising Russia, one in this town and one in that, because it seemed funny to make so much of them when a few years ago nothing was too bad for them. Diplomacy, I suppose.[5]

Laski states his views very clearly in *Where do we go from here?* It is the first expression of war aims I have read, and he has certainly given me another viewpoint. Up to now I have had no idea why we were fighting except that we wanted to crush Germany and Japan and to hold our own possessions, and perhaps to rescue occupied countries who didn't seem to have any desire to have anything to do with us. We might also have been fighting to rescue the Jews, but it seemed that only a section wanted to rescue Jews or anybody else. I did not know why we were fighting, but concluded some men thought they did and the majority joined up because they hadn't the courage to object or were too ignorant to think and so just obeyed. Not belonging to the monied classes, I had no particular interest in a fight to retain India, but being English I preferred, in order not to be unduly disturbed, that we should win. The hostage system also made me think that the Germans were worse than ourselves. Laski, however, does suggest that there may be something which makes the fighting worth while and which, in fact, turns

---

5   *Salute to the Red Army* was broadcast 4.15–5.00 p.m. on 21 February, and was part of a concert in the Albert Hall, organized by the Ministry of Information, to mark the twenty-fifth anniversary of the founding of the Red Army. The principal speaker was Anthony Eden, the Foreign Secretary, and the cast, besides the two mentioned, included Laurence Olivier and Ralph Richardson. Malcolm Sargent conducted the London Philharmonic and BBC Symphony Orchestras, and the bands of the Grenadier and Scots Guards also played. This was a time in the war when the alliance with Russia was taken very seriously, and favourably, by the British authorities, many of whom had not long before expressed very different opinions of the Soviet Union.

it from an utterly evil thing to a Christian one. Please don't take this for my sudden conversion. It may be, but one cannot form an opinion on one man's views, and this is the only book, as I said before, I have read. I have, however, a heavy load of cynicism at the back of me which accumulated mainly between the two wars and had got me, at the beginning of this one, mistrusting everybody. It may seem strange that I trusted the internee, but in that case it was not a matter of trust but merely one of knowledge. Laski makes me understand why people have clamoured for a Second Front – I presume many of them have been afraid the government would 'fight the war to the last Russian' so that Nazism and Communism would wipe each other out and British Imperialism would survive. More like than not, I suppose, that is what will happen in the long term. The war may be a big convulsion but I can't imagine that the 'City of God' is going to establish itself on earth in our time. Men are not ripe for that, neither are women, including myself.
…

Wednesday, 24 February

… A delightful newspaper cartoon today with a thin man called 'Labour Rank and File' displaying a white poster 'Social Security for All'. A little way off stand caricatures of Bevin, Morrison and Attlee, in the garb of parsons, and underneath the words 'The fellow's a heretic! He believes in what we've been preaching.' …

Somewhat of a coincidence that Gandhi is on a dangerous fast in prison at the same time that Churchill is in bed, apparently with pneumonia. If Churchill got too ill he might not be able to release [Mahatma] Gandhi even if he would. It is a pity in my opinion that we did not give the Indians their freedom before the war, despite the fact that our upper middle classes wanted jobs with big money and their wives wanted crowds of natives to run about for them. Such women are parasites and their husbands fools and neither British working people nor natives should be called upon to support them. Even lately I heard of a nurse going out East to take charge of a British hospital, and the government fitted her out with a marvellous outfit, like a wedding trousseau, for her off-duty social life, so that she could attend social functions and keep 'face' with the natives. 'Face' be damned.…

Thursday, 25 February

Anybody reading this [diary] would think I haven't a good word to say for anybody.[6] That may be because my lack of interest in life makes me notice

---

6 Some of her remarks the previous day, not reproduced here, had taken various people to task.

only the bad patches, or it may be that I mix with the wrong people. Tommy, for instance, although his 'responsibility to his neighbours', if ever it dawned upon his consciousness, would give him a tremendous shock, and though he is either mean or has to account to his wife for every penny he spends (or even both), has good points in that he is not vicious and is 'willing to live and let live'. Gooch I should think is kind and will make a pretty good man by the time he is 40 and I should consider him straight, honorable and reliable, but at the moment he is in some ways narrower than Tommy, despite his better brains. He has always been in public assistance, in a job where promotion could come with work and study, and where he had security of tenure, he has married a girl in a better position than himself and been careful and made arrangements for the future and present security, living moderately and within his income. What he has done he does not realise that many people cannot and have not had the opportunity to do. He has brains but also a lower-middle-class touch which distinguishes between himself and the poor.

I think I prefer the educated working classes to any. Some of the lower working classes, even if honest, are uncouth and rude and noisy and perhaps gossipy, and refinement oils the wheels of life, so I shrink from the lower working classes. Their views too are often limited. Often they are generous and pay attention to their diet, so that a lodger would be quite well fed. The middle classes are smug and intent on keeping up appearances. Their dietary is very often inadequate because they economise on that, spending their lives in niggardly little economies, studying (in peacetime) every stick of wood to light a fire, every lump of coal placed upon it; horrified at what they consider the wastefulness of their scullery-bound, badly-fed maid, who probably was brought up in a home where there was enough to eat and so far as food and firing were concerned (though she might have been deprived of all else) a feeling of plenty. Where such middle-class persons have plenty to eat themselves they frequently economise on the maids, giving them inferior foodstuffs and as little as possible. They spend a great deal of time on their animal pets and in discussing the terribleness of their maids. My nerves object to living with these economical people, for it peeves me to live in an atmosphere of such attention to petty details because I like, though I am not wasteful, to live in a land of apparent plenty and devote my attention to more important things. We are all, however, now the war is on, spending our lives in petty economies, though it has now become necessary owing to the fact that there is a shortage of goods and labour.

I wish the internee would arrive so that I can have a talk with him about our future, and find out if mine is likely to run alongside his or not. Actually, as I am 47, there is nothing I can do to secure my own future, for even if I learnt a dozen languages and book-keeping or anything in the business line I should not be wanted in the business world at my age. The war may be run by a man (Churchill) old enough for the old age pension, but the less arduous duties of a typist require someone not much older than 25. There will be a terrible lot of work needing to be done after the war, but most of it will be social work for which no funds will be available. The newspaper today gave a translation of a speech by Hitler, who is stated still to be out East. We mostly refer to him as an uneducated man, but even in a translation his words give vital meanings, and if he composes his speeches himself [they] show a very much deeper education than we credit him with. I can quite understand that his speeches go a long way in keeping the unity of his people. I do not think he will beat (in war) the Jewry of which he talks, but I think he is yet capable of holding the allegiance of the bulk of his people.

A few years before the war I met a Jewish woman and a German one in a room. The Jewish one was resentful and apparently hated the German. The latter was open and humorous but there was one thing I objected to and concluded might cause trouble. She thought it would be marvellous to have colonies and high adventure to get them. To my mind the fact that we were pirates centuries ago and gained them was something to our shame but a thing of the past we would not stain our hands with in present more civilised times, and it seemed strange to hear her talk as if we did wonderful and exciting things when we got them. A year or two later a similar subject came up with a French-Swiss girl and she seemed to think it was no worse for the Germans to want them than for us to have wanted them previously – with neither girl did there appear to be any idea that civilisation had now advanced beyond robbery and capturing slaves. It made me wonder if we British might not be more civilised than Continental people, despite our lower standard of education, and despite our reactionary governments. Still, France also had reactionary governments, so in that we are not solitary, and judging by the hovels I once saw in Belgium I shouldn't think they have a government at all!

There is a heading in newspaper today, 'Six million pounds to improve life in West Indies'. Well, I'm glad they are doing something, but it seems a paltry amount for the whole of the West Indies. Probably Sainsbury who keeps pigs and horses etc. in a Suffolk village could have given that sum without noticing the loss of it, and there are plenty about like him in regard to cash.[7] Most of them, of course, hold it tightly, for as a rule the more a man has the tighter he grasps and the more he strives to increase it. Why, I do not know.

Gandhi is reported as going along pretty well, and Churchill as improving. He has refused to release Gandhi. We may have sufficient reasons to keep the man imprisoned, but if so it is a pity we English are so modest that we do not explain our reasons and instead of doing so allow our enemies to broadcast everywhere what a criminal lot we are to do such things. It is unfortunate for our government that Beveridge, the catering affair and Gandhi all came in a lump, putting them (the government) in such an unfortunate light. Clearly,

---

7   Members of the Sainsbury family lived at Little Wratting, and Sainsbury's had a factory at nearby Kedington for processing food.

of course, in the Beveridge business, the government are in the wrong, for a healthy, vigorous, disease-proof and intelligent people would do a great deal more for the future of Britain than a disease-carrying and mentally defective sub-stratum of slaves.

As I came out of the Shire Hall today in the bitter cold stood a very thin, hungry-looking child. She was dressed fairly well (the Women's Voluntary Services often supply clothes) but she looked too fragile to withstand the weather and she certainly looked miserable. Free milk is a blessing, but they can't live entirely on that. She *looked* as if her mother received about 6s. a week to keep her on. Joan Burton says lots of the children living Hill 60 way here, where the council houses are, look half starved, and Gooch says it is because their fathers will have beer. Maybe. This irresponsibility of the male sex is, of course, a very big problem.

I wonder if the internee still smokes a good bit. I lectured him and refused to send him cigarettes because I said it was a luxury he could not afford and money should be used for more vital things than smoke. He informed me that whatever I said would have no effect and everybody did it. I retorted that it was no less a vice for that fact, at which he laughed and agreed. This was in the internment camp last spring. I think I ought to write to the kid again – it takes a hell of a long time to get him fixed up in a job and the waiting must be at least as trying for him as for me.

Yet I ought to go into the other room and wash up and go to bed and there are other letters I ought to write, and if I don't sew the sleeve of my black fur coat in it will come apart from the coat entirely! I went round the Shire Hall bike stand tonight to pump up my bike and felt energetic enough to feel a desire to ride it but did not. When I got home I felt energetic enough to go shopping but did not. Then a wave of despondency made me ask – what was the good of doing anything except going to bed? Then I lit a fire in this room with a view to carpet-sweeping it, but it was too dark to sweep where the carpet doesn't reach and so I've merely had tea and written this. My energy may have expressed itself so early this period because each day I have drunk a mixture of sugar, milk powder and the equivalent in powder of about two eggs. The clerk told me today that his chickens last week laid 51, so he is quite well provided with shell eggs. I got one the other day, after several weeks without, and haven't yet decided what to do with it. I don't quite fancy them boiled and scrambling needs toast and makes a dirty saucepan, and I can't be bothered to spend half an hour trying to get bacon to fry with it. If I could have bought ¼lb cheese the other week in Sudbury I would have got it, but as I have to get cheese in one particular shop it meant taking a long walk after I got back in Bury St Edmunds, so I didn't get the cheese. So of my cheese and bacon rations I think since Xmas (to 25/2/43) I have bought ¼lb of each, which is not extravagant in two months! I try to reduce my shopping for rationed goods to once a month and sometimes on that occasion I am not out of cheese and the shop is out of bacon. It is easier to shop in Sudbury but of course I cannot get my rationed goods there but only bread and cake and vegetables and so on. It would be easier if one were not tied to one shop, of course.

Friday, 26 February

Every day brings its bits for this diary, but I wish they didn't take so long to write! It must be the effect of my egg powder, milk powder and the sugar tonic, for so far tonight I've cleared up two grates and lit a fire, filled oilstoves, washed up, washed some clothes, used a carpet sweeper and swept up a bit of floor and had my tea, and it's just 8 p.m. I've also washed a brush and comb. I'd better buy some more egg powder, but the sugar is getting low so my one tin of golden syrup must come into operation!

Bury St Edmunds meeting today. Nice to walk instead of going by car and the day was sunny. Fairly pleasant meeting. Cragg suggested paying 12 guineas out of 15 towards a surgical appliance for a poor housewife but quickly repented and brought it down to 10. He is also on the borough council with my revered landlord, R.A.C. Ollé. After anybody else, including the chairman, has ventured a remark, Cragg says 'Well *I* think', as if that clinches the matter. And often it does, though even Tommy these days will intervene occasionally with 'That is not enough'. He did this morning in the case of a child of 14 who is so deformed the doctor says she will never work, and by so doing he raised her allowance from 5s. a week to 7s. 6d. – her mother having a widow's pension. Her mother could have had the pension for the child (5s.) continued had the child remained at school, but it was said that the village school where she lived only catered for children up to 11 years and already she had had her schooling there extended and the Education Committee would have nothing further to do with the case. She is not mental, which perhaps for her is unfortunate. It seems to me there ought to be some sort of school which would teach such a child to earn her living by means of her brain. Still, we do not desire intellectual attainment or spiritual or moral development in this country, things alien to our race....

Cragg even upset the chairman today, who after the meeting was mimicking him with a relieving officer. There was another child in the same house as the deformed one and it was stated that she came into this town daily, being apprenticed in one of our largest draper's shops, and that she earned 12s. a week and paid nothing at home for her board and lodging. Cragg harped on the fact that she had 12s. a week for herself whereas she should help to keep her deformed sister. It transpired, however, that she paid her own fares and paid for her own midday meal out of it, and after the meeting the relieving officer, the chairman and Tommy all agreed she wouldn't have much to spare. I agree, remembering my own youth. At that age clothes need renewing every year and wear out very quickly, and owing to the fact that one has been in the habit of growing one has no reserves. After I became 25 I found that my dress bill was comparatively nothing, for by that time I had a store of shoes and underclothing and one or two decent costumes and winter coats and gloves and it was only a case of buying one article now and again, not an entire rig-out. At the present price of clothes I don't know how anybody can afford to buy any. Fortunately, like the chairman, I shall be able to make my pre-war or early-war ones hang out until the war is over....

Leggett the relieving officer took me back from the meeting in his car. He said that now he knows what the committee is like, if people make application for things he thinks they will refuse he does not bring the applications before them, but the committee makes him feel sick sometimes, with their thousands, sitting there screwing people down to the utmost farthing [a quarter-penny]. I said he saw the squalor and it was a pity they didn't have to put their noses in it even if it choked them. He thought it might do them good....

Helpings in the British Restaurant have been larger lately. A boy walked along with me after lunch today and offered to fix up my wireless if I arranged about electricity. He is working in the electricity works here and as I must ring him up about an altered date for the gramophone recital I will ask if the company now has a meter to spare for me. If Bostock is paying for Mrs Nudds' electricity there seems little point in my paying her and I don't see that I can offer to pay Bostock himself such a weekly trifle! A trifle that is from his point of view, not mine. Nor is it satisfactory to share a meter which does not register how much each use has had.

The local paper notices regarding Major Heilgers are amusing. The Guildhall was large enough for such an insignificant person as Professor Harold Laski, but not nearly large enough for the Conservative MP. Further, on page 6 there is a flaring announcement of it with the words underneath reading; 'Chairman, His Worship the Mayor'. Now to have as chairman so distinguished a personage as our mayor puts this meeting on a very high pedestal. It ought to be amusing and pompous....[8]

Saturday, 27 February

... Gooch was saying that some years ago when West Suffolk forced its relief cases to work for the money, hedging and ditching and road works and other work, the government objected but the council opposed them and continued. In Great Yarmouth, however, it was impossible to find work for them. He thought this was about 1922 and he was working there. Said they had orders

---

[8] This notice was actually in the *Bury Free Press*, 27 February 1943, p.6. (This is further evidence that Winifred's dating is sometimes muzzy.) Elsewhere in this issue (p.1) it was reported that 'the venue has now been changed to the West Suffolk County School (the Athenaeum not being available), thus considerably increased accommodation is available for those wishing to be present.'

to give them relief and almost anything they asked to avoid a revolution. He also added (but this I did not understand) that they rammed all the food tickets up a chimney – the staff did that, I presume – and laugh about it to this day.

The gem of today's newspaper items is G.B. Shaw on Gandhi. He suggests the King should release Gandhi unconditionally as an act of grace unconnected with policy, and apologise to him for the mental defectiveness of his Cabinet. I think that's lovely. Don't suppose G.B.S. will get his head chopped off for it, being G.B.S. His wit gives him great privilege.[9]

Close together in the paper [p.1] are two articles. In one the Bishop of Berlin protests against totalitarianism, the execution of hostages and persecution of Jews, and does it well. In the other it states that horse-racing was banned in Germany, 26 February 1943, and beer will be banned from March 15th. It seems to me that a country capable of banning two such things is capable, despite the horror of their hostages and persecution, of a morale to which we ourselves are hardly likely to attain. They may now feel 'backs to the wall' but it certainly requires unity to defy jockey clubs and brewers, and self-discipline to go without alcohol. We have not, apparently, beaten them yet.

10.10 p.m. Back from Major Heilgers' meeting. Pretty good, on the whole. I called to see if Miss Osborne, the one and only borough health visitor, would go, but she was ironing and was not keen to hear the Major. I told her the mayor was acting as chairman, so she said, then she certainly did not want to go. I said I did not really know the mayor, having seen him once only sitting in front of me at an Adelphi Players masque in the Abbey Gardens. She said 'You must know him; he always walks as if he has done something in his trousers'. When he walked on to the platform I had to agree with her.

For the first twenty minutes or so the meeting was a wash-out. The mayor got up with a paper he had prepared (or got somebody to prepare for him) on the Beveridge Report. He was against the Beveridge Report, and said so in detail. People kept coughing as he went through item by item giving his opinion on each. Perhaps he is honest enough to say exactly what he thinks, in season or out, but it was all tripe. At length he shut up. I said 'Thank God for that' and the man next to me laughed. Major Heilgers got up. Unless he had arranged for the mayor to disagree with the report so that his own

---

[9] According to the *News Chronicle*, Saturday, 27 February 1943, p.4, 'The chairman of the Tagore Society has received a message from Mr G. Bernard Shaw in which he says: "You may quote me as declaring that the imprisonment of Ghandhi is the stupidest blunder the Government has let itself be landed in by its Right Wing of incurable Diehards.... The King should release Ghandhi unconditionally as an act of grace unconnected with policy, and apologise to him for the mental defectiveness of his Cabinet.'

agreement would be enhanced, he should have been feeling pretty awful all this time, for the audience couldn't have stood much more talking like the mayor's without walking out. They had no oranges or rotten eggs and were too respectable anyway. Quite a sizeable audience.

I should judge Heilgers to have had just the upbringing that every man ought of right to get – plenty of food and exercise and full opportunity of physical and mental development. I imagine him just average plus the best environment. Without favourable environment he would have been nothing, but with it he has turned out pretty good. Nerves steady and he is able to laugh. Very agreeable with everybody. He took the view that the government had accepted most of the report and were holding the rest up because it needed further consideration, but that the government had explained their position badly, particularly Sir John Anderson, whom he considered a man of the highest integrity and unusual honesty. Perhaps he ought to have called him just a great fool, but he did not. Major Heilgers is not, apparently, in the habit of summing people up like that. He would probably have found something nice to say about his own chairman, who sat there, peering at the audience, his coat buttons unduly on duty, and he himself looking like a Humpty Dumpty. Heilgers explained the report fairly thoroughly and the coughing had died down as soon as he started, which he did by telling them the Prime Minister was improving.

At the end lots of people questioned him. One got him to pledge to do his best to get Beveridge through. As he said nobody could guarantee employment after the war a woman asked if Beveridge had been given the opportunity to make a report on employment as well as unemployment. No. (They would hardly, of course, like him to publish one, I suggest.) The mayor at the beginning asked each questioner to give his name. I should have asked why, but nobody else did, and they all gave their names. The audience clearly favoured Beveridge. There was some talk of the disillusionment after the last war, a little about vested interests. Heilgers said he was sorry no doctors managed to catch the Speaker's eye when the debate was on in Parliament. He thought voluntary hospitals good and London County Council hospitals good. Said he was sure everybody there thought the West Suffolk General Hospital excellent, and there was not the slightest murmur of agreement. One man said the present Minister of Health was the worst ever known and Heilgers thought him quite good and was surprised to hear other people took a different view. He (Heilgers) called Herbert Morrison the Dictator of London. This had some bearing on his job as Leader of London County Council. Heilgers said he would always follow Churchill.

Arkwright (Fabian Society) got the biggest applause of the evening. He let other people question first each time and as a result did not get going until the end. After the burst of applause I think he got one more question in, but the chairman began to be afraid he might gain more expression of approval from the audience and perhaps spoil the favourable impression given by Heilgers, so he closed the meeting quickly before Arkwright could say any more.[10] In that, of course, he showed good chairmanship. As the Bible says, 'The sons of darkness are wiser in their generation than the children of light' – or something like that. I haven't seen my Bible for about 25 years and it probably got sold recently with other of my belongings when my stepmother's sister sold our house up, so I can't look the quotation up....

Heilgers is so average he is bound to be popular. As a speaker he is entirely eclipsed by Laski of course, but he is agreeable and appears to have a happy disposition. If he has any axe of his own to grind in Parliament he certainly hides it perfectly. It would need an exceptionally taking man[11] on the other side to wrest his seat from him, speaking of them as individuals, and I think if he does ever get pushed out it will be merely because people vote for the other party and not for the man.

The recent reports on drugs for the Prime Minister's pneumonia bring to mind an episode of my nursing days. Several people had died in the hospital from pneumonia and as I took a doctor to see a patient suffering from the same disease I asked if that one would die. This was probably 1932. He answered that a certain drug would save his life but that it would cost about fifty pounds and so that was out of the question. I wondered then how much a man's life was valued at, it not being valued so highly as £50.

The government are frightfully frightened there may be outbreaks of trouble between us and the Yanks. Heilgers last night stressed the point that we *must* keep friendly with them, individually. Well, the Stars and Stripes banner floats at the bottom of this street, but I should not think anybody worries. Some of the girls will be most pleased. If they get so numerous that they come and turn us out of our houses, then we *may* object! Owing to their bigger money and all that goes with it, I suppose our soldiers may get an inferiority complex and the Yanks may 'lord it' and the British 'object', but then the British Army has had the same complex with the Air Force and it does not appear to have upset the Air Force; so why worry?

Sunday, 28 February

Afternoon. I am going for a walk. I feel I haven't had a walk for about a year. Sunshine this a.m. made the country enjoyable. My housework can wait until evening.

---

[10] According to the very detailed report on this meeting in the *Bury Free Press*, 6 March 1943, pp.1 and 13 (five and a half columns), 'Mr Arkwright urged that we must organize for peace as much as for war, and then all the problems we had to meet could be met – (applause) – the Member replying that he agreed and that was what they were trying to do.'

[11] A 'taking' person is one who is charming and attractive, even captivating.

After the last of her sixty-seven diary pages for February, some of which are in typescript, there is one final page with the following words:

To the reader of all this stuff. When I read this myself just now, it struck me as if it had by accident become laughable. Are all the diaries you get just as amusing? (*Signed*) W.M. Challis

Tuesday, 2 March

The day has been pleasant enough, but tonight again there is still no news from or of the internee. Curses won't help, for I could turn the air blue and nothing would happen. It is no good writing or phoning or telegraphing because nothing would bring news and if I went to Douglas I shouldn't be allowed in the camp, so there is nothing to do but wait and hope for the best. It's a sad life, and I don't like waiting. I am impatient, but life is so short that one wants to achieve things, not just to wait and wait in hope and fear. I am afraid of that strip of water; I was afraid (except when I was on it) for myself and I shan't lose fear until the internee has crossed it. Once he is on the mainland I feel my fear will have vanished, for then life will to some extent have returned to normal. In some ways the waiting is not so bad for him, for at least he should have some idea what is happening whereas I am entirely in the dark. He is dealing with the tangible (I hope), I with the intangible, and I loathe the intangible.

I hate my own impotence for here is a situation in which I am as helpless as if I were imprisoned and tied hand and foot with bonds. Perhaps internees who are keen to fight with democracy in this war feel much the same as I do – that thought had not struck me before because (perhaps because I'm a female) I have never really been interested in movements and political parties or religious strife but only in individuals, and so physical fighting for anything would not have appealed. It was in my nature perhaps to have died for a man, a woman, or a child, but not for masses, or causes, etc. In these days I am half afraid there will come a time, during this war or after it, when a cleavage will arise and I shall be forced on one side or another, either on the side Laski calls 'privilege' or on the side of the Communism which through the Russians is giving Germany a hiding. So far in my life I have escaped having to make decisions. As nobody proposed, there was no decision to make as to marriage and therefore none about sex or whether or not to have children. As I was not a man, in neither war have I had to decide whether I would kill or not. In fact, I've had no vital decisions to make ever, the only ones I've made being business ones such as which out of two or three jobs to accept, or whether to leave a job or stay, in which case I believe I have always left, preferring risk and adventure to getting bored.

My talk of fear tonight follows my walk home, which was dog-haunted. Half the way a Pomeranian barked sharply (I caught sight of it once) and I nearly wished somebody would murder it for making such a row, and then in the darkness a big dog suddenly barked at me and I jumped and let out an 'Oh!' and a man, fortunately having it on a lead, pulled the lead and told it to shut up.

Tommy took his wife with us today. She thinks Heilgers will get knocked out of Parliament next time and that he is too much of a 'yes' man. Says she certainly won't vote Conservative next time because she won't be on the same side as the mayor, Mr Lake. She said she told Heilgers she knew nothing about the Catering Bill but that after the war employers would get their own back and that in these days everything was done for the workers and nothing for the employers who kept the country going by paying its taxes. Said she forgot to tell him mental defectives ought to be put out of life. She told me she thought there should be opportunity for cultivation of the brain power of the country so that money and position did not run it. Strange how many different kinds of people these days want education thrown wide open to all.

I said in a previous note I thought it a good idea for a Co-operative candidate to stand here, but now I'm not at all sure. In any case votes will be split because some people still call themselves Liberals. If they got a really first-rate socialist perhaps the Liberals, the Co-ops and the private traders could go over to him. Tommy's wife said she thought Mrs E.C. Wise a marvellous woman, which was strange as I've known Tommy [to be] very rude to Mrs Wise. She said Mrs Wise's two sons (one dead but previously an MP and the other just lost a seat as socialist) jolly good and I rather gathered she'd like the latter to put up here....[12]

I saw my youngest brother, who was having a 10 days' leave. He is always very well dressed and looks the officer rather than the tommy type. I told him I had not yet seen him in khaki and he laughed and said 'Didn't you see me in the Home Guard?' I said 'I didn't know you were ever in the Home Guard'. He said that being an air raid warden was by far the worst job of the three from the health point of view, and he certainly prefers being in the Army. Thought there was a possibility of his going to North Africa but not just at present. He looks very fit now he is getting East Coast breezes. I don't think Eastern county people thrive on the South Coast.

At the February Newmarket meeting it was passed by one vote that a woman and four children should be granted 50s. instead of 40s. a week.

---

[12] Mrs E.C. Wise was a JP and councillor. Her son Major F.J. Wise, 'an old boy of King Edward VI School, Bury St Edmunds', had run as an Independent Socialist candidate in the recent King's Lynn by-election, losing to the Conservative candidate by 10,696 to 9,027 votes (*Bury Free Press*, 13 and 20 February 1943, pp.1 and 5 respectively). Winifred was later told that Mrs Wise, after being widowed with two children, 'kept a small drapery shop to bring them up.... They got to where they are by winning scholarships at school' (20 April 1944).

Several clergymen there and they are more generous on the whole then the others. Tommy thought 50s. too much so arranged for a fresh voting to take place yesterday (2nd March) and as a result the 50s. was reduced to 45s. though some members still considered it ought to be 40s. The woman's rent is 9s. 6d. for five people but she has an Air Force man billeted on her who pays 27s. a week for board, lodging and washing, so the committee thought she would make 5s. to 7s. a week profit on that....

Sunday, 7 March

Weather today made life worth living – so long as one could be out in it. I went out this morning but had to spend a few hours after lunch cleaning. It is unfortunate, but I do not like dirt in a house, and this place seems to collect a six months' supply every week. Even Bury St Edmunds was on the borders of being lovely today, though I'd have liked to be back at Bexhill. Only the sea is lovely at Bexhill, but my housework was a much simpler and happier affair and the sun came in, and I went out when I wished. My landlord called it a picnic, and I suppose he was right.

Mr Jex, Norwich boot and shoe trade unionist, was interesting last night. A rather charming young corporal did not see why it was necessary to gather up the pieces and patch up a capitalist system, thinking a socialist one the thing to strive for. Mr Jex thought the majority of people in this country still wanted a capitalist system. I think the chairman's name is Mr Palmer. There is a kindliness about him and about Mr Arkwright, as well as brain power. Mr Crowe, the secretary, is younger and well dressed, and also rather good-looking. I should say he has a very keen intellect but judging from appearances I prefer the other two. The glance he gave me was devastatingly keen. I am afraid I only like the very cream of socialists. I first lost my faith in human nature listening to certain members of a Co-operative Society but got it back, for a time, in a munitions works, where the management were not so grasping and hard. I do not yet know where to place Mr Crowe. I like his wife....

Another shopman talking about our mayor said he used to run the town and so did his father before him, but after this war he would find things changed, and even now people here could afford to be more independent, and a good job too. I have heard that his brewery people are treated quite well....

I hear that lots of our county girls sent into factories get a sort of nervous breakdown through fright. I simply revelled in a fuse filling factory last war, but one girl here got a nervous breakdown over going to a factory of that kind. Nobody at the Shire Hall wants to go into factories but I like the life and should prefer it altogether to the Forces, but they shun it. As they know nothing of factories, perhaps it's snobbery....

I am booking two seats at [the] cinema for *Gone with the Wind* at 4s. 9d.

each. Mrs Nudds says they are compelled to charge high prices and she doubts that soldiers can afford to go.

Tommy was saying I would not believe what this town is like at night. Air raid shelters are used for sexual purposes and made filthy, and he thinks the Americans we have, like our evacuees, are the lowest types. Still, as far as I know, evacuees everywhere were mostly like that. There must have been a colossal number of slums in London but I myself know they were not only in Bermondsey etc. but in Catford, Kentish Town, Camden Town, the West End, round about the Zoo, and all over London. Tommy says that every night the shop fronts here are fouled and you have to pick your way across the roads with a flash-light because in the darkened streets the Yanks and others do not trouble to find public conveniences. Gooch said it was not only Yanks, for before they arrived people from an opposite pub used the gratings at the back of the Shire Hall and if Tommy remembered they had had to have the front letter box put up higher because it was being used as a lavatory.[13]

Tommy also said that the hotels in the place had had to take down all their fittings because everything was broken just out of a craze for destruction.

I hear that one of the maids in the annex of Everards Hotel [in Cornhill] has been sharing her bed with a soldier or soldiers, and that the case is coming up in court and the mayor has been notified.[14]

---

[13] In February 1944 Mass-Observation commissioned a report on Bury St Edmunds, which found that 'Local inhabitants say that the war has made little difference to the town, except for the influx of evacuees and American soldiers. The principal employers are still the brewery firm of Greene King and the local sugar-beet factory. Some Irish labourers have been imported to work on the new aerodrome outside the town. There is a history of antagonism to London evacuees' (M-O Archive, FR 2035, pp.2–3). The 'flood' of American servicemen into a town of some 17,000 residents inevitably caused problems. 'There are a few service clubs and canteens, but in general the soldiers appear to have a boring time in the town with little to do in their spare time but go to the pictures or flirt with the local girls' (*ibid.*, pp.14–15).

[14] This M-O report from early 1944 recorded the views of a middle-aged woman who kept a café. 'There's a lot of immorality goes on in this town. I've seen some sights in this café. Early in the mornings I've had young girls, 14 to 17 years old, waiting outside my doors with Americans for me to open so they can come in for some breakfast. You could see they'd been out all night by the bits of straw and hay all over them.' Her 18-year old daughter, who was with her, agreed. 'But what else is there to do but go for walks in the country? There's three cinemas here, and they're always full. If you go to a dance it's too crowded and full of Americans. There aren't any nice clubs to go to. There's only the pubs and country walks.' (MOA, FR 2035, p.15.)

Whatever the reality, Americans and sex were often discussed. On 9 July 1943 a well-off woman spoke to Winifred of girls having 'illegitimate children, usually fathered by Americans', and on 5 August 1943 Winifred recorded some of her own thoughts on the subject. 'The USA soldiers I have seen have looked quiet enough and seem specially fond of children. Other people (except young girls) appear to despise them though the same people speak very highly of the Poles. The Americans are frequently accused of sexual intercourse with children well under 16. Prostitutes are in many cases making much money out of them.' More concerned testimony was evident

Wednesday, 10 March

One of our planes crashed in Chevington, Suffolk (I presume it is Suffolk as it is not far from here but I don't know the village) late last night or early this morning, burning fiercely and dropping bombs which, if they have not yet (6 p.m.) exploded or been put out of action, may explode at any time. About 50 people were evacuated to one of our county council rest centres nearby. I have not heard of any casualties.[15]

The Women's Voluntary Services got to work quickly enough to pack sandwiches for the working-men starting at 6 a.m. for work. They augmented the iron rations in the Rest Centre by their own produce and sent to our Public Assistance Department for bread and a few other necessaries, which we always keep at the Public Assistance Institution for use in emergency. Tommy, the public assistance officer, went to Kedington today taking a couple of 'visitors' to report on some of the mental defectives there, and the rest centre job fell to Perrin, the superintendent relieving officer.…

I thought Tommy was piggish over a case last Friday but these people have the workhouse tradition in their bones and in any case in these days we are a sort of 'Lost Legion', for whereas labour exchanges and assistance boards are run in the light of present-day events and their instructions are continually altering, we in public assistance still take our instructions from laws made

---

at the end of this month. 'There was a meeting this afternoon about Americans, Blacks and other troops. Many clergy from different parts were there, also women speakers. It is considered that ten times as many girls will need rescue houses during the next three months. One speaker reported that in her district the black men were the biggest attraction and even bus-loads of married women came in to walk and lie down with them. It is thought it may be possible to get a ruling for Yanks to be in by 11 p.m. It was said our police are not allowed to control the Yanks, or to say anything to them. The meeting is making another try to get women policemen here, to look after the girls.' 'As I came by the Corn Exchange', Winifred wrote a few lines later, 'there was a dance band playing and in a way I could understand young girls being attracted by the troops like moths to a light' (31 August 1943).

Winifred revisited this issue after the war. 'In going around the town tonight', she wrote on Sunday, 10 February 1946, 'I realised for the first time how utterly dead Bury is.… I did not pass a single American and became conscious for the first time how much of our population and noise and drunkenness and love-making had been occasioned by them. Couples were no longer falling in and out of Everards Hotel and there was no dance and so no lights or gaiety in the Corn Exchange.' Later in the following year she thought that local women had by then changed tack to service German POWs in the area. 'I am glad to note that Bury girls have some idea of their own value. They are asking Germans five shillings a time for intercourse. The price to Americans was twenty shillings and to the Poles ten shillings' (3 November 1947).

15 A fully loaded RAF bomber crashed in a field in this parish on 9 March. 'The whole area had to be evacuated because of the danger from the unexploded bombs scattered around the crash site, and the village hall and feeding centre was used as accommodation until next day an RAF bomb disposal squad moved in and made things safe' (R. Douglas Brown, *East Anglia 1943* (Lavenham, 1990), p.35).

probably in Elizabethan-to-Victorian times, and our idea of 'relief' required is still to give as little as will prevent people dying immediately from starvation and exposure. Nobody 'at the top' troubles about instructing us, probably thinking we shall soon be wiped out and so we don't matter. Mrs Ramsay was saying that the taking over of guardians committees by the county council had in her experience been an unqualified success, nothing being lost and much gained. Honestly, I think women do outshine men on our committees. If I had my way every committee-man would first have to take a course in housewifery and East End settlement work before being allowed to become a member of a relief committee, and I would also stipulate that members dealing with staff should have proper business training or knowledge of the handling of people and of the work to be done. There are such people in the world, but our Public Assistance Committee haven't the least idea how to deal with staff, and here again the women are a little less helpless because most of them have at least run a few domestic servants.[16]

Elsie Foulger was spouting the other day about our being behind every other European country, laughing and asking if in any other country we should be compelled to sit and look out on all the junk we now had to. Her 'junk' was a large area of ancient tombstones, numbers of them enclosed with rusty iron railings, which comprise our large and charming churchyard – which, however, does eventually have a somewhat depressing effect. She thought the reason even Bury St Edmunds was dead set against voluntary hospitals was their knowledge of their own and the cinema pictures showing marvellous USA state hospitals and the Russian ones, which made them ask why we couldn't have such things here.

Gallup Poll on 'What We are Fighting for' is interesting today, 78 per cent thinking they do know and 22 per cent thinking they don't. It seems to me that 22 per cent is large, for surely after all these years of war more than four out of five should think they know what we are fighting for. Also, 31 per cent thought we were fighting for justice, peace, freedom from aggression, security, self-determination of nations, and I suspect that many who said that were merely repeating newspaper stuff parrot-fashion and had never in

---

[16] A few months later (28 September 1943) Winifred summarized a conversation she had had at a Workers' Educational Association class. 'I ran down public assistance (some of the amounts given at Bury today were really scandalous) and some of the members getting still further in their dotage and the majority not troubling to work out the amounts suggested for relief but voting for the lowest proposed figure if they were mean or for the higher if they were on the generous side. Mobbs just bumped through cases as quickly as he could, not stopping to present them properly, and Tommy ignoring Ministry of Health instructions, which he has never really read', and some committee members, she complained, discounted the need of those on relief for clothes as well as food. Discretion, according to her (and she reported many specific cases), was rarely exercised on the side of generosity.

their minds gone deeper than that.[17] The last war was 'The War to end War' and the present one has all the way through been 'A War for Peace'. When this one started it was a joke among people I met that when Hitler, Mussolini and Chamberlain, after their meeting a year previously, had returned to their respective countries, each one was acclaimed as the person who had saved the peace, and I suppose ever since, the 'fighting for peace' expression has been a sort of joke. In fact if all those words were examined carefully, apart from 'self-determination of nations', I think they would fall a bit flat. 'Justice' – for whom? 'Freedom from aggression' – impossible. 'Security' – we could have had that before the war had we wanted it. At least we could have had improved social conditions, but in this world there is necessarily no such thing as security. Quite recently I have gathered from books that the British Communists are fighting to help Russia establish her regime and to destroy our imperialism; I have learnt that the Labour Party are desirous of procuring socialism as far as possible but fight because they prefer Democratic-Capitalism to Nazism or Fascism, which they consider Capitalism without the Democracy. Presumably, therefore, Conservatives are fighting to preserve our 'Status Quo', while those of us who are left are fighting in order not to be beaten by foreigners, or because 'everybody else is doing it'.

It is rather interesting that sections of the populace fighting for such widely divergent reasons should have amalgamated to fight the one foreign foe. There are also people fighting (strange as it may sound) to put Roman Catholicism back again on its throne. The percentage in USA who don't know what we are fighting for is 32 per cent, which doesn't say a great deal for their propaganda. Ours at the beginning was so terrible I wondered if they had reprinted it from newspapers before and during the last war, but probably it has improved somewhat since, and the same may happen in USA. It feels better if one has some idea what people think they are fighting for, because otherwise one is apt to think the whole world had merely gone insane.

Suggestions in newspaper that Hitler has gone mad. I shouldn't wonder, though in the circumstances a good man would go mad sooner than a villain would, for it might worry a decent man if he thought the whole world blamed him for the wholesale massacre of humanity, whereas the villain would ordinarily care neither for humanity nor public opinion. He might, of course, go mad if he thought his own skin were endangered, and in that case it looks as if we have won the war.

I wonder how far M-O can rely on the public opinion passed on to it. I am reckless and feel I don't care a damn what happens to me, and therefore to some extent I put my feelings (for what they are worth) in this diary. But

---

17 The standard reference source on these polls does not confirm that this question was asked at this time, though it had been asked earlier, in June 1941 (George H. Gallup, ed., *The Gallup International Public Opinion Polls: Great Britain 1937–1975*, 2 vols (New York, 1976)).

I know quite well that 9/10ths of my time I do not *say* what I really think when in conversation with other people, and in these days when anybody can be imprisoned for dropping a careless remark I think most of us must say what it appears expedient to say rather than what we think. It is the only safe thing to do. For instance, I have only heard one person say the least thing against Churchill (no, that is wrong, two persons). Now, however popular Churchill may be, it seems to me that if we had our pre-war liberty of speech back again I should hear more adverse opinions, even if Churchill were a veritable angel. There is, of course, a fairly general idea that the brainpower of the country is so non-existent that if we lost Churchill there would be no one capable of taking his place, just as there is a feeling that nobody except Beveridge is capable of planning anything. I noticed that particularly at Major Heilgers' (or the mayor's!) meeting....

Friday, 12 March

... I see in today's paper we have destroyed a half million books in Munich. Nobody I spoke to thought it anything to be proud of. It makes me realise how ancient civilisations managed to get destroyed.

Now [that] I've studied the Duchess of Grafton and Mrs Weller-Poley at length together in the British Restaurant today, I feel I shall know them apart. They are about the same build and both in the same kind of green Women's Voluntary Services uniform. Neither is at all good-looking or outstanding, though both are tall and probably robust. I should think both are admirable women, in an ordinary way.[18]

I have changed my back room round again and prefer it. It became possible because I found that the mattress I had covered and arranged on the floor as if the room went up a step, could be rolled in three and covered with some Eastern sort of tapestry carpets to form a seat in the centre of the two high windows. Most of the furniture in this low-ceilinged room is diminutive. Low divan, low Chippendale stool, an oak stool and ditto stool-table, a knee-hole desk of normal height, a low oak chest and a low easy chair. None of the bigger furniture will come through the door anyhow, as it is very narrow, with the result that the other room contains four large arm-chairs, for which fortunately there is ample room. There are also two fairly large and one small table there and an antique bureau, all of which leaves plenty of space. Planes

[18] Lucy Eleanor Barnes (1897–1943) was the second wife of Charles Alfred Euston Fitzroy, 10th Duke of Grafton. Their ancestral home was Euston Hall, twelve miles from Bury. The duchess was active in the town's affairs. Captain Edward Hall Halifax Weller-Poley, MVO, JP, owned the Boxted Hall estate and was county councillor for Sudbury North.

are throbbing overhead as if many are outward bound. The hour is much later than I thought.

Sunday, 14 March

Conversation in a (small) stationer's shop. Customer: '*Daily Worker*? – what's that paper? – never heard of it'. Shopkeeper: 'Surely you remember when it was banned? There's a lot in that paper the other papers won't tell you. That's why it was banned.' Customer: 'Then I'll have one of those'.[19]

Last night at the Fabians' meeting regarding Beveridge Report I got a 2d. pamphlet by Dr Eva Black, *Health and Medicine in Soviet Russia*. It is a record of much already achieved and *ought* to convince our self-centred politicians that if they cut out their vested interests and ran this country by common-sense and not oppression they would breed fighters incomparably better than we British are at the present day.[20] For it is clearly evident that notwithstanding our tremendous good fortune in this war, so far as fighting goes, on the whole we have been almost complete failures. With (in many cases) fools at the head and apathy within the ranks, the result is understandable. It is almost unbelievable that a country of slaves and untaught brutes such as Russia was in 1918 should in these few years have got their medical services 200 years in advance of ours. This pamphlet makes the Beveridge Report look very elementary and modest and it makes the Rushcliffe Report look rotten, for the Rushcliffe Report attempts, by increasing salaries of the few to ridiculous heights as a bait to the masses they hope to inveigle into the nursing services, to carry on the nursing services as they are by luring fresh entrants into the criminally inadequate, sordid, unhappy, unhealthy, badly-run hospitals and institutions which now exist. The Rushcliffe Report may be only dealing with the financial side of the question (our country worships the farthing or quarter-farthing and can never see beyond it) but at least it could have shown that other aspects of nursing required to be dealt with. As it stands, it looks like a report issued by the employers' side in which all the muddle and confusion of the nursing services has been hidden out of sight but will be maintained to their utmost ability. It will 'gloss over' but it will eradicate no evils. What was good enough for the world in medieval times is good enough now, in the opinion of the committee which evolved that report. Judging by the names on it, trade unionists, NALGO, local authorities, medical and nursing, it looks as if our national characteristic of compromise did so much compromising that the result was nil. It is an evil report, worse than useless.[21] ...

---

[19] The *Daily Worker*, organ of the Communist Party of Great Britain, had been banned between January 1941 and August 1942.

[20] This pamphlet, which was published for the Russia Today Society, was reissued in October 1942 as *Soviet Health in Wartime*.

[21] The Rushcliffe Committee, set up in October 1941, was charged with investigating

I have not yet heard from or about my internee. I do not want to write and enquire of Bloomsbury House what is happening if I can avoid it, and it would only cause still further trouble if I wrote [to] the Home Office again. I think at any rate they might allow internees to use the sort of field-cards soldiers used during the last war, so that their (the internees') friends could know whether they were alive or dead, well or ill. But here in Bury St Edmunds I remain, gnawed with chagrin and furious at my own complete helplessness. I, just a puppet to be played with, with no rights of citizenship, no claim on justice, just something to be crushed out of existence when it suits the policy of the rulers of the country or the whim of some powerful person in it. I, who am nothing, less than nothing, for I must take my bread and butter from their charity and possess nothing of right. I, an average English woman, treated as lower than the refuse of the gutter, and only endured now because wartime shortage of labour makes my labour of advantage in the waging of war. I, who after the war will be chucked on one side to starve and perish, because I am 47 years of age and therefore no good to charm or breed. My thoughts read rather unpleasantly, but this shutting up of harmless and friendly and clever people and guarding them as if they were worse than criminals and treating their friends the same stirs all the anger of which I am capable. It is better that I say no more. As it is, this internee's detainment may have been lengthened already because I have published my fury to them. All the fury in me at the moment focuses on this point. Meantime, just to prevent myself from going mad, I attend Fabians' meetings and poke fun at county councils and mayors and corporations, none of which (with the exception maybe of one or two people in the Fabians) interest me at all. Perhaps after the war I can emigrate to Russia! I think, however, I'd find it too cold. I am wondering if some of our British medical people have helped to bring Russian medical services to such a high level, or who has done it. If one says that the people themselves have done it I don't think that can answer the question, for they must have had almost miraculous leadership, and I see no reason why all the brain-power of the world should have been inherent in Russians, and none in Britons. Perhaps the British could do in that country what they were not allowed to do in their own.

I really do not understand why our own ruling classes are so decidedly averse to social improvements. If they wanted to decrease population it would be easier understood, but apparently they want an overcrowded population living in filth and poverty and ignorance and sickness. Why, unless to provide cheap labour, I cannot think. I suppose that is actually the reason, but it appears a most short-sighted policy, and one which is in the long run likely

---

nurses' salaries and recommending pay rates and conditions of work. Its recommendations, *First Report of Nurses' Salaries Committee* (Ministry of Health), had just been published.

to destroy them as well as their slaves. It seems strange that they haven't enough brains to realise this.

Monday, 15 March

Winifred frequently complained of the arrogance or stuffiness or incompetence of her superiors in the West Suffolk County Council, and on this day the principal target of her displeasure was Perrin, the superintendent relieving officer, with whom she had had a quarrel. Then, after recording some of her complaints and frustrations, she continued in a more benign spirit.

… Yet, despite all I say in this diary, there is a certain friendliness among Shire Hall people. Blossom would do anything for anybody. The county assistant solicitor (Mr Jefferson) would help anybody over a stile. Hinnells, accountant (under Mowbray), is very nice and helpful. So are the county medical officer and the county architect. There is, however, an unusual amount of petty back-biting, and I think there is a reason for it. In an ordinary commercial firm where employees come and go and have nothing to do with each other outside office hours, people don't to any extent get on each other's nerves. In local government, however, where people have worked together for years and expect to do so 'until death do us part' or retirement allow us to part, and where after the day's work they meet each other again 'On Control' or in the Observer Corps, or in chapel, or wherever it may be, even if they attain a certain amount of friendliness they do 'grate' on each other. Moreover, as the jobs are 'safe', little petty rivalries enter in and things become more childish than they would be in a less secluded world.

I trust that anybody utilising this diary will alter the names of persons and places. It is easier for me to give the real ones but I don't want to be had up for slander! …

No letter from the internee. If only he were out and working and we could endeavour at least to make some plan for after the war then all the Perrins in existence wouldn't concern me one straw. I am from a personal point of view wasting my time at the Shire Hall, getting nowhere and achieving nothing – as usual. Unless, of course, this diary may at some time become of use, in which case the Shire Hall life may have served a useful purpose. In this life one never knows what might become of use. So far as I know, in 47 years I've achieved nothing at all worth while. I've amused myself by floating around as a shorthand-typist and that's been the beginning and ending of it. I've been too nondescript to achieve anything by personality. I've created nothing. By holding a job I've merely deprived somebody else of it, so there's no achievement there. I've produced nothing for myself of anybody else. But for the fact that there's a handful of people alive to whom I might in some way be of service, on the face of things it looks as if the only really sensible thing to do at my age would be to commit suicide. I shan't do it because my cussedness wouldn't allow me, because any form of future life would have no appeal, because I'd be far too much of a coward, and because it seems a duty, once we're here, to stick it to the bitter end. And yet I've a feeling, daft though it may seem, that the most wasted life may, unknown to the liver, in some way have been worth while, and though one's efforts appear to have been fruitless or the results entirely destroyed, that some force behind the world is utilising things for a good end. I suppose that's 'faith'! It may, if anybody reads this 200 years hence, seem strange that in these times when the whole horizon appears to be bombs, and bombs, and yet more bombs, and all death and destruction, an irreligious person like myself can still write about 'a good end'.

The only cheerful thing in the newspaper today is an account of the sort of world Shinwell wants after the war [*The Britain I Want*, 1943]. As the price is 10s. 6d. I'm not likely to read it.[22] There is a public library here but all it contains is a small selection of old-time light novels, just good enough for light literature for housewives who like a little amusement sandwiched in with domesticity. Boots the Chemists have a very much better selection but I shouldn't read enough to make a subscription worth while, so what I don't buy I don't read.

With all the talk about planning for peace one might think the war is going to end in a year or so. Yet that seems impossible, for if it ended now, it would have achieved nothing. Before it can end surely there must be one vast uprising of people throughout the whole of Europe? Surely there must be a far more terrific clash than anything which has happened so far? Surely the foundations of Europe must give way to allow something new to grow up and mature out of the wreckage? Almost in the death of the world, a new birth. Surely things cannot again go on as if this war had never been, in which case in a few years it will be war again? We plan, many of us, thinking life will be after the war just like it was before but more poverty-stricken and harsh. People say they remembered what happened after the last war and if people don't get together to prevent it things will be the same again. Yet it does not seem possible. If things have not altered, how can the war end? If Germany collapses at the most it will mean a period of so-called peace during which she would arm again. We should never know if we were beaten (which God forbid) and the Yanks haven't had a good fight yet so are fresh, so I don't think the war will end on that account. It would be a calamity if it did end, only to be resumed in the near future. If it ended now the conditions which caused it would still be with us and cause another. Of course, it may be that human beings just fight until they are too war-weary to fight any longer, and so wars are inevitable and eternal. I hope not, but it may be so.

---

22 Emanuel Shinwell (b.1884), first elected to Parliament in 1922, was Labour MP for the Seaham Division of Durham. He became Minister of Fuel and Power in the Labour government of 1945.

History suggests it, if ideals don't. In our personal lives, too, we either evade quarrelsome people or are compelled to fight them, and certainly personal relationships strongly suggest that wars will never end. Perrin tonight, for instance, would gladly see <u>me</u> bumped off, and I could see him go with the greatest equanimity!

Wednesday, 17 March

… Figures in newspaper today gave percentage of women between 20 and 24 who had babies before first eight months of marriage as 33. I used to wonder how many marriages took place for the sake of appearances. If you put it as one girl in three it seems tremendous. I'd have guessed 1 in 20. A pity children can't grow in a garden so that sex could be dispensed with! I am aware that plants have some sort of sex life but I am ignoring that fact, for life would be so much nicer and easier without sex. I am aware it doesn't concern me at my age, but it was a blinking nuisance from 17 to 33, and did rather upset my whole life in consequence. The trouble is that until one is about 33 one can prepare neither for matrimony nor business properly, because one doesn't know what is going to happen. Some women seem to make a success of both, whereas I fell between the two stools, getting nowhere. And really now I don't know (and never have known) how to launch out to make a living. I've thought and thought, but what is there I can do? If only I'd been born with an income of £1 a week, I could have done all sorts of things, painted and written books and learned languages and studied much and flitted from office to office at will in England and abroad. One could do almost anything so long as in the background there was enough to keep one from starvation. I've never had enough guts to risk starvation and that may be one reason I've got nowhere, and until I got too old shorthand and type-writing guaranteed me a living if I hung on to that instead of venturing into more remunerative spheres. I never liked the idea of starving in a London garret and developing tuberculosis. One needs to be exceptionally robust to risk such things, and besides I have never felt I was a budding genius!

I am just a woman who does not like women's work. When it comes to practical things, I might have liked being a painter and decorator or an architect or something of that kind, in which one could see the result of one's work. I'd hate to be a cook or a housekeeper or housemaid or companion or nurse or nursemaid or laundress or dressmaker or milliner or hairdresser or lady's maid or hotel receptionist or to run a restaurant or draper's or grocer's shop. In fact rather than those jobs I'd prefer to look after machinery in a tin mine! I went over one in Cornwall where the running of huge machinery rocked the place and it thrilled me. I am very fond of a typewriter, too. After 18 months of nursing I craved for a typewriter as well as for a landlady and an office. At the end of three years I left hospital and when I could no longer afford to look for a clerical job accepted one as a nurse in a private nursing home, whither I eventually went feeling like a little servant maid embarking on her first job. Before I went, however, a cyst under my armpit became infected (I'd been doing some terrible cases in hospital) and as I'd had the cyst about 15 years I wondered if it were a cancerous lump. I knew I'd just accepted a nursing job but my chief worry was that an operation might mean I shouldn't be able to typewrite! It was only an ordinary cyst. However, after three months nursing I got a temporary job at 30s. a week in a Whitechapel office (minus 12s. to 15s. a week fares from St Albans) and wasn't I glad! The flowers in life again began to spring (from Whitechapel pavements) and the whole world cheered up. Then I found I could earn 1s. an hour overtime and so I worked a good many evenings and some Saturday afternoons and Sundays and by so doing earned about 50s. or so a week (a fairly normal sum). It was heavenly – after nursing. I had not been so poorly paid since before the 1914–1918 war and this was 1933–1934, but I felt I'd 'got back', or was on the way to it. I did find, however, that my spelling and English had deteriorated during my absence, and I don't know that my English ever regained its former preciseness – little things had been forgotten. On the other hand, after a brain-rest for three years I felt I'd a lot more stamina physically. I was quite happy in that job, and liked the boss and the staff, for nine of whom I acted as shorthand-typist, and then the boss went through the stuff and dictated to me a revised version for the printers. He is a very clever man, and it is pleasant working for a man who is capable of dictating good English and recognising it when he sees it, the latter in my opinion being of more importance than the former, because I hate typing ungrammatical letters just to please the dictator, as one so often has to do.[23]

I am cross-stitching an old costume to make it wearable – I like cross-stitching, though I'd dread having to make a garment by sewing it. If I'd to sew a sleeve into a coat, for instance, it would get on my nerves to such an extent that I'd never have enough patience to finish it. I like knitting costumes and shop ready-made costumes etc. fit me, so I can manage without making clothes, thank heaven. I think the only garment I've made in my life with a sewing needle was a dressing-gown, and I've never in my life seen anything so badly made. I shall do nothing tonight for it's 10.20 and I haven't washed or washed up yet. Well, there's nothing really urgent in the employment line before I get a letter from the internee. I'll be glad when he's out.

Sunday, 21 March

Wish I'd left writing to internee until tonight, but then I might have interested the censor too much, so I couldn't have written anything worth while. Not

---

23 On 22 August 1946, she summarized her thinking about gender relations: 'It's a man's world all right, and we women only exist for their benefit, whether we marry them or work in their offices'.

that one can write anything worth while to an internee, for one is just as likely to upset as please, whatever one says. I wish the boy were out of that camp and as free as the rest of us – we may not be free but our chains are longer, and so don't gall so much. If he got to the North of England and wired me to go, I feel at the moment I'd drop everything here and go. I don't say it would mean happiness or contentment if I did, for we'd probably squabble and wouldn't like our jobs, or get horrible lodgings or none at all, but it would be somebody to talk to and laugh with. I feel I haven't laughed for years, and not over a long period at a time for about twenty years. You don't laugh if you have no friends to laugh with, or play with.

Saturday I called on the borough health services – no, not quite, for I think in addition to the one and only health visitor there are school nurses and so on, and I called on the health visitor, to see if she would accompany me to hear Oliver Gollancz on 'The Future of Party Politics'. She was too tired as she'd been walking from one end of the town to the other all the morning, had a baby clinic in the afternoon (or vice versa), and had fallen down a couple of steps on her bedroom stairs and then fallen down some cellar stairs. She does that sometimes but never seems to know how it happens. She looks very robust but is 64½ and some years ago had a breast off for cancer and later an accident which made a leg bad for a long time. Is worrying about her job because she can't cope with it and knows that babies are probably suffering because she can't get round to them. Also, her doctor in charge is a very old man who has been ill a long time and she has either been without a doctor or the locums have come and gone rapidly. She wants to stay in the job until September in order to get her 20s. a week pension, when she hopes to get a flat in Cambridge.

So I called on Miss Westell, welfare worker at the Moral Welfare Home. She is about 55. She was too tired also. Has neuritis in her arm which keeps her awake at night and wants a change she can't get. Her matron is in the same boat in regard to a change. They are not allowed a maid or a charwoman and so the matron has to be both. She is 42 or 43 and was a missionary in India. Very nice, but Miss Westell thinks she expects too high a standard from the girls and won't get it. I said if it would help I'd go and stay at Easter and let one of them get away, but don't suppose they will accept because I can't do a lot of housework and I can't cook at all for other people than myself.

So I went to hear O. Gollancz by myself! Despite the subject, I think in a way one studies the personality of any speaker most of all. This one did not sound entirely English, but was quite likeable when one got use to him. Tall and somewhat student type, might have been good-looking but just missed it. Spectacles and perhaps a sort of squint, but otherwise eyes quite nice. Long fingers and sensitive hands. A few Communists in audience. Talk of splintering Labour Party by the members of somewhat similar groups putting up at elections. Labour still refuses to accept Communists. Talk of Labour leaders. As at the Conservative meeting, the impression was that we have no leaders who are any good in any party. Chairman (Mr Arkwright) suggested that Morrison might have been given his 18B job by the Conservatives to make him unpopular but Gollancz did not appear to have that view, but said nobody but Churchill had gripped the people's imagination. I said nothing all the evening but I do think people hang on to Churchill because there is nobody popular enough to take over. Besides, when the executioner Morrison stands in the background ready to behead anybody who says a word about Churchill, people must perforce praise Churchill. As a body-guard Morrison could not be surpassed. Rev. Pelly asked what about Cripps for a Labour leader and Gollancz thought he would not do, his heart not being sufficiently Labour. Gollancz was not at all dogmatic and all discussion was quite friendly. At end of meeting Co-operative Society man (a Mr Bennett) asked if we would go to hear a Co-op Party secretary talk on Beveridge Report Wednesday at Guildhall, particularly with a view to names going to Parliament or something of that sort in order to push Beveridge forward....[24]

Gollancz also (like Heilgers) thought it vital we should keep friendly with USA. Years ago somebody remarked to me that in his opinion before this war ended Germany and England would be together fighting against America. That sounded to me far-fetched but certainly one would suspect that our government feels that the situation now between us and the Yanks is very delicate. There may be more in it than the people realise I suppose. There seems to be a big gulf between us and Russia but that apparently does not worry the government but only the Communists. We have two flags flying in our town, the Stars and Stripes near this house, where there is a USA Services Club, and a Union Jack on top of our grandest modern building – the brewery. The latter may be flying because this is 'Wings for Victory' week, and the mayor (of the brewery) is in charge. There is an exhibition of planes in the Guildhall but I have not been in because planes have never interested me and I don't know one from another anyhow. I liked the wood-working department in an aeroplane factory I used to work in and I liked the factory, but I don't even know the names of the planes they turned out there (last war). 'Wings for Victory' gave the mayor and corporation an opportunity to attend church in full glory last Sunday – silly fools. I don't know why men are such idiots about dressing-up. Vanity, I suppose. Still, I daresay people turned out to look at them. I've a little book here which says there are nearly a million 'backward' school children in England and Wales, and of course we have plenty of grown-ups of the same calibre, and such grown-ups would doubtless be delighted to see a procession of any kind. I preferred the old-time circus processions myself, particularly ponies and elephants....[25]

---

[24] Oliver Gollancz (1914–2004), an artist, was a cousin of the left-wing publisher Victor Gollancz. There appears to have been no press coverage of his speech.
[25] A 'Wings for Victory' week was designed to stimulate National Savings in aid of the

Monday, 22 March

... *Babies.* The downstairs tenant (Mrs Nudds) referred to Churchill's remarks regarding increasing the population and thought present-day girls wanted a good time, not babies.[26] Said a good many single girls would have babies, but for the 'shame' and having nothing to keep them on. Someone she knew had done so and refused to marry the father, not being interested in him but wanting the baby. She herself would not have minded a baby every year, though she'd prefer them more ordinary than her boy, who is a highly imaginative child, very charming but requiring a skilful upbringing. She had always wanted to have a baby to see what sort of one she could produce. I told her I had never wanted one – which is perfectly true. I think babies the most fascinating things on earth and if I'd plenty of money would perhaps adopt one, but I've never felt a desire for one of my own but rather a thankfulness that I've never been responsible for the birth of one. I'd feel so sorry for the poor little brat if I had to watch a replica of myself running about. Nephews and nieces are much more interesting, and I can watch bits of myself cropping up in them without accepting any responsibility for it myself.

I think there must be two kinds of women, those who want love affairs and those who want babies. If I'd had a love affair I can imagine I might have liked a baby for the sake of giving the man the baby, and also because, being in love with him, I'd have thought there was something in him worth reproducing, in which case I should doubtless have been passionately fond of the child. I wonder if the difference shows itself in childhood in that some little girls like books and some like dolls? I liked the books, not the dolls; wanted to paint, not sew; studied book-keeping as an excuse to evade housework. I think when I grew up one or two boys might have been willing to marry me had I suggested I was interested in having a home and pretended I could run one, but I certainly had no wish for a life as a housekeeper/bed-partner, which was about what they desired. Boys are funny creatures. They seem to roam about looking for a suitable wife, and several might have been willing to marry me before I'd any personality at all and just because they thought my parents respectable and in a comfortable, even honoured position. Even

---

RAF's war effort. The *Bury Free Press*, 20 March 1943, p.2, carried a long account of the elaborate ceremonies. Bury's target was £180,000; in fact, some £242,000 were raised.

[26] In a broadcast the previous day ('Postwar Planning'), Churchill had pondered the implications of a continuing low birth rate. 'In 30 years, unless present trends alter, a smaller working and fighting population will have to support and protect nearly twice as many old people: in fifty years the position will be worse still.' To preserve Britain's place in the world, he said, 'our people must be encouraged by every means to have larger families'. While avoiding specifics, he declared that 'well-thought-out plans for helping parents to contribute this life-spring to the community are of prime importance' (*Churchill: His Complete Speeches*, VII, p.6761).

young boys are mercenary. However, nobody ever wanted to marry me for myself, so here I am. I certainly had no ambition to be married for my womb or my housekeeping ability. If I'd fallen in love I'd have managed the house-keeping with ease, but otherwise it seemed senseless when the lower strata of women were there to do it for me if I did not marry. I suppose I was 40 before I preferred my own rooms to other people's houses, and even now it may be because half the stuff is the internee's and some of it is beautiful. I suppose some females grow up with the aim of expressing their personality by having a house and a baby or babies, and in that case they would decide to marry some fairly ordinary boy in their sphere and on that foundation achieve their own aim. Probably they are wise. I probably wanted a Robert Browning!! ...

Friday, 26 March

The last two or three days have been very full and will take hours to relate. So I put aside the housework, cooking, washing and sewing and letter-writing, and start on this job. I've a lot of Beveridge Report to read up for tomorrow evening, too.

Wednesday evening I went on my own to hear Mr Bailey of [the] Co-operative Party explain the Beveridge Report. A poor audience, partly perhaps because the meeting was a party one arranged by the few (it is a new branch of the party) and not sponsored by the society itself. It was a pity, because the speaker might have been termed 'inspired'. He was excellent in replying to questions and he explained the report altogether better than Laski or Heilgers had done. I know nothing about him but he seemed to have a perfect 'grip' on his subject and a wide knowledge of other matters, such as population questions and so on which in a way were outside the scope of the report though loosely connected with it. He explained very clearly too what had happened over the report in Parliament and why it was essential certain measures should be taken. Apparently he was used to dealing with the average citizen, too, who wanted to know if her 'free policies' and so on would be honoured if the scheme came into being.

I talked to a woman too whose menfolk had been in Dunkirk and were now pilots and/or in Malta, and I realised (perhaps for the first time) that the internment question was not the only worry in this present world. It creates much more frenzy but not necessarily more anxiety.

A resolution is being sent to our MP, to Herbert Morrison and various other such people, urging that the Beveridge Report should be got on with at once and announcing our objection to the government attitude.

Thursday we went to Sudbury Home and Children's meetings. Not many members there but quite decent ones.... We interviewed Alice Sylvia Smith, in the board room. She looked typically Poor Law and had no powder or paint on. Occasionally an independent toss of the head and she is not unat-tractive to look at. Mrs Stafford Allen handled her marvellously and very nicely and surprised me. They asked her what she would like to do and she said be a waitress. They asked if she would like to go in the Forces when 17½ and she very definitely said she would. They are all keen to go in the Forces and the committee always think the discipline will do them good. I can't see how discipline can alter but that is the general idea about these parts. They don't like factories. Alice probably thought the Forces meant 'men', which it will, and she loves men. She very definitely said she did not like the laundry-work she was now doing and so she is to go into the kitchen to help there for five months until she is 17½ and can go in the Forces. Her old hag of a mother thanked Tommy and said (in different words) that the girl would now have a good chance and was too good to be a prostitute. That was probably soft-soap....

I made my lunch-hour [on Thursday in Sudbury] expand because I saw the M-O [book] *People in Production* in a shop which was closed for lunch hour (some shops in Sudbury keep open on market-day) and waited to get it. I find it very interesting and from my knowledge of factory life, true to life.[27]

Thursday evening I went to hear gramophone records and the Waddington boy (son of the rector of Hawkedon and Somerton) was there with a few friends. I saw him at lunch in the British Restaurant today and he asked if I could go to Hawkedon to his organ recital Sunday, in which case I could go about 2 p.m. and have tea at his mother's. I thanked him but as I don't know the way and there are no signposts and my bike has no lamps and I hate cycling in the dark (I'd be nearly scared to death!) refused and suggested he'd better arrange another for a Sunday afternoon instead of 7 p.m.

This morning was the Bury St Edmunds guardians relief meeting. Present: Hunt (chairman), Cragg, Redness, Col. Harmer, Major Ackroyd, Page, Mrs Nevile, Mrs Hunter, Mrs Harrison-Topham. Tommy got up several times and objected to their decisions and again remarked to me what a mean lot they are, to which I agreed, and complimented him on standing up to them. They spend over half an hour deciding that a man earning about £3 [a week] who had offered 2s. 6d. a week towards his mother's maintenance should be asked for 4s. a week and a magistrate's order taken out against him immediately if he refused. Tommy's particular pet, however, was the Holt case. Here a small farmer had had to give up some years ago because his wife got rheumatoid arthritis, and he took a job at about £3 10s. a week, out of which he supports himself, wife and three children, and a woman to look after his wife partly at least. Good type people. A surgical appliance has been recommended which would enable the wife to walk – price £15 15s. They asked for help to pay [for it] and had in all the world savings of £2. Tommy did not want to deprive them of their £2 but the committee was unanimous that they did. Tommy

---

[27] *People in Production: An Enquiry into British War Production. A report prepared by Mass-Observation for the Advertising Service Guild*, a Penguin Special, was published in 1942. It is a study of industrial relations and efficiency.

spouted well but it had no effect. All the members were wealthy, some very wealthy. So after the meeting Tommy decided to get some of his friends in the Woolpit (where the people lived) to look them up and see if they could help. Hunt (chairman) afterwards expressed his disgust about Cragg's meanness but said he had improved, for at one time he used, when pressed, to agree to increase a family's relief by sixpence a week – 'Well, I would agree to put it up another sixpence'. Mrs Allen, however, had cured him of that, with her 'You and your sixpences!'

Leggett afterwards said he had many cases receiving money so low they could hardly exist on it, but knowing the committee he did not bring the cases forward for revision. He instanced one invalid receiving 16s. a week out of which she paid 3s. a week rent, and a family of man and woman and two big children on relief of 24s. a week for the lot. He had told his wife (a school-teacher) the night before that he and she could invest in war savings but these people could scarcely exist. Leggett also said that after the war things would alter. I said 'If we make them alter'. He said 'Whether we do anything or not'....[28]

One must find occupation for people in this war. The British Restaurant here has nearly become a picture gallery of photographic pictures showing a girl washing up and a man putting coal on the fire or not turning out electric light, and so on, all this waste of labour and paper being with a view to impressing on people that they must save fuel. It is all so silly. If you freeze, you catch cold, and if you go out walking you wear out shoes, and housewives can't afford to waste fuel at any time. I don't think I've used a third of the coalite this winter I did last, but the winter has been so very much warmer. I used about a ton last winter and I doubt if I've used five hundred weight this. I had very few fires before Xmas and very few since, an oilstove (or two) supplying enough heating and being cleaner and more serviceable for cooking and heating water. More often than not the fires I have had were composed mainly of pine logs, of which I have burned nearly 10s. worth as logs and kindling. There is a lot of wood in this district. My fires, of course, are in any case only lit in the evenings and at weekends.

Mr Arkwright is going to lend me some books, and so is the boy who is due to start his organ recital in his distant village within 15 minutes from now, but I haven't got them now or I'd read and darn some stockings at the same time....

---

[28] 'After Thursday's meeting at Sudbury', Winifred wrote later this year, on 25 September, 'one of the relieving officers remarked that if our public assistance meetings were samples of democracy it would in his opinion be a jolly good job when the civil service took us over. Actually, of course, they are run by the ruling classes.'

Tuesday, 30 March

I am feeling much more happy tonight, but that won't elongate my evening, so I must get to bed as soon as I can. The internee has written saying he is really hopeful about being released and should know shortly and he will in that event be released without a pre-arranged job. So I am hopeful too, my thick mass of doubt having become much thinner and for the moment going nearly out of sight. It seems too good to be true but at least there is a possibility that it is true. All through 1943 I have been half afraid the authorities would change their plans about allowing him to accept a job and tonight I was half afraid they had before I opened the letter whilst the other half of me hoped the news would be good; which it was, one might add, 'almost decidedly'....

Sunday, 4 April

6.10 p.m. Life has seemed rather hectic this last week. Monday I felt 'Mondayish' and as though I wanted my own life, not public assistance. What is my own life? A miserable ghost of a thing which has never developed; not so much stunted as crowded out. It is now aimless and perhaps never found an aim and in any case it is too late to expect much now. Yet it is a ghost which occasionally haunts me and makes me despondent over my lost, or unborn, soul. This isn't life. The existence I have is not worth being born for. People who are born should live to the full, not merely exist and endure. Of course I don't know how to live to the full, and from the appearance of most folk they don't either. I went on a train journey from Newmarket to London when I was 21 and studied the faces and forms of people, and couldn't see one person who looked in any way physically perfect or really happy. At the time I wondered if it was that most of them were the offspring of lust and not love, though I can't blame lust in my own case.

All day at intervals very heavy bombers have flown low over these houses. They rather frighten me for fear they hit something and crash. I get annoyed and then tell myself I suppose they must practise. They are so low that the houses and streets vibrate as they go over. We live here in the midst of a war which might touch us at any moment. I use this house rather as a hole to crawl into for safety, and become the ostrich in that I do not look outside and in here, for no reason at all, feel safe. Actually, the safest place would be a trench in a field, but we can't live in trenches in fields! I have certainly had the ostrich mind all through this war, and before it, at Bexhill, when I enjoyed being out of London with its 'rumours of wars' and got a tremendous surprise when war was declared. The previous year I expected it, but not when it happened. I don't remember reading a newspaper during the eight months I was in Bexhill, having no money for luxuries. Before Bexhill I used to feel I could not endure another war and in a way 'having an internee' has

8. Men of the RAF with their band taking part in the Warship Week march in Newmarket, a photograph taken 8 March 1942 in the High Street. The real HMS Newmarket was originally the United States destroyer USS Robinson, launched in 1918 and transferred to Britain under the Anglo-American Agreement of 2 September 1940. Most of the fifty such destroyers were, like HMS Newmarket, given the names of places in both Britain and the USA. © Imperial War Museum, CH.5120

been good for me in that it has taken my thoughts largely away from myself, and so made life easier…

My sister-in-law at Newmarket said she wanted the government to finally settle what they were going to do about the Beveridge Report, because there was so much controversy about it she didn't want to trouble her brain until it was all settled. Her mother looked vaguely troubled when I mentioned lectures in this town and the daughter said they weren't interested in such things in Newmarket, and were having none. To my mind, except for fresh air, Newmarket is a most terrible place to live in. I saw it on Friday again, and its little boxes of houses where the ordinary inhabitants live, and I wondered that anything good could come out of such a little, mean existence. I could never have married a man and brought up children under such conditions. I don't know what emotion it is that that town gives me, but perhaps it is fear, a sort of fear that because I was born and brought up there I too, had the last war not allowed me to escape, might have had to become part of it – or perish. I needed a somewhat roomier world than that.…

Saturday afternoon saw *Gone with the Wind* for four hours and got hotter and hotter, coming out in a bath of perspiration and with a slight headache. It was an ordinary picture extra well done. The scenes from the war between North and South America were enough to cure anybody of war-mongering, but I suppose it doesn't affect some people to see ghastly physical suffering. Probably, like small boys who torture animals, they enjoy it. I myself always keep the thought of the terrible sufferings now going on out of my mind, and live, so long as I and mine are untouched, as though a war were not raging. It will rage itself out, I suppose, for there seems no way of stopping it any more than there was a way of preventing it. We are in the storm and pray it will pass over our heads. The last war should have taught us to prevent this one, but it did not, and now our yearly two minutes of silence, when one might have thought prayer went up to God, showed itself a useless thing, whilst the emotions called up by 'If ye break faith with them' etc. and the poetry published seem to have been the essence of futility. Still, why should I write thus? Are not ideals childish things which crash one after another as we grow up, so that in the end reality is the only good? There are fair things in poetry and the daffodils on my mantelpiece are fair, but is the whole scheme of life any more than one huge blundering to caverns of destruction? Surely this world is hell? What else could be so unreal?

Yesterday morning I heard that the internee's friend Mr R. had died on the 1st, it being cancer, not rheumatoid arthritis. He was a very nice old gentleman and I had rather hoped that if the internee and I started business he would come in with us. He was a refugee with very little money but he had a big reputation in the numismatic world and, moreover, I think he would have had enough wisdom and understanding to make the internee and I understand each other better, whereas I myself feel rather like a woman presented with a son aged 21 or so whose temperament she had not studied from his childhood. To me it always seems so much easier to understand people older rather than younger than oneself. This boy teased me too, which makes things worse. However, death has decided that question for us.

I went to tea with Miss Osborne last night. Then as she was short of tea and I of sugar we exchanged! At 7.30 Mr Arkwright and Mr Powill gave a very interesting talk on the Finsbury Health Centre. One doctor was there – Dr Bett.[29]

Today I've done nothing but cook and write and go out. The butcher had closed last night when I got there but the grocer found me a little thick chunk

---

[29] The Finsbury Health Centre, which had opened in October 1938, was set up to provide a full range of clinical and other services and was innovatively designed. It was the subject of an extensive pictorial essay in the *Architectural Review*, vol. 85 (January 1939), pp.5–22: 'The purpose of the building is to co-ordinate all the health services, which were previously scattered over different parts of the borough' (p.7). Lorraine Lees at the Islington Local History Centre aided our research on this subject.

of bacon to boil. So I had that and boiled onions which had started to grow and a little 6d. cauliflower and potatoes, and they didn't go too badly. There is enough left for tomorrow.

Sunday, 18 April

My diary is a long way behind, so I will try to remember what I can....

Women's Voluntary Services here started a scheme for exchanging children's clothes...

On Saturday, 10 April I registered as a nurse at the local office of the Ministry of Labour. Only four others there (all in mufti) at the time and one said to me 'What a farce!' I replied 'It won't be a farce if they take us' and she laughed and answered 'No, it would be murder'. I myself am banking on the fact that the doctor would not pass me. I could not now do the hard physical work involved and I have never held a position of responsibility as a nurse, so should be ineligible for a matron's work. I'd hate it, too. So far as administration goes, I ought to outshine most matrons, but it's the hospital 'atmosphere' I loathe, and the domesticity, or worse, of the job. I hate the shapes of the wards, the lines of ugly iron beds, the sameness and deadliness of white counterpanes, the bareness, the windows all along, facing each other, mealtimes, the horrid germy uniforms with the much more horrid stiff caps, the stiffness of the nurses, the linen cupboards, the filth, bluffing the public, treating the 'lay people' as idiots, the professional smugness, the unhygienic methods and surroundings, the routine, the horrible 'etiquette', the walking up and down, the noise, the rushing, the worship of the doctors and addressing them as 'sir', the danger of making mistakes through ignorance or tiredness or having no time to think, being cut off from outside life and thought, having no leisure or self-interest, never being free from dead and dying, fear of infection, the feeling of always being covered with germs, the homelessness, the landladyness, having no office and no quietude, never getting away from other people. No, even war does not inspire me to return to a life like that, and in any case one could do more for the nursing world outside it than if crushed beneath it as a nurse is....

Miss Osborne says her clinics in Bury St Edmunds (maternity and child welfare for the borough) never get any sunshine, but when they were built by the borough nobody who knew anything about clinics was consulted.[30]

---

[30] These were centres 'where mothers could get advice on the ordinary day-to-day questions of their babies' feeding and general care. The clinics were run by local authorities or voluntary organizations and were staffed by the health visitors and voluntary workers, and a doctor was usually in attendance. Mothers were encouraged by the health visitors to take their children to the centres for regular examination. Furthermore, most of the centres tried to attract the mothers by maintaining a friendly

This is a marvellous sunny day, with most trees except beeches in green leaf and the wide sweep of gorse around me as full with yellow blossom as ever it can be. The sun has hardly gone in at all the whole of the day. Last year about this time I could not keep warm sitting in fur-lined boots over a big fire. Today I sit on Hardwick Heath and nearly roast.

After the war I lose my job. Elsie Foulger will have to give up her job as case-paper clerk and become the case-paper clerk's typist. Ruth will have to give up running the boarded-out children and become typist to the man who returns to her present job. It seems silly but there it is. The man who should take over my job has had a fortnight's experience in it, and perhaps it is well I shall not remain to become his typist, because I might get bored.

I had a note from Mrs Rappaport regarding her husband's recent death. It reads: 'I am convinced that it would have meant happiness for my husband to work with you and Mr Luther'. Well, cancer has decided against that. Whether Mr Luther and I ever make a living or not out of numismatics, it is rather unlikely that I should get bored, for there would be a world for any initiative I could develop, and I could certainly never get to the end of learning all the subjects which border on coin-collecting and selling.

Last time I was at Sudbury Mr Kiddy the relieving officer was saying that in the last three years his son had earned more in farming than he himself did in a lifetime. Said he kept afloat during the bad years before the war by becoming relieving officer as well as farmer. Said he thought laws of supply and demand would operate after this war and he would advise farmers to sell out when this one ends. As an instance he mentioned clover seed. Just as English farmers were ready to sell this year, a big lot came in from America and the price fell, and he thought if the government dared do that with a war on they would certainly do it after the war.

I also talked to Day the relieving officer. He thought we should have another war about 15 years after this and could see no way to prevent it. He thought the bulk of the people wanted other people to do their thinking for them. He also talked about poor relief and the cost of getting in contributions from 'liable relatives'. Said the Sheffield public assistance officer had recently opposed all legal authority by refusing to charge Poor Law patients' sons who were married 'towards the cost of their parents' maintenance', on the plea that laws were made for the man and not man for the laws. He (Mr Day) now thought other authorities had the opportunity to follow this lead, for even sheep could follow. Plainly Mr Day considered our West Suffolk Committees to be sheep.

---

social atmosphere' (Sheila Ferguson and Hilde Fitzgerald, *Studies in the Social Services* (London, 1954), p.146).

Monday, 19 April

Shirley (aged nearly ten) said on Saturday on the subject of my being conscripted as a nurse 'Oh, well, I should think you've forgotten all you ever knew about nursing', as if she considered that settled the matter....

I have never seen Gooch so emotional as today when he called this town 'soul-destroying'. He said if anybody with enthusiasm came into it he would have it knocked out of him either directly or indirectly. His remarks came up because the new Congregational minister is Welsh and cannot understand the apathy of his new congregation. Joan, who also attends said she thought people went from habit and that very few indeed were really Christians, but she did not know if that related to other towns than Bury St Edmunds, which is the only one she knows much about. I assured her Christians were rare everywhere, as far as I know. After Gooch's remarks on enthusiasm Joan remarked that the people here seemed to get along all right, and Gooch and I laughed and remarked that they weren't really interested in anything, either because they hadn't any brains or because for centuries they had merely obeyed and so had never had a chance to develop brains. I thought the lack of intellect operated in many other towns as well, though probably this district would be a sort of 'star turn'. Later I shall be writing of Ely, Cambridgeshire, but for the moment will only say that Ely now has a Communist League or something there, whilst Bury has not....

The other evening I met my typist Ruth in the street and she asked me what the apparition was coming towards us and was there a fancy dress ball anywhere? It was a man in cloth gaiters and bright yellow velvet trousers and rows of coloured military ribbons roaming half over his chest. I answered that I had seen another such at the door of the Guildhall and thought it was something to do with the mayor and corporation. She laughed and said he'd got the corporation (stomach) all right and what rot all this dressing up and tradition was. I agreed. Later I learnt that the mayor and corporation were entertaining English and American officers in the Guildhall and that the two lots of yellow trousers (pantaloons, breeches, or whatever they were) were the mace bearers. I can but hope that the Yanks were duly impressed – 'What fools these mortals be'.

Tuesday, 20 April

... 8 p.m. and I've come to bed. I've washed clothes, crockery, self and my hair, and I just can't do any more manual labour, not even knitting. The apple tree among the chimneys and roofs from my window is in pink and white blossom – quite pretty. But it merely reminds me that yet another spring of these fruitless and weary years is here. I get the same thought each year when I see blackberries and golden corn and think yet another dreary winter has got to be lived through. Both these rooms are crying out to be swept and dusted but there is only one clear evening left before I go to stay at St Elizabeth's Home for Easter and a bit longer, until whenever it is the superintendent returns from holiday. I am going to stay there so that she can get one. They don't charge me for my board and I usually give them a present and perhaps take some rations with me, the home being a voluntary concern.

Miss Osgathorpe from the Home called on me Sunday evening to ask if I would go to London this Saturday (Easter Saturday) to collect a couple of girls and drop one at Ipswich and bring the other here. The latter was sent to a Home near Brighton but is being returned as she repeatedly ran away, so she is to remain in the Bury St Edmunds Home I presume until we can fix her up elsewhere. So far as I know there will be about six girls and four babies in the home. Suppose I'd better take my thermometer. Last time a girl got a 104 temperature on her return from the maternity hospital, owing to breast trouble. She had to wean her baby and had enough milk for two. Girls cannot always get jobs where they can take their babies and so often have to put the children with foster mothers perhaps miles away from themselves. With a little attention and a breast pump this girl recovered in a day or two. Had a certain sister in Hertford Hospital some years ago used a breast pump instead of Epsom salts and a cruelly tight bandage I expect my own sister would still be alive. Unfortunately then I knew nothing of maternity cases and dared not undertake the job, and that was the result. It is true that owing to getting wet through my sister had contracted tuberculosis and so was not entirely fit and could not feed her baby on that account, but the sister need not have killed her off with Epsom salts etc. even so. She had a separate room and in consequence the baby (my nephew John, now apprenticed at De Havilland's) had been born about a half hour before anybody looked in to see if she wanted anything, but despite that the actual confinement went beautifully and it was only the lack of a breast pump which killed her, plus the Epsom salts three times a day. She said the bandage was altogether more painful than the confinement. I think I shall never now let anybody go to a hospital if I can keep them out....

I wonder what effect the difference in dress of the American and British soldiers has on them. Our men in comparison are dressed woefully badly, the ordinary American soldier being dressed as well as our officers and their own. Great Britain is very definitely the Poor Relation of not only her own colonies such as Australia and New Zealand but also of USA. The poor old mother seems to have become so poor that she is only just outside the work-house, whilst her sons put up a very brave show of well-being and prosperity. Queer, when we have been accustomed to think so highly of ourselves as in the forefront of nations.

I returned Eric Newton's *European Painting and Sculpture* and Laver's *Whistler* to the Waddington boy today and he half unconsciously remarked that it was remarkable I read such books. He was equally amazed the other week when I said books on architecture interested me, and I cannot say I feel flattered at his amazement. I must try to ask him in what way he considers the fact remarkable. Perhaps it is in Bury St Edmunds, but he has lived in other places.

He has books on birds, too, I found out today, after I had paid 12s. 6d. for a book on British birds for Shirley on Saturday with which she was delighted as she had found difficulty in getting one for school. She had 20s. for pocket money when she came on holiday but had bought a present for her mother and one for the aunt with whom she is staying and paid for a few dinners at the British Restaurant and 10s. of it had vanished. The first thing she did in Ely Cathedral was to put 6d. in a collection box there, as though that was the correct procedure on entering any religious building. She is much more grown up and very much nicer than I was at her age. I was rather taken aback, however, after meeting her at Ely railway station and after she had talked for some minutes, to have her turn suddenly to me with the question, 'Well, what are *you* doing with yourself these days?' I could only answer, rather weakly, 'Poor relief'. She is nearly ten. I think she enjoyed her day and the bird book was the crown of it. I showed her on the river bank how to manipulate the microscope I lent her, and being practical she at once wanted to make her own slides rather than to find interest in those I supplied. We spent a lot of time in the cathedral and she was afraid she couldn't take it all in and would get it muddled with Norwich Cathedral which she had visited the previous Sunday. She thought Ely was nice for one day but too old to live in, though of course it might be better if one got used to living there. I told her I thought it would get worse if one lived there.

Ely is different from Bury and I enjoyed the change. Green trees suitable for Corot and fruit trees in blossom and the grass very green and the fens flat as billiard tables. I like the flatness as a change from Bury and Sudbury and perhaps it is to me a bit homelike or blended with my experiences. I like the river lying as still as a mirror between its low banks. The weather was perfect. Everywhere almost, of course, one gets views of the cathedral. The city is different from the town of Bury St Edmunds, and more asleep. Bury is varied, sharply differentiated, reddish in colour, and somewhat grotesque. Ely is quietude and simplicity and is old and brown. There is much more pretension in Bury. I imagine there is more aggressiveness and roughness, and there is the 'county', the mass of tradesmen forming the mayor and corporation, and the poor. Probably most people in Ely are poor, and if the Church people who dwell in the ancient and larger buildings immediately around the cathedral are well-to-do they seemingly are not pretentious but form part of the unit which is the city. One gets the impression there that class distinctions are lacking. If one goes through Bury St Edmunds at sunset the age of the places makes all its varieties blend into a living, almost fairy-tale unit, but

Ely needs no sunset – it definitely is a unit at all times. The old little roof tiles are brown and the walls are brown. The cathedral is grey.[31]

I know nothing of the life of Ely, but it apparently has a Communist League, which Bury has not. A labouring man was talking of having a bit of 'sparrowgrass' (asparagus), which word is common in Newmarket also. It is not considered the luxury here that people in various other counties consider it.

I like Ely Cathedral extremely and there would have been much less in Bury to interest Shirley. The mirror in the Ely waiting room had been stolen and the lavatory attendant was tearing short strips of lavatory paper up to hand to people as they went in because in these war days the rolls get stolen. The official in the cathedral explained that the lady chapel has to be kept locked now because it had been used as a room for boxing and as a lavatory. So apparently such conditions are the same at Ely as at Bury, Newmarket and Sudbury, and probably elsewhere. The city, however, seemed very quiet and quite unruffled.

It is easy to get food in Ely, and I think Shirley was delighted with her dinner. It was a hard-boiled egg with salad and salad cream, roll and butter and mashed potato, lemonade, and two jam tarts in custard. Said it was the best dinner she had had for a long time – and there was more of it. Said school dinners were all right sometimes but cost 10d. whether good or bad. I asked if they were about like British Restaurant ones and she said they were. Later I told her the meal (including a cup of tea) cost 3s. each so ought to have been all right, and she said it was worth it – it was a good dinner.

Winifred then abandoned diary-writing for three whole weeks.

---

[31] 'I am an outsider here', Winifred wrote of Bury the following year, on 17 September 1944, 'and I'll be glad never to come here again. I have not let the town impress itself on my mind any more than I could possibly help. It is a grotesque, Grimm's fairy tale kind of town, with wizards and Gothic gargoyles, and it might "catch one" unless care were exercised. No, I am not mad, but it is not a town one could love. It is not strictly beautiful although sometimes a dancing sky and the sun on its old, crazy red roofs give it a certain eery loveliness. It has also an East wind and dust, and an air of aggressiveness. The houses nearly all need painting and some are falling to pieces. They are old houses, big and small, shapely or erratic, all lumped together. All styles of houses – and probably few which have not been altered throughout the years, so doors and windows often come in unexpected places and the doorstep may be at the side of the front door instead of in front. Mr Boyce does not like Guildhall Street, though like most Bury streets it winds and has an irregular charm, with roofs all over the place against the sky – crazy roofs of all shapes and as if drawn by a painter who was drunk. He says the street always makes him think it was the scene of murders.' Two years later she wrote of Bury's 'gloomy tunnel-like streets' and compared it unfavourably to Newmarket (2 December 1946).

Wednesday, 12 May

So long since I wrote this diary up that the task in front of me seems colossal. I stayed ten days or so at St Elizabeth's Moral Welfare Home and have since been cleaning white paint (nice clean white paint and a grey ceiling). Some of it still wants doing but the strong soda water has roughened my hands so much I have to desist for a day (or evening) or two.

I tried to get a book on Ely in Bury St Edmunds before I went, but no shop had one. Bury is only interested in itself.

School-teacher in British Restaurant said friend of hers who has travelled around since she was evacuated concluded Bury had more reverence for money and the people who possessed it than anywhere else she had been to. The school-teacher said Bury was aghast at the lack of discipline (as they know discipline) in the schools evacuated from London.

Woman in small general shop said she had come from London but was seriously thinking of returning so that her small daughter should not miss all chances of being educated. Said nothing was taught here and the children were very dull though that might be due to lack of proper teaching. I said the powers that are would most strongly object to educating children to any standard of independence because what they wanted was unthinking robots to perform their will.

Talking to a wool merchant in the restaurant the other day I realised he had received no depth of education, though he had been to an expensive school. These people can appreciate one art only – music – and ideas are foreign to them....

I saw the two biggest tanks I have ever seen and the noise was terrific. I thought they must be in danger of tearing up the roadway, which they practically filled. Then I concluded my nerves were not so steady as they ought to be, for the effect of the noise and the thought of the tremendous scope they had to crush humans (so great as to suggest a mesmeric quality) caused my eyes to fill with hysterical tears. I suppose I was afraid of them and the spirit of destruction they embodied.

A week or two ago there seemed increased war activity and planes flew so low that one felt them vibrate the ground or one's bed. Mine is a vibrating bed and often I can feel heavy traffic that way before I can hear it coming.

USA soldiers seem to like giving sweets to children. One of them offered to pay for my late landlady's greengrocery as she purchased from a cart at the door and on her refusal followed the cart and paid for another house-holder's. The greengrocer said if the Yankee followed him round he would do a roaring trade. Perhaps some of them realise our native poverty. At any rate, it is *practical* social service.[32]

---

[32] After a further year of exposure to the presence of Americans, Winifred's comments were much less charitable. 'Last night four American officers stood outside this house

Mrs Stafford Allen asked if we could supply an overcoat to a man who for years had been receiving insufficient cash from us to buy clothes, and Tommy very quickly said 'No' and closed the matter. I suppose he thought it would create a precedent, though we do supply clothes sometimes to London evacuees because they have been used to receiving clothes and expect them, whereas the local people expect nothing, and usually get nothing....

On 7 May 1943 I had a letter from my youngest brother saying he was going to his Army headquarters to await embarkation somewhere or other. It gave me a shock as I did not expect it yet and thought he might remain on the English coast. As consolation he reminded me the war could not last for ever. I wrote him a hurried and inadequate letter, but what can one say? There is a great deal in blood relationships and I realised it then. For the first time since the war started I felt an urge to do something practical to help our fighting men, as if I could go to some war front and nurse wounded and do my bit regardless of the mess the peacetime and wartime nursing services were and are in and my disgust and despair at and hatred of the authorities who have permitted such a state of things to drag on so many centuries for meanness of spirit and purse. I have no intention of obeying that urge, but I record it. It is not fear of danger or ammunition which keeps me back, I think, but the fear of blank endless years of boredom and self-sacrifice, weariness and uncleanness and horror, and nothing to keep alive my own body and soul. The performance of duty does not keep one's soul from dying – unless of course one reaches a climax when all the fear and chartless voyaging turn not to the madness one expects but come out into some clearer atmosphere of living. I was afraid of that lonely, chartless voyaging to an unknown port and came back with relief to the flowers of earth as a shorthand-typist. Besides,

---

wetting the pavement', she reported on 16 February 1944, 'and two other drunken American soldiers got hold of my new downstairs tenant and had to be pushed in the gutter. Some of them broke the window of the next-door house.' The United States, she complained on 6 June 1944, 'is not "grown-up" but more like a lot of untamed hooligans enjoying themselves very noisily. Well fed and with boundless energy; but no culture such as continental people have, or even England has.' Moreover, 'the Yanks keep almost entirely apart from British Forces', she wrote on 22 June 1944, 'and on the whole have no interest in anything British – sex and cinema being, so to speak, universal. I am told that black Forces are not allowed to enter Bury unless they are driving lorries through, but that they are allowed in most towns such as Cambridge, Ipswich, etc. This killing blacks when they rape white women is fiendish. The Yanks are an utterly uncultured nation for the most part, though the few are as good as the British. They are like spoiled children.' Several lines later that day she seems to have reminded herself of the existence of Americans more to her taste. 'The decent ones attending the Fabian Society all visit Mrs Crowe's house and are keen on her writing to their mothers. She gets five of them.' There were, she acknowledged, distinctions to be made. 'I like decent Americans but of course meet mainly the riff-raff brought along by war. They are such a mixed crowd, too, all nationalities, but proud of being American citizens' (25 July 1944).

I could not go back to the wearing of a head-dress or a filthy and servile uniform, with its stupid apron, stiff collar and cuffs. I belong to the world, not to a cloistered so-called 'profession'. For the first time I suspect I may be selfish in my attitude to nursing. On the other hand, I don't know much about the job and girls can soon be trained – an intensive course of three months would teach as much as I learned in three years.

I do not like my brother to leave England and it will mean anxiety for us and possibly hell for him. On 7 May I felt almost certain my internee would be released as my brother went away. It seemed impossible that my emotions could stand the hopelessness and despair of the internment situation together with a living sympathy for a youth going into the hell of tremendous mechanical and bleeding combat. I have, by the way, had several letters secretly from the internee, who is still hopeful of release though the strains of waiting must be intense. He will, if he comes, bring with him a landscape he has painted for me and a mother Manx cat which he says is so attached to him she would in his opinion die if left alone. On the 7th I wept, though that was largely due to the nervous disturbance created by menstruation. The war had put out its poisonous fangs and touched me personally. I thought if any men had been consciously responsible for launching it an eternity of torture would not be too severe a reward and that I would willingly walk round hell later on and watch them writhe. But underneath I thought it was not the few who had engineered it but that each of us in our own degree had been responsible and that war results when all our little individual sins, ignorances and negligences mass together and create an explosion. In which case, we get paid out here.

British Restaurant is certainly used for a social gathering place. Today I had lunch with Peter Waddington and his friend who is wife of a Scottish doctor. She was a 'Plymouth Brethren' but considers religion is a way of life and only by living it all the time can we do any good. She is very downright and says Peter has many good points but some bad ones. She is about old enough to be his mother, as am I also. He said his amazement at my reading architectural books was that he never read them but only bought Penguin books to be able to lend them to the several friends who borrowed books from him. Mr Arkwright has asked him to give a pianoforte recital in lieu of our gramophone records and Peter thinks it a good idea because then he can practise on the London County Council school piano he hopes, it being a good one. Owing to fire-watching etc. he often does not go home at night and I asked him what was the good of having a home, to which he answered it was useful to get an occasional change of clothing.[33]

His lady friend had personality. She wears a large crucifix round her

---

[33] The British Restaurant was, for Winifred, a place to connect with people. On 3 September 1943 she wrote of various 'encounters' there; at one of these the 'small child of the soldier's wife from Plymouth came and put her arms round me and kissed me and told me her daddy was home'.

neck which shows to the world. She talked religion to me for nearly an hour with an occasional chip from him and one from me. I suppose she is deeply serious and she made me think of a sturdy oak tree which had grown up in plenty of space and had room to develop. She has been a journalist but what she does now I don't know. There was almost the force of an ancient prophet about her. He laughed and said conversation with her was a monologue by her and the subject invariably religion. The subject was far too large for me to form any opinion of her ideas. She enlivened me, anyhow. She says she is very hopeful that after the war we shall be more Christian, because she thinks ordinary people will realise that our winning the war will have been because we were a more Christian nation than Germany and treated the Jews well, and that therefore God was with us. She believes in the Bible of course whereas I don't. I might have suggested it was not God but American money, but did not think of it at the time. Anyhow, she says ordinary people are now turning to God. Peter reminded her of a group in a shop who were hoping we would slaughter our recently captured prisoners but she said that was only an isolated instance and things in general appeared to be getting more Christian. I told her probably she mixed with different people from those I mixed with, as I had concluded that our good luck in the war merely made them smaller and more selfish. I suppose if she wrote an M-O diary it would be totally different from mine. ...

At last Newmarket meeting an estimate was submitted from a firm of engineers I worked for in last war. Made me feel 'homesick' and I felt that if the head of that firm had appeared and asked me to go back to his employment I should have left the county council without a pang. Queer. ...

I see that the Women's Institutes have published *Our Towns – a Close-up*, Oxford University Press, 5s. It is a record of the 'submerged tenth'. I ought to get it.[34]

When I left our vault-like office this evening I realised the weather was warm, even hot. And I wished myself back in town so that I could have a garden to sit in and not be boxed up in a room. I do get starved of sunshine in this country town. I am wanting to hear from the internee again. I do hope they will let him out and are not just telling him things so that they keep him going from hope to hope for the entire period of the war.

Thursday, 13 May

Tommy told me today fighting had now ceased in North Africa. That at least is good news. My mentally defective newspaper vendor has not left me any

---

[34] *Our Towns: A Close-Up*, which had been published in March 1943, was subtitled *A study made in 1939–42 with certain recommendations by the Hygiene Committee of the Women's Group on public welfare.* It dealt mainly with those problems of urban poverty, such as inadequate sanitation, that had been exposed or at least highlighted by wartime evacuation.

newspapers for a couple or three weeks and of course my wireless cannot be used without electricity. I might give up these rooms any week so it does not seem worth while to trouble about electricity. I wonder if the small amount of savings I have will be rendered valueless when the war ends – several people seem to think so. In that case it will mean a reversion to the dole, next time unrelieved. I shan't be alone, anyway. Perhaps the internee and I can go to USA after the war and see if a living can be earned there – if we can make up the passage money, that is, and he has been released. I wish I were 24 and not 47, for then I could get a job almost anywhere. All avenues are closed before [i.e., 'after'] one gets 40, except during a war and then it is only temporary work. It will be a hell of a mess when all this wartime activity is over. Life is a hell of a mess. I don't know how women dare have babies, for either the world is 'red in tooth and claw' and the only sensible teaching for it is complete selfishness and ruthlessness, or one becomes a Christian for the apparent fate of being crucified. Neither of which appeals to me, or ever did appeal. Anyhow, I should not pass it on to a helpless infant and I am very glad indeed I have none.

Saturday, 15 May

Curious the thoughts which come in flashes. The other night when a crash woke me and I lay in bed waiting for the next and realising my clothes were not near at hand, I decided to hang one or two things on the door so I could grab them quickly if a sudden plunge to the cellar appeared essential. As I did the same thing just now I thought of a friend who was killed in a raid and decided my life was too full of interest for such a thing to happen to me....

Before I got up this morning I wrote to the borough education secretary and suggested I should sell tickets for plays to be given by the Adelphi Players in September, hawking them from door to door. Incidentally I made a few remarks regarding mental defectives, malnutrition and/or lack of educational facilities.

Women's Voluntary Services on behalf of the borough are finding out if in event of a blitz we have fixed up to take people in or take shelter elsewhere. I filled up the form provided, stressing the primitive conditions under which I live and the dilapidation of the attic which makes it unusable for a bedroom, though this town is crying out for accommodation.

This afternoon bought four books, i.e., *Dachau* (exposing the concentration camp so we shall know what and whom we are fighting); *The Faithful Years* by Robert Storr;[35] *Soviet Science* by J.G. Crowther; and *Village and Town* by S.R. Badmin. I called at St Elizabeth's but neither [friend] wanted to go to the Fabian's [meeting]. It happened that the night Miss Westell did

---

[35] She may have erred here: no author by this name has been found.

go two or three people who asked questions at the end did not approve of Churchill, and I could see by her face she objected to that.

I looked at the Dachau book. There was no letter this Saturday afternoon from Martin and a sentence in the Dachau book hit me in a vital spot. It was this: 'They survive the physical tortures; the disappointed hope of freedom kills them.' If they don't let my internee out soon, will he ever recover?

I went into the streets, full of young people looking very happy, but I felt (despite my utter helplessness) forceful. I thought it a pity God was not strong enough to stop this war by entering the hearts of every man at the same time, because such a revolution of feeling would prevail. But there was nothing I could do about it.

I walked into the Fabians with Mr Emil Davies, one-time chairman of the London County Council and our speaker. It was a really excellent speech and a very enlightening one. The title was 'Alternatives to Private Enterprise' and he covered a very wide field. A very good audience. Gooch was there, also Mr Spencer of NALGO. Lasted from 7.30 to 9.45. In question time a man voiced what I wrote recently but have never heard said – that this war was caused by the amalgamation of all our personal failings. Nobody disagreed with him.[36]

Mr Crowe, the Fabians' Secretary, went round the town today and ten newsagents agreed to sell Fabian literature. I should think that is about all of them. It may be of course that the Penguin books are in short supply and they are glad of something to sell.

Mr H. (chairman of our Bury Institution Committee) remarked on Friday that marriage of mental defectives had not been stopped yet because we were not awake yet. I don't know if any of these people ever do air their views to MPs or anybody, but they certainly never resolve in committee to disturb the status quo.

… There is a lot of banging about 12.15 (past midnight) but in this house I never know bombs from other noises except when something as loud as a distant landmine makes the place suddenly reel. Think I'll go to sleep. Some of our own planes are throbbing and swishing loudly. I suppose with North Africa over the war may be more on our doorstep or over it now.

Sunday, 16 May

9.30 a.m. and I recognize the national anthem on the wireless followed by a preacher. No, I think he is a soldier drilling men, supported by bugles. I must get up.

---

[36] Albert Emil Davies (b.1875), chairman of the London County Council in 1940–41, wrote on political topics and was honorary treasurer of the Fabian Society. He advocated public ownership of key industries. He had recently published *I Wander* (London, 1942), a memoir.

I'd like to say that the Douglas camps at the present time are better than Dachau. Whatever they were in June 1940, they are better now. There were sadists among nurses from 1930–33 so I presume they are everywhere (one of the delightful human instincts, no doubt) and in prisons such sadists would consider they had an additional excuse in gaining their personal satisfactions that way, but apart from the fact that in many cases the prisoners are on show precisely like animals in the cages of the London (not Whipsnade [Bedfordshire]) Zoo, I imagine things are now better. I was not shown over 'P' Camp, of course, but judging by the outskirts of it I should say it is very definitely the best there. I felt, too, that whatever the Home Office muddle, the military command was the 'saving grace' of the place. There were the usual good-humoured, decent British Tommies, and so far as the military were concerned, I got a feeling that the sadism I did sense – hear and see and experience – so far as physical torture was concerned, was held in leash by the control of the military headquarters. Some of them in 'P' Camp would go out of their way to shatter the nerves of their prisoners and by word and action try to reduce them in their own opinion to the lowest of the brutes (their own level), but the sadist cringes to authority and I do not think in 'P' Camp they would dare to give physical punishment. Much of this sadism appears to be jealousy of persons who have finer instincts than brutes, and a desire to kill what they cannot understand. Reading the book on Dachau one asks if the human race were ever in their history more despicable than now. Perhaps in these days it is out to commit suicide and so save any God there may be the necessity of destroying it. That is rather a pity, because a God could destroy it so much more effectually, quicker and more painlessly. It is the aftermath of war that is so very terrible.

Tuesday, 18 May

I'd like to clear out of Bury St Edmunds. I've nowhere in particular to go to, but I'd nevertheless like to shake the dust of this town off my feet. I am damned crabbed and simply wasting my life here, and I am just not interested. Besides, that blasted old ice-cream factory belonging to my landlord has now started making revolting smells, very much as if gas taps in this house have all been left on. I think it is animal carcasses they use in the place, or the procedure of utilizing them....[37]

---

[37] 'I've had a pleasant week', she wrote on 30 October 1943, 'and yet I've cursed the old ice-cream works in my back garden. The machinery now goes night and day and the last two nights my windows were wide open and the noise nearly drove me potty.' Despite her feelings of malaise in Bury, she was not always negative. 'I have never been happy in Bury St Edmunds, but life here has been bearable. It has been fairly pleasant and on the whole people have been pretty decent. A good many of them are

A little bit strange today. Ruth is on holiday so Tommy brought me in a letter from the Care of the Mental Association (that's not its proper title). Dorothy Davison is to be examined again as to her mental state and they wanted particulars of her early history for the doctor. Tommy had suggested our mental defectives' place at Kedington as a 'place of safety' but the county medical officer said she was too high grade for that and if there was a vacancy would be better at Colchester. I did the letter and Tommy was quite pleased with it, which surprised me as I hadn't thought he would pass it. I gave school reports for two years which were as good as anybody's reports could be. Also two letters from a foster mother she had been taken away from which spoke highly of her and a pretty good one from the headmaster of her next (senior) school. Unless Tommy has information outside the case-paper I don't see they can certify her as insane. I understand she made eyes at Dr Turner when he examined her and she has been rude in domestic service and stolen small articles from her mistresses and her mother is in St Audrey's Mental Hospital, Melton. Besides, the life the poor kid has had has been enough to send anyone insane – torn from the house in which she had been brought up and not allowed even to visit it, and thrust into jobs as a domestic with occasional intervals at Sudbury Public Assistance Institution. But where are grounds for certifying her? The matron at Sudbury has recently used her as a maid in her house and the last report from the master is that she has stolen some perfume belonging to the matron and some cigarettes and lipstick of his sister's who is staying in the house, and one table napkin, and she is insolent and he wants her removed as soon as possible. Damn their perfume, cigarettes and lipstick, say I. And of course everybody in due course at Sudbury gets insolent and the master and matron want to get rid of them, so that is nothing fresh. I think if I were in the girl's shoes I should want to destroy their silly vanities and probably also break their windows or crockery!!

Two student nurses wanted to resign from Sudbury. They said they were getting no tuition as the sister tutor was ill (seriously) and there were no social amenities. Miss Penly Cooper was sent along and suggested they should form a social club. Later Dr Roger and Tommy conferred and Tommy made out a report for Mrs Stafford Allen's approval, telling me it was confidential. I think he thought he was taking a very big step and didn't want it discussed in the office. He suggested a wireless set in the nurses' quarters, use of the board room for socials, whist-drives and dances, and keeping two tennis courts, one in the institution's grounds and the other in the master's garden, for nurses' use and the getting up of tennis tournaments. This last encroachment, of course, was amazing, but he remarked that as there was no social life for the nurses in the institution, what else had they to do in their spare

full of kindly little actions and some are willing to be friendly. Nevertheless, I do not "live" but only exist' (23 August 1943). For the most part she did like her work.

time but to go on the streets and find soldiers? I agreed it must be frightfully dull. He said the master and matron had a lovely garden and their own friends to visit them but cared nothing at all about the nurses, and I agreed to that emphatically and went on to say that the trouble so often was that there was no class distinction between the master and matron and nurses and therefore the former were so much more inclined to create a gulf.

Fred Coppen has gone to 'Heathside' as odd job boy and they are very pleased. He had been designated unruly, a ringleader and quite lazy, but 'Heathside' think him marvellous and amused Tommy by saying they make him lie down two hours in the garden in the sun each afternoon – he is delicate and asthmatical.

Patrick Bull has won a free place at Sudbury Grammar School so flags ought to fly tomorrow to think that one of *our* children has achieved such heights.

The lady who talked on religion accompanied me home today. She remarked, without being invited to, that from the portrait my internee looked a very nice boy but there was sadness about it. I think she was amused at my back room, thought the whole place very old and quaint and the front room (which was the tidy one of the two) a room to be happy in. She said the furniture was just right for it and the general effect was a room of character. I did not say that the internee chose the furniture, so I have probably got credit for the 'character' unworthily!! She says she lost her husband in the war and then they were bombed out and the practice (medical) at Hastings went and she can't get a war pension because her husband had neglected to make some payment to the Indian government and she paid her £2 5s. a week board and lodging for herself and her son and had an offer of two unfurnished rooms at 20s. a week and an offer of a job as nursery governess. The boy is now away at a public school and she says he is fine and the only thing she has been able to do for him is to give him a fine character, to do which she found she had herself to act finely and that talking alone had no effect.

… In my own view all Dorothy Davison has needed was somebody she liked to guide her and be interested in her, instead of which cold and un-psychological treatment brings her to the possibility of being certified as insane, and in any case has brought out a don't-care, insolent attitude, and a habit of using other people's perfume and lipstick – I presume this did happen at Sudbury, though they may not actually have any proof. In her domestic jobs she has been good enough to start with and her faults have showed themselves later. From a letter she wrote Tommy (and which he is not literary enough and so on to appreciate) I should say she is nearly intellectual enough to write an account of her life and the places she has touched, and I think it would be well worth reading and of use. I have never seen the girl.[38]

---

[38] There had been ongoing debates about Dorothy Davison's intellect. A report of 28

I have been warned by Tommy not to mention to the master and matron anything about the nurses' social possibilities. I told him – I hope pointedly – that I never have had a talk to the matron beyond saying good-morning.

Thursday, 20 May

The nurses' recreation business went well. Apparently it was all pre-arranged as the matron said they had put wireless in the nurses' quarters from one of the wards and she offered their own tennis court, balls, and tuition to those who could not play. The master was pleasant enough but is still a 'bundle of nerves'. His wife on the other hand always appears entirely self-possessed....

Mrs Nudds has been asked by several persons in this street to put her name to a petition against our unpleasant smells, and she says she is doing so. I think with a war on we may have to bear them. Tommy said, with an air of pride today, that if his friend Ollé could find a way of making money he would find it. I agreed.

Friday, 21 May

Very nice letter from Mary who concludes Harry sailed somewhere last Sunday. She says he 'accepts' the army but does not like it and feels he is in a dream – yet to meet him you would conclude he enjoyed the life. I don't suppose he wanted to leave a very pleasant home and very pleasant wife. She is headmistress of an infant school but now has in addition to teach a class of 45 – this is in Cambridge....

I asked Mrs Nudds where people were going to send their protest regarding

---

April 1942 from the county medical officer stated that 'although Dr Rae, Public Health Department, was of the opinion that the girl was neither feeble-minded nor of unsound mind', a meeting of the Children's Sub-Committee of 30 April 1942 thought it 'advisable to send her for a further examination as to her mentality to Dr Turner of Colchester', who later recommended that she 'be dealt with under the Mental Deficiency Act' (meeting of 4 June 1942). At the Sudbury Area Guardians Committee meeting of 3 June 1943 'The clerk submitted a letter dated 2 May 1943, which had been sent to the Secretary of the Home Office, London, by Mr H.N. Davison, 30 Hunts Hill, Chelmsford, and also a letter dated the 1 June 1943, from the East and West Suffolk Joint Committee for the Care of the Mentally Defective, stating that Dr Atkinson was not prepared to certify this girl as a mental defective, and that the detention of the girl in Sudbury Institution as in a place of safety was being withdrawn on that day. The clerk further reported that he had asked Mrs Davison, an aunt of this girl, to attend at the institution after the meeting of this committee, when it was proposed to discharge the girl to her care' (Suffolk Record Office, Ipswich, WS 123/11).

smells and she said to the borough, so I suggested Ministry of Health as Ollé was on the borough and county councils and so nothing would be done.

Today is also my niece's birthday, so the 21st this year is quite eventful. I sent the internee (or ordered to be sent) two books of illustrations of several hundred pictures (Continental) in National Gallery.

Leggett at meeting said he had allowed 8s. a week to woman with illegitimate baby. Mrs Wise queried if enough and he said she was living with wives of two soldiers and he thought it enough. He had on two occasions told the woman to get work but she had refused one job by saying house too large for her to manage the work and had not gone to labour exchange until quite recently and the baby was six weeks old. It did not happen to strike anybody that soldiers' wives should not be expected to help keep her or that she was not fit for heavy work before the end of six weeks. She had now, however, signed on at labour exchange so would be getting I suppose about 15s. She is Dorothy Talbot, who was at St Elizabeth's, so I must ask Miss Westell about her.

Cragg was really generous today and beat Col. Harmer by 5s. on one relief case. Cragg was also good over a girl we had sent as farm and domestic worker to Mr Waters, farm bailiff, and his wife. They seem to be nigger-drivers and the wife is due for another baby and so wants our girl away before some Italian prisoners arrive for farm-work. I should not care to be an Italian prisoner on some of these farms. We take the girl away tomorrow as we also don't like leaving her with the Italians owing to her previous record. The other girl with Mrs Waters is a very nice girl about 19 years old, strong enough to work from 6 a.m. to 11 p.m. without losing cheerfulness (and she says there is plenty to eat) but she has an illegitimate child, so again, what about the Italians? Again, regarding this second girl, I must let Miss Westell know.

Saturday, 22 May

… I was just going to tea with the borough health visitor when Mrs Nudds handed me a letter from Martin. He has not yet heard about his release but hopes day by day. The shoes were sent merely because he could not get them repaired in the camp. Says if he is released it will be for London so a weekend with me can be fixed to suit *me*. Mrs Nudds offered me loan of bed-linen if I wanted any and the health visitor offered both linen and bedroom! She has two spare bedrooms and a bath, but I think Martin would prefer to 'pic-nic' here. Says his cat has a lovely yellow angora kitten and is very proud of it. I don't know what an 'angora' kitten is but as there is only one I have asked him to bring that also as Shirley would adore it. He also wanted a tube of raw siena at once, so maybe that's the shade of yellow. I have also advised him to send what luggage he can, in advance, for he probably doesn't realise our present scarcity of porters and taxis, and I can just about picture him struggling along with heavy trunks, and oil painting, a gramophone and two feline creatures. Even without that lot he is the sort of person artists ask if they may paint.

The borough health visitor says … she can't cope with all the work and administration she gets and Dr Stork (in charge) is too old and not an administrator. In addition to herself there are two school nurses, but they don't visit schools and instead hold a clinic, and one of them is not a trained nurse. Recently they applied for more money and Cragg said they were only part-time and so didn't earn any more. She has correspondence to attend to and various baby clinics and swarms of mothers, half of them mentally defective, call at her house for advice when the infants look like dying through neglect, but she prefers that type to the group of middle-class mothers whose doctors send them to her so she can weigh their babies and who want to talk and ask all sorts of questions. The point is, I suppose, with all the rest in the background, she has no time for their conversation. More than ever I notice the late hours at which children here are on the streets. She worries about the youngsters and says she will be glad to retire and if she had her time over again she would not be a nurse. She will have 20s. a week superannuation and 10s. old-age pension and she hopes the pension will soon go up but is going to live in Cambridge and if possible take part-time work in the food controller's office or some such place. She is looking forward to doing arrears of sewing.…

Tuesday, 25 May

I am back from Newmarket and feel sorry for Newmarket civilians. There is a cottage hospital – reserved to all intents and purposes for stablemen. The public assistance institution is merged into an emergency hospital – for military and evacuees. The townsfolk have nothing. The relieving officer had been called into a household because the assistance board could no longer make an allowance to the niece of a man aged 79 as his housekeeper because she was ill. I remember her as a very talkative, laughing, good-natured young woman. Today she has cancer on the spine, or near it, and cannot walk. Out of the pittance they were living on they had paid a woman 20s. a week to look after them, but she has left and today there was nobody even to give them a meal. Well, I suppose the pair of them will have to go to Bury St Edmunds Public Assistance Institution (now called St Mary's Hospital) to die. 'Heathside' would suit them, but 'Heathside' again is only for evacuees, though situated in Newmarket. So they have the bleak prospect of a distant workhouse. A pity suicide is not easier and more fashionable.

I visited Dr Ware Monday morning. A lot of people in the surgery for him and his two partners. I believe he is looked upon as a 'man's doctor', whereas O'Meara (Tommy's doctor) is looked upon as a 'ladies' man'. In consequence I have much more faith in Dr Ware. I talked on the subject of menstruation and he gave me a form for the chemist for a mixture containing ergot. When I am clear again I am to visit the surgery so he can examine me, in case there may be fibroids or worse. I don't somehow think there is anything so abnormal, and I decidedly hope not, but on the other hand I certainly bleed profusely. It may be due to diet or to worry or to inheritance. My sister, ten years younger, is the same and when doctors prescribe iron for her she just gets worse....

Wednesday, 26 May

Another event to date back to the 21 May, i.e., a letter received this evening from Martin is dated 21/5/43. Fortunately I had decided to do no housework this weekend, for he requires of me a visit to shoe repairers, chemist, art-shop, book-shop and post office. Says afraid he is asking a lot, so leave it if I cannot spare the time. Actually, I have asked for it so certainly cannot complain, but I have often thought he puts me in the place of his mother, for if he needed 100 things to be done, he would ask other people for one of them and me for 99! ...

Very good collection of records at the recital in the little schoolroom tonight. There was a Congregational Church picture on the wall with a Union Jack flying and a list of people (including Dr Stork and soldiers, etc.) to be prayed for. The first names were the King, Queen, and princesses, and including underneath 'The Mayor of Bury St Edmunds and the Mayoress'. Alluding to the mayor, Mr Arkwright laughed and said 'He needs it'. Mr Arkwright is reading M-O's *Pub and the People* and is enthusiastic about it. He is arranging a lecture by someone who is something to do with the Minister of the Interior in France to lecture when he returns from a trip to Algiers with De Gaulle. I introduced Peter Waddington to the Rev. and Mrs Pelly today, and he met Miss Strickland and arranged to borrow songs from her. She used to go to school with Kathleen Long the pianist, who when tiny would say 'If you will help me with my sums I will play for you', Kathleen Long being pretty hopeless at most things other than music. She is supposed to be a marvellous pianist.

I am having a fairly lazy time and feel very tired, but it may be largely nerves, for I forget the tiredness when talking to other people and only 'flop' when on my own. Think I will be examined on Monday and get that bit over. Life is a worrying affair and why the Almighty cursed me with a womb I fail to understand. Still, I can't see that the excretory system bestowed on all flesh is any more of a gift to arouse enthusiasm. Life is damned queer, though not too bad when everything is in perfect working order. I feel as though this examination will almost murder me, but Dr Ware would never have guessed it when I calmly agreed to it, making no more fuss than if I had been accepting a bottle of tonic. I hope I am as phlegmatic about it during the actual process. It must be done, however much it hurts. My God, if it is a bi-manual examination he may put his whole fist up.

Sunday, 30 May

I ought to start at 28 May 1943 but if I don't write this bit I'll forget it. Met a woman pushing a child in a push-chair type of perambulator. She had seen me somewhere and wondered if I made soft toys but I told her it was in the British Restaurant. A healthy-looking, fairly young woman. She has a commercial licence to collect toys from the makers (private persons) and sell to the shops and was afraid the makers were getting a poor deal and the shops over-charging. Said she came from Portsmouth and had been bombed out and was billeted in a home with two other families who were quite decent. Said in Portsmouth people were helpful but the 'graft' in Bury St Edmunds was against her principles. Said some of the restaurants and snack bars here were making fortunes but there was a reasonably-priced snack bar or café in John Street which provided dinners on Sundays and she went there as it was cheaper than buying and cooking her own. Said she preferred the British Restaurant, the only thing being they didn't give her enough to eat and seemed amazed when she asked for more potato so she made up with their bread. She liked its cleanliness but in other places she usually took her own cutlery for the child, her husband having been very keen on hygiene. I thanked her for the information about the place which caters on Sundays and she advised me to get there by 12.30. She said she had never been so hungry anywhere as in Bury St Edmunds but of course she was walking about all day. She was supposed to share a kitchen with the other people in the house but did not as it was so awkward waiting for saucepans and so on and everybody having to fit in with everybody else's cooking. Said sometimes she took home fish and chips and the fish and chips shops were a godsend. It would be interesting to know how many bombed-out women and soldiers' wives spend their days pushing perambulators around the country.

I heard from Martin. I had asked him what he wanted and in reply he told me but added it seemed such a lot that if I couldn't manage it I was to leave it. He is still waiting his release daily. Would ever anybody imagine anything could be so slow? I only hope he gets it. He wanted white flake or zinc white oil paint, which I got. The illustration of a certain flowerpiece I could not find, and I don't know which *Burlington Magazine* he wants me to order. Marcel Proust's *Time Regained* is a guinea so I have asked him if it is worth it. The book I sent him at Xmas had apparently never been dispatched by the London booksellers so I have made enquiries about that. And the distilled turpentine he asked for I could not obtain so sent him some American turpentine in case that may be of use – supposing the small bottles (aspirin bottles) don't break en route. I took a pair of his shoes to be repaired but the shop had a notice up that they could not accept any more that week and the shopman told me if I took them Monday and would wait three weeks for them they would accept them. So I have promised to take them Monday, which is tomorrow. I see Dr Ware first, however. I shall be glad to learn that all is well with me.

Sunday, 6 June

Staines (Middlesex). I have arrived here. Trains were packed with HM Forces and holiday-makers. Weather is a bit better and it is pleasant to be back where there are modern conveniences, sunny and airy rooms and a garden. This is a small house on a fairly new estate [at 17 Fenton Avenue]. The rent and rates are about double what I pay for my two rooms in Bury St Edmunds but the value is incomparable. Here there is cleanliness, a long and pretty garden secluded enough to have meals in, and at the bottom a sort of common so I am not hemmed in with houses as I am in Bury St Edmunds. Compared with this, my amenities at Bury St Edmunds are equivalent to those of slums. I can also get a bath here which I cannot there.

My brother-in-law (in Army but now sleeps at home) shares an allotment on the aforementioned common with the tenant of the next house, who is on war-work. They do not have a piece each but work on it according to the time at their disposal and I presume take from it according to their needs. They also share six chickens which have a run in the neighbour's garden and a chicken-house in this one and are fed by the two families. They are right at the bottom of the garden and some cockerels may be added for next Xmas's dinner.

My niece heard yesterday she had passed her Middlesex Scholarship to continue at the Eleanor Hollis School at Hampton free of charge. My sister thinks the school fees she has paid out of her capital the last year have been worth while as the elementary school here had only seven free places for all secondary schools in the district and there were 110 entrants. However, two out of the seven successful were friends of Shirley (the niece) and her remaining school friend, who was already at a secondary school, has also passed, so there were no disappointments in that little circle....

Dorothy Davison was released from Sudbury Institution last Thursday, when Tommy carried out a bit of bluff. The uncle of this girl had complained to the Home Office and this letter had arrived from Dr Atkinson with the latter's report that the girl's mental quotient was 100, the standard of education low, and he could not certify her as insane and she should be released at once. Tommy told the aunt that after consideration the committee had decided to release Dorothy and that she (the aunt) could see she had achieved nothing by writing to the Home Office, as all such letters were always forwarded to the county council. He told me there was no change of expression on the girl's face when he said she could go and that showed how daft she was, and she only said 'Thank you very much' and he said 'Good afternoon' and nothing else to her. He has been her 'guardian' some years. He thinks she will join the Forces and be back pregnant within a year....

Tuesday, 8 June

My sister and most of my relations and 'in-laws' are about like the majority of German women in that whatever their country does is unquestionably right. For that matter, nearly everybody I mix with is more or less the same, women predominating. The British government is undeniably right, in their opinion, because the fact that it is the British government makes it right. They hate conscientious objectors and the whole of the German people are cruel savage brutes.[39] I used to imagine at one time that in 1900 odd the world was Christian and civilised, but my imagination was greatly at fault, for we are still races of untaught, unthinking slaves, run by governments of one kind and another but governments which thousands of years ago were just as now. And I am one of that mob of slaves. At the same time on my sister's table she has a *Daily Herald* and it contains an article 'Labour Friendship for the Soviets' by Ernest Hunter [8 June 1943, p.2]. It describes events which took place after the last war but of which I knew nothing at the time, and describes our government's attempts, after financing other people to fight the Russians, to draw our own country into conflict with them. No wonder our government threatens death to any who speak against them. The times are such that they induce such laws as 18B. Revolutions such as the French, American and Russian don't seem to achieve anything in the long run, owing to the inherent wickedness of men, but sometimes I feel as if only a revolution following it can wipe out the horrors of this war and make men 'men' instead of idiots. It seems that the Almighty never intends the human race to wipe itself out entirely, but they certainly live a grovelling, unworthy existence. My sister will not read the Hunter article. She is pleasant and easy to get on with, rather superior in appearance to most people one meets in the streets, and her orthodoxy is probably a natural shrinking from unpleasant things and thoughts plus an idea that English people and English governments are all as good and generous and well-meaning as herself.

As a theory, I prefer democracy, and I suppose even in practice I prefer it, because at least it allows one to grumble. Yet the worst elements of human nature crop up in democratic institutions. Co-operative societies as an ideal are perfect, but they are often imperfect in practice. People running them may be doing so to serve their own personal interest. Others in big positions thieve what they can and then set up in private enterprise. Some societies are run so

---

[39] 'I don't know if I am singular,' Winifred wrote a little over a year later, on 25 July 1944, 'but I have never yet felt any hatred at all to the German people. That may be because I've met no unpleasant Germans.... The few people I've actually met colour their particular countries for me.'

badly from an accountancy point of view that there are all sorts of loopholes for graft. You get loads of selfishness, ignorance, jealousy and grabbing.

Staines Co-operative Society at the moment appears to be flourishing from a monetary point of view and today the grocery shops are marvellously tidy and clean and well set out. Their old employees are leaving and after 30 to 40 years' service go out empty, to wait for the poorhouse. Men who join the Forces are not only sent out empty but if they want a day off beforehand to settle up their private affairs, their wages for that day are stopped. My brother-in-law was their furnishing manager and may be glad to go back to them after the war. On the other hand, unless he gets another job he too will be left high and dry in a few years. He is 36 or 37 and by the time the war ends there won't be many years before he too is pushed off as too old. There is an offer of a postwar job in the North of England, but my sister prefers the South.

Miss Schofield [a nurse in Staines] says she always wears an overall over her uniform when dealing with infectious cases.

I suppose we shall soon start the war in full force – it is thought in two or three places at once. The PM still emphasizing our cordial relations with the Yanks – perhaps for their or German benefit, for I shouldn't think the average Britisher troubles about it. There must be something behind the anxiety. The Yanks I have seen, though many of them were boozed, seemed friendly enough and quite pleased with British girls and small children. Whisky at £3 a bottle seems plentiful in several towns I know, and the Yanks buy it. In the train they were standing in the corridor and passing the bottle one to another.

I have no news of Martin yet. Perhaps they do intend to keep him 'for duration'. It looks like it. I wish I knew what to do about it. I want to curse.[40]

I ought to say that my [abdominal] examination was nothing at all. The doctor merely pressed me below my stomach and put her finger in my anus (back passage). She told me to take the little pills before my next period, these to contract the womb. Lots of women I meet get this near-flooding business, the married and the single, and any age over 30. I am glad to be on holiday. It has rained all day.

There was a letter from my brother, written from his boat, so of course we don't yet know where he is.

---

[40] A little over a year later she revealed one of the reasons for her attachment to Martin. 'I hope I hear soon again from Martin. I wondered today if my anxiety not to lose him in any way was due to the fact that I don't want to drop to earth and realize I am merely a temporary local government clerk cloistered perhaps for life in a little dull town; a very dull, untalented, rather lifeless and colourless individual with no possibility of security, happiness or enjoyment or achievement. Looking at Martin and realizing his power of achievement, I can forget what I myself am' (30 August 1944). 'He stands for everything in life I consider worth while', she had written a few months earlier (23 February 1944).

Wednesday, 9 June

Spent yesterday in Windsor. Excellent British Restaurant and of course plenty of other cafés. Several shops closed for the whole day. Not much of interest in the shops and prices for most things sky-high. A small bottle similar to those sold containing boiled sweets in peacetime for a few coppers was empty and had a few flowers painted on, and the charge was 4s. 6d. Most things 300 per cent advanced in price but suitcase gone up from 7s. 6d.–15s. to £5–£7. I mean those which used to be about 7s. 6d. were £5 and the 15s. sort were £7. So we did not spend much....

Edith has had her war grant money reduced by 2s. a week, presumably because she is now receiving 21s. a week for her husband, who is living at home though working elsewhere in the Army. They are at present getting on all right. She spends her Army allowances on food and buys clothes and pays for all extra expenses out of her capital, and her husband keeps his Army allowance for cigarettes and probably plants for the garden and allotment and to take his wife and child to theatre or pictures occasionally. Doctors' bills for herself and the child are also paid out of capital and the rent (the house is on hire-purchase) does not get paid at all. Just as well she got about £180 from father's money, for I don't think she and her husband had ever saved anything to speak of.

Windsor was pleasant. There was a full house at Ivor Novello's play *Full House*. It was amusing and even clever and seemed to me to be mainly a characterisation of a borderline mental defective running family life in the West End and getting saved from disaster by marriage.

All the youngsters about here seem to be getting skin rashes of various kinds.

Friday, 18 June

I am surrounded by unanswered letters and housework. Since last evening the internee has asked for a loan of £2, the Fabians ask me to collect towards a hospital in Stalingrad, the Shire Hall collected for a girl's wedding present and now M-O would like some cash. Actually all my spare money goes on the internee. It is true in return I am collecting his furniture and I merely state a fact. I suppose he has cost me £100 since he got interned and there is about that value in furniture. Thank heaven the latest news sounds a bit more hopeful, for the doctor has passed him as fit for clerical work which he says means that his release is certain and he may be released in July. He must earn his own living when he gets out and live down to it. As my sister says, present-day children have no idea of the value of money. It is time, however, that Martin got a chance to learn it. I hope that just for a time he gets exactly so much a week and no more, sufficient but not too much. He has doubtless grown up in many ways since internment. Meantime I keep hunting round for turpentine in order that he may continue to paint.

I met that other youngster, Peter Waddington, nearly outside my door last evening. I had just bought two copies of illustrations of National Gallery pictures so lent him one and also came upstairs to lend him my one of coloured reproductions. With the milk on my stairs was Martin's letter, so I opened it in front of Peter and remarked that I must get Martin some more turpentine and I thought like himself (Peter, who shops for the village and buys books for other people to read) I appeared to be very useful. I was laughing and he replied he feared he only did things for people when it pleased him to do so....

Sunday, 20 June

Following my remarks on women's happiness [on 18 June], one [neighbour] was talking about her two sisters and said one of them would have made an excellent wife and mother but her first fiancé 'let her down' and now she just lives a flippant life drinking in her leisure hours with a man she is friendly with. The other sister has quite a nice husband and no financial worries but she does not like sleeping with him and they have no children. The speaker said she told this sister it would be her own fault if the husband found another woman and she answered that she would not mind much so long as she had Micky. Micky is the speaker's child who was evacuated to her care and she thinks the sister was somewhat in love with her husband, who is now dead, somewhat to his wife's relief. She said the sister loved cuddling the eight-year-old boy in bed and the doctor thought that might have caused his enuresis. Micky, now back with his mother, has not wetted his bed for five weeks, and now sleeps alone. He looks more robust, too. The dead husband was, like the child, charming, and wonderful in the house and in his manner to his wife as well as other people. Her married life, however, consisted of a series of paying up his debts, mainly gambling ones. He would borrow money from her friends and she would scrape and save to pay them off, so it was a relief when he was dead and could borrow no more. She is nearly terrified that her boy may have inherited his father's temperament. The sister spoils and demoralises the boy.

Wednesday, 23 June

A Mr Jacques of the Workers' Educational Association spoke at the Fabians tonight. It gives one a feeling almost of warmth and comfort to realise that just here and there isolated individuals would have courage to face death for things they considered right. I should judge him to be one such. He is the third person, or perhaps the fourth, of that calibre whom I have met since the war started. It is almost like a fire inside these people which could perhaps burn them up physically and gives them the effect of inspiration such as the old prophets may have had. This man could laugh and was fairly solid when one got near to. In speech he did not spare his brain, going deeply for the incisive phrase, and usually producing something original. He was out to make his listeners realise their responsibility for world events and stripped war naked to the bone in emphasizing the fact.

Later I read Laski's *Marx and Today* [Fabian Society, 1943] and was much surprised to find that in most respects his views on the Labour government coincided with mine and were just as unfavourable. I suppose Laski is another man who would risk his life for freedom of speech. There are a few, it seems.

Then I thought of my niece Shirley. I have always been glad of her since she was born and in a way grateful to my sister for accepting the responsibility of bringing her into being, though before her birth, had I been asked, I should have advised against bringing new and innocent life into this jungle of thieves and liars and murderers for monetary gain and crushers of the poor. Tonight, for the first time, I felt really afraid for the child's future. Our own generation has been pretty bad, but what hope is there for the next? The present-day child is a barbarian compared with whom we, though dull, were child angels. Today they are untaught and with no respect for parents and no standards of right and wrong. To be a gangster is to be a hero. Between 14 and 18 most present-day girls are amateur prostitutes, untaught and beyond the control of parents, and floating about the streets in all their spare time, or having babies all over the place. They will produce fodder of some kind for the next war, but they won't be capable of bringing up even ordinarily decent citizens, for the bringing up of a child is altogether more difficult than our rulers know – or care. And I was afraid for Shirley, who is good and generous and capable of self-sacrifice. Her mother strives to have her educated and developed to her capacity. Perhaps she will go to a university and take up some creative form of work. And by then she will be an isolated girl, without brothers or sisters, fighting her way in a world of ruthlessness where ignorance, insanity and extreme poverty are all around her, and moneyed power threatens her annihilation. It is more likely that this will happen after the war than that we shall get together and make a better world. We who could get together are woefully ignorant of the wiles of the Devil in human form. We are just the trodden on masses, and without courage....

This war is terrific. So many, many millions of dead soldiers and still it goes on and will go on, for the end is not in sight. Planes here are terribly noisy, day and night. Germany must be shambles. If they were winning I feel they would bomb us as we are bombing them, instead of sending over only a few most nights.

Sunday, 27 June

I feel better now, having spent 2¾ hours cooking, eating and washing-up. When I got home at 6 p.m. I felt I wished I had wings to fly away! Rather pleasant day, picking black currants (with break for lunch) from 10.30 to

5.30, and earning thereby 3s. 6d. – much less than I did with apples. Easier than apples but I was fagged out to a state of irritability. Came home cycling with Miss Hinnells, an admirable young woman, good-looking and healthy. I noticed it specially one evening when she came into a concert and made all the previous entrants look passé and powdered up to preserve. She is cheerful and has nice eyes, but in my irritable state she was too goody-goody. At first she did spare-time land-work free but as Burrells preferred to pay she keeps it for the Red Cross. She does not go away for holidays because the government has asked us not to. She was going home cheerfully to bottle and jam 12 pounds of black currants. By that time I felt I had seen enough black currants for one year, would not bottle anything, and would make plum jam – being the easiest. I wasted about ½lb or ¾lb sugar the other evening stewing bottled greengages and as they had fermented I spent the night being sick! I did not greatly mind being sick, but I did regret the sugar and time I had spent bottling the things!

I suppose I ought to buy some coalite for next winter, but I keep hoping either that the war will be over or that I shall be somewhere where I shan't require coal. Wishing, however, won't keep me warm next winter if I am still here. I suppose also I ought to enquire at Post Office for a form to get 'priority' paraffin.

I have collected 14s. or so towards a British wing for a hospital the Russians are building in Stalingrad. Tommy and Perrin gave me 2s. 6d. each, very generously. Tommy went on holiday Saturday.

… I wish the war would end. Though I certainly look forward with some trepidation to my own future when it does end. The security I have now will then have vanished. Blossom today said she hopes to leave the Shire Hall after the war and start some tea-rooms. She is on the permanent staff so need not leave but would like to. Her father, like myself, will then be out of work, and as he was a grocer perhaps he could help her. Miss Hinnells is also at the Shire Hall but I imagine is in comfortable circumstances financially.

Miss Osgathorpe at the Moral Welfare Home lost her bicycle recently and it was found abandoned at Ipswich. A 16-year-old girl at the home took the lock off the door and escaped with the bike and food and a few oddments. She was intelligent and illegitimate and looked upon it and subsequent court proceedings as a joke. Somebody told me recently the Marquis of _____'s family were the same, even going as far as murder for a joke in one case. This girl biked to Ipswich, got to London and through Liverpool Street station without a ticket, stole a purse containing money from a child and eventually attracted the attention of the police at Euston – she was trying to go to Scotland. She is now going to an Approved School.

I have asked R.H. Ward of the Adelphi Players if I can sell tickets for them for September. The secretary of the Fabians thinks he may be able to sell some too. They are very good actors and it seems a shame that only a handful of people will go and see them. Winnie Wharton, a 'Strict Baptist', and shorthand-typist at the Shire Hall, won't go because she considers all actors agents of the Devil, and the Adelphi Players as the 'thin edge of the wedge'. Shakespeare in her estimation is very good read but should never be acted, and Nativity Plays are bad and quite unnecessary. She comes from Norfolk, not Suffolk, and is to be married shortly. The Adelphi Players are dividing their time between the Cloister Gardens and the Congregational Chapel, and are playing *Ghosts*, *The Duchess of Malfi*, and *Robin Hood*. They and the Fabians just keep my soul alive, thank God....[41]

A child aged eleven at St Elizabeth's now – I don't know why. She is such a typical Anglo-Saxon ('not Anglo but Angels' variety) she made everybody else look un-English. Her fair hair (flaxen) stuck out at all angles, too, rather in Ancient Briton style! She is pretty, like many of the girls who get to the home.

Wednesday, 30 June

Until 10 p.m. the skies were amazingly peaceful tonight, and even now (10.30) it is only a very occasional plane flying low which breaks the stillness. Joan Burton said on Tuesday night they kept her awake. I said they got me to the point of praying they would bomb the guilty, not the innocent. Gooch said they would as they were going to Germany and I answered 'Yes, a crèche of babies, or something of that kind'. I can but thank God it is Germany, not England, getting bombed so terribly, but I cannot quite understand how we came to escape so much that the rest of mankind are experiencing. We have been lucky it seems beyond our deserts.

---

[41] The players performed in early September and, according to the *Bury Free Press*, were enthusiastically received (11 September 1943, p.10). Winifred was again inspired by their work on stage. 'This Company does much for me in that it lets me know there is courage and intellect in human beings and that spiritually one is not fighting entirely alone. Shall I call it a sense of comradeship?' 'Tonight in the play', she wrote later, 'I wished it would go on for ever; that time would stay still. It is only when these players are here that life in this town is worth living' (3 September 1943).

Afterword

Winifred continued with her diary for another five years, writing at least a third of a million more words. During these years her writing was mainly personal, opinionated, and gossipy; and passages that highlight social observation are few and far between. The most informative and interesting of these passages with regard to West Suffolk are reproduced above, in some of the footnotes to her diary, and below in Appendix C, which presents most of her writing about VE celebrations in Bury in May 1945. She made some new acquaintances, and Martin Luther was released from internment in November 1943. He later went his own way, disconnected from Winifred. She enjoyed a number of intellectual and artistic events and pursuits. She anticipated peace with mixed feelings, for she continued to be pessimistic about her postwar job prospects.[1] And she became moderately politically active, joining the Labour Party in 1944 (with the goal of making it more genuinely socialist) and working for it in 1945 in both national and local elections. She still thought of herself as something of a displaced bird of passage in Bury St Edmunds. Often she was highly critical of others just as she was sometimes critical of herself. And while there was a part of her that recognised her own talents and felt a sense of intellectual superiority, there was another part that condemned herself as a complete failure.

Winifred's views of Americans wavered during the last year of the war, usually depending on whatever evidence or tales (often lurid) had recently come to her notice. Sometimes she saw Americans as sorts of modern savages, on other occasions she was impressed by their merits, including generosity and friendliness. 'The Americans are entertaining all our county children, boarded-out and in homes, to a Xmas party,' she wrote on 1 December 1944, 'and will send conveyances all over the county to fetch them. They are certainly amazingly fond of children, and the kids will have the time of their lives.' Three weeks later she reported that the 'Americans are gathering up our West Suffolk children in thousands and entertaining them, and the children love it', and she went on to portray their wartime presence in a relatively benign and good-humoured light. 'Apart from the Yanks who are interested only in sex relations, the Americans are easy to get on with and we and they

---

[1] On 19 November 1943 she thought that 'it is practically certain that after the war nobody will employ a typist who is about 50, and I'm no good for any other kind of employment, having insufficient brain to forge my way through life as an individual doing something creative, and yet too much to become a contented beast of burden'.

chip each other about our respective countries and get good laughs about all the matters which our rulers consider we shall fight each other about. A few minutes after meeting one, these Yanks show photos of all their family, including aunts and uncle and cousins and so on. I suppose it's their way of effecting an introduction' (21 December 1944).

Winifred also had mixed feelings about her diary and her merits as a writer. 'Most of the stuff I write seems utter piffle,' she declared on 31 January 1947, 'but if it is it merely means that that's the way life actually is in this place'. She then remarked on what many diarists might say when they come to reflect on their years of diary-writing. 'Had I not written this diary, I should have thought nothing at all had happened since 1940. Perhaps nothing has, and yet a remarkable number of small events are penned here' (31 January 1947). Once (19 August 1944) she reflected on her literary leanings. 'A letter from a writer received this week thanked me for a description of wartime Bury St Edmunds and said one of these days I'd write a lovely and very readable novel. Writers have told me such things for many years, but they don't understand my limitations and don't realise how infinitely easier it is to write a running commentary than to create something which has plot, theme and form. Besides, a typical typist earns more than a novelist does. If somebody would bequeath me £3,000, I'd start on a novel right away!!'

Winifred, clearly, was acutely class-conscious. This is hardly surprising – perhaps most British men and women at this time were. What is more unusual is that her perspective on class was that of a woman who did not really fit in anywhere socially, or, to put the matter differently, whose sense of self cut across social boundaries. For her identity was in some respects working-class (she sympathized with some workers and her own income was sometimes barely enough to live on), in other respects lower middle-class (family, friends, salary in wartime), and in others still fairly genteel (especially her cultural aspirations and interest in the arts, a product of her own curiosity and strivings). She was highly sensitive to social slights and had a sharp eye for the posturing of members of the elite and their lack of empathy for the struggles of the unprivileged. After the war, recalling her months at Hillcroft College in 1936–37, she said that 'I learnt [there] that the professional classes jealously guarded their ranks from penetration by the working classes' (13 February 1947). On one occasion she spoke, bluntly, of 'class distinction (curse it)' (25 November 1943). Living in Bury St Edmunds and observing close-up the conduct and attitudes of its people of property and influence undoubtedly fuelled her sense of protest: 'I simply boil at all our snobbery and injustice and lack of democracy', she wrote on 23 May 1944.

As World War Two ended, Winifred continued to work at Shire Hall. During the following three years she appears to have enjoyed better health than during the war and more self-composure. 'I am more contented these days', she wrote on 19 March 1946. 'I don't look at Bury St Edmunds with such distaste as I did. I think the fact that the war is over and I am still in a job brings subconsciously a feeling of hope.' She made a close male friend (they were probably not lovers) – 'I am not likely to be asked to marry, but the attraction is sufficient on both sides to make us want to be alone together as often as possible' (3 November 1947) – and she befriended German prisoners of war who were still kept in the area (some of whom she visited in West Germany in the 1950s). In the summer of 1948 she got a position as a secretary in Newmarket Hospital[2] and moved to Burwell, eleven miles from Cambridge.

When Winifred retired in 1961 she moved to a bungalow on Centre Drive, Newmarket, which was designed by her architect nephew to unusual specifications – she wanted a small kitchen (she disliked cooking) and a large living room to accommodate her books.[3] But the bungalow did not appeal to others and was demolished after her death. Her former neighbours remembered her as both 'very nice' and 'highly intelligent'. In the early twenty-first century those of her kin who remembered her portrayed, in some respects, a person very different from the woman who revealed herself in her wartime diary, for she was recalled by them as a fundamentally happy elderly lady. She was given credit for holding the widely scattered Challis clan together, thanks to her frequent and long letters, up to forty pages in length (as were some of her diary entries).[4] She is remembered for her family parties, especially at Christmas when she served lavish quantities of home-made wine. Certain eccentricities stood out in their minds – she used up half-tins of paint on the walls of her bungalow which gave them a harlequin look, and she wore distinctly unfashionable clothes. Winifred does not seem to have spoken of her writing for Mass-Observation, which nobody who was contacted by the editors and who had known her knew anything about.

Winifred Challis died in a nursing home in Cheveley near Newmarket on 10 October 1990 in her ninety-fifth year.

---

[2] Her opinion of Newmarket improved with time. 'I went to Newmarket for the weekend', she wrote on 2 December 1946, 'and it looked a very nice clean, light and green little town after Bury St Edmunds.' She also found public assistance in Newmarket more generous than in Bury (24 April 1944).

[3] This paragraph is based on Peter Searby's conversations with Winifred's nephews, Andrew Challis and John Boorman, and her one-time neighbours on Centre Drive.

[4] Sadly, none of these letters seem to survive excepting that reproduced as Appendix B.

Appendix A

Mass-Observation

Mass-Observation, the social research organization for which Winifred wrote her diary, was established in 1937. It was created to meet a need; and that need, in the eyes of its founders, was to overcome Britons' ignorance about themselves in their everyday lives. Mass-Observation – it was often referred to simply as M-O – aimed to lay the foundation for a social anthropology of contemporary Britain, and to contribute to a better understanding of the behaviour and beliefs of the majority of the nation's citizens, not just the élite. Mass-Observation, according to a sort of mission statement in 1937, 'will encourage people to look more closely at their social environment than ever before', for M-O, it was said, 'shares the interest of most people in the actual, in what happens from day to day'.[1] Its goal was to help found a 'science of ourselves', rooted in closely observed facts, for a proper social science, it was assumed, had to be based on evidence, methodically and laboriously collected.

In order to pursue this science of society, M-O recruited hundreds of volunteer 'observers'. These observers were asked to collect facts, to describe, sometimes to count, to listen – indeed, even to eavesdrop – and perhaps to ask questions of members of the public. Their efforts at social recording were thought to be akin to those of an anthropologist working in the field. Mass-Observation, with hundreds of data-collectors working voluntarily in different parts of the country, was especially interested in casting light on matters of social life that had previously been largely ignored, such as jokes, superstitions, pub-going, betting on football pools, fears, habits of spending and saving, personal grooming, smoking, and 'Doing the Lambeth Walk' (a new and very popular dance).[2]

While M-O's volunteer observers were normally expected to collect facts, an opinion developed among M-O's leaders that observers could also function usefully as subjective 'cameras' that captured their own experiences of living. This acceptance of the legitimacy of subjectivity in social observation

---

[1] Charles Madge and Tom Harrisson, *Mass-Observation* (Letchworth, 1937), pp.29–30. In 2006 Mass-Observation dropped the hyphen from its name and became Mass Observation. In this edition we have retained the pre-2006 usage.

[2] The range of M-O's interests is evident in a Penguin Special from early 1939: Charles Madge and Tom Harrisson, *Britain, by Mass-Observation*.

was a major reason why diary-keeping came to be promoted as a promising vehicle of both social reporting and self-observation. A diary was another way of recording, especially of things as they happened. The writer of a regular diary would be well placed, while memory was still fresh, to report on actions observed, rumours that were circulating, conversations overheard or taken part in, and other external events, not to mention the diarist's own immediate thoughts and feelings. From late August 1939, with another war on the horizon, M-O decided to encourage its volunteer observers to write regular diaries – some people initially called their writing 'Crisis Diary', later 'War Diary' – in order to convey, as they thought fit and as suited their temperament (no explicit directions were given), their own experiences of living in wartime. This was, we might say, an invitation to speak out; to give voice to one's own thoughts and feelings; and to put into words one's own outlook on living, whatever that might mean for each writer. A diary both encouraged and permitted an individual to see the world from his or her own angle of vision, and each person's vantage point was thought (in the eyes of M-O's leaders) to be of interest, and every perspective to have value. (M-O was a project infused with democratic values.) By 1945 some 480 people had produced diaries for Mass-Observation, though many of these lasted for only a few months, and most were not particularly rich in detail.[3]

We do not know why Winifred Challis decided to start her diary when she did, though we have some basis for suggesting why she may have been attracted to diary-writing and kept at it for half a dozen years. She was a person who liked to write, and was not at a loss for words. Moreover, she had time on her hands; she was often lonely, if not actually friendless – the life of a middle-aged spinster left much to be desired – and her diary almost certainly gave her an outlet for complaints, doubts, comments, and ruminations that, in different circumstances, might have been directed to the ears of a family member or confidant. Winifred's diary was her confidant; it was there that she deposited thoughts that (for the most part) had no or few listeners in her actual social world. Her diary was certainly, in some respects, a private, self-disclosing document, but she knew that it would be read by at least a few other people, and she accepted that one of her tasks in putting her writing before M-O's small group of readers was to describe and record those aspects of everyday life in wartime West Suffolk that she observed directly or were brought to her attention by others. In doing so, as her diary

---

[3] One other M-O diary from East Anglia has previously been published: Robert Malcolmson and Peter Searby, eds, *Wartime Norfolk: The Diary of Rachel Dhonau 1941–1942* (Norfolk Record Society, 2004). For a useful anthology of writing by these observers, see Sandra Koa Wing, ed., *Our Longest Days: A People's History of the Second World War* (London, 2008). James Hinton has drawn upon some of the best of these diarists in his excellent *Nine Wartime Lives: Mass-Observation and the Making of the Modern Self* (Oxford, 2010).

makes clear, her observations were usually coloured by her own sceptical and strongly-held opinions, many of which were not shared by a lot of her Suffolk acquaintances. One of the merits of her writing is that she noticed and attached importance to incidents and attitudes that would probably have gone unnoticed by others. A more conventional diarist might well have been less engaging, less animated, less probing of accepted wisdom.

In 2005 the Mass-Observation Archive was given Designated Status by the Museums, Libraries and Archives Council as one of Britain's Outstanding Collections. Much information about Mass-Observation, its archive and its current activities is available on its website: www.massobs.org.uk.

Appendix B

Winifred Challis's early life

The following life and times of Winifred Challis, as recounted by her, was written in a letter of 23 June 1982 to her nephew, John Boorman, and his wife, Janet. Winifred, aged eighty-six, was then living at 36 Centre Drive in Newmarket.

I was a Victorian – 1896. A first-born and probably spoilt. Flo (your mother, John) came third, barely a year after George, and by then we had no nurse-maid but I believe my long-widowed grandmother was living with us. Flo I think was more of a Challis and much more popular than I – better-looking too. She had been a much more contented baby and that could have been that patent foods were by now on the market and she therefore got enough to eat. We were all big babies at birth. I walked at 18 months, when I became much better-tempered, but shy. I went to school aged four – we went then from aged three to five. I had expected to go to a Newmarket private school called Glenwood College. In the Doris Street area families with few children sent them to private schools; those with a lot sent them to St Mary's Church School which at some period was taken over by the council or government board. Father at some time had a lengthy illness when money was tight, and it *could* have been now. Anyhow, St Mary's was close and therefore convenient and I found myself there.

For the next two years all went well. I wondered what good it was to have toys on a platform when we were not allowed to play with them. The teachers seemed mature. Sitting next to Dora Moon, I thought she was lucky to have such a short name to write. Listening to a five-year-old newcomer howling when her mother left her, I thought what great babies five-year-olds were and the three-year-olds never made such a fuss. So it was better they should come at three.

However, my troubles started at six. My paints were taken away and I had to go to the top class and learn to sew. Here the boys and girls were divided into two blocks and I got my first notification of sex inequality! True, the boys were not allowed to paint, but they were allowed to draw, while I had to sew.

Newmarket seemed to me a hotbed of class-distinction. We saw a lot of Edward VII and fairly often Alexandra. Aristocracy came and lodged among us with their carriages and later cars and chauffeurs. Princess Mary's husband stayed three doors from us. The Prince of Wales who later gave up his right of kingship for the American he married used to stay at the corner house on the other side of the road. They were all right as far as they went. They never wanted food on a table twice, so lots of children were fed better with the left-overs. Also, many women paid their rates out of profits in taking lodgers. Small boys earned sixpences by rushing to open or shut carriage doors.

The next rank in class-distinction was the trainers and some jockeys. Then came the ordinary people of which I was one. Last came the stablemen. It was more complicated than that though. Church and chapel did not mix too well, and there were the slums in Grosvenor Yard, Icewell Hill, and The Rookery. When seven I was moved to the Girls' School and here the chapel-going teachers favoured the children who attended their chapels. Possibly it worked the other way round. We attended St Mary's Church on Sundays.

In school we children could not mix well either. There was the problem of clean and dirty children because we were near the slums and some of the dirty ones had fleas in their hair. Edith Seal, it was said, had no mother, and by the time she vanished to have something done about it she was sitting quite on her own and the fleas and nits had made quite a nest on the top of her head. In any case, when outside school, we played with very few children except those of our own immediate area, where we knew the parents as well as the children. We had a day out at the seaside yearly through attending the church Sunday school and as the church had no Band of Hope we attended the Congregational chapel once a week to go to their yearly outing to the sea. As a small child at home I had plenty of toys and books, and preferred books to dolls. My mother, her mother and her family, and my godmother, had all been excellent needle-women, so I had plenty of clothes. Sweets were provided so we had little pocket-money to buy more.

Which brings me back to the teaching I got when aged six. Possibly well-meaning people thought our lessons should suit our station in life and there seemed a lot of stress on the Church's 'Do your duty in that state of life to which it had pleased God to call you'. I was very early reading Victorian novels and anything else I could lay my hands on, and there was much stress on the gap between servant and master, and I got the impression that to be a domestic servant was the lowest possible way of life. To sew or cook or do anything in the domestic line was therefore to be avoided whatever God and the Church thought about it. The young teacher was no friend of mine and she seemed to work that way. One day she was describing the difference between rich and poor and asked me 'Are *you* rich or poor?' Now when going to Haverhill father's brothers and sisters used to give me sixpences and shillings instead of my customary half pennies and pennies, so I felt quite triumphant with my answer. 'When I am at home I am poor but when I go to my grandfather's I am rich.' She did not attempt to challenge it.

So, you see, if it had not been for one good teacher in the Girls' School who taught me in classes one and three, I was likely to be a problem. At twelve, in class 7, I had mumps, diphtheria and appendicitis followed by six weeks at Lowestoft to recuperate. The day I returned to school the teacher was holding a spelling bee and to her annoyance I won it. She presented me with the prize – a silver thimble which I soon lost happily.

I was already doing shorthand at home and the only lessons I could see of possible use were English and arithmetic. This, with a very few girls in X7 attached,[1] was the highest class and such a thing as a scholarship unheard of, and the poor woman wanted some night-dresses made for her, so for three weeks we were on needlework. The night-dresses had lots of tucks and I could see her sitting up in bed in them while I decorated them with feather-stitch I think it's called. At the end of the three weeks I was 13 so I had a talk with my mother, said I was learning nothing and wanted to leave school. I left on my 13th birthday or next day and wheeled our baby about the streets for a year. By now mother had twins but the boy baby died aged six weeks. The girl (Lilian) lived to be seven and died at the end of the 1914–18 war.

As I approached 14, letters began coming in from firms wanting milliners, dressmakers and shop assistants. I turned them down. When I was 13 mother had suggested I went to Bury St Edmunds County School, but I was aware I'd got to earn a living somehow, so why go to a school which would do little towards it except teaching me tennis? So I had turned that down too. As a last resort, and doubtless after talking to father, she said the head woman in the Co-op cash desk was leaving to get married. There would be a vacancy in his office for a shorthand typist later, but it would mean first going into the drapery department for a month and then into the cash desk while waiting for the office job. 'Would I do it?' 'Yes, I would.' I did, until I was 19, by when we had been at war some time. I wanted a change from Newmarket and to see the outside world. War made it possible. Father gave me my return fare.

Winifred then went on at some length to describe the job she had at a munitions works between Luton and Dunstable and the people she worked with. This was a happy time in her life.

Generally speaking, it was the most friendly place I knew. We also visited one another's houses. We all went about weekly to the same theatre. We had our concerts and went to others held by Vauxhall and Commer cars, and they came to ours. The Kent family (from the owner, George Kent Ltd, who also owned their Biscot Road engineering works and a HQ place in London) were always helpful and pleasant when they visited us. I was sorry to leave them for Newmarket and more wages in the Royal Flying Corps. It was

---

[1] X7 was short for 'Extra 7'. The school leaving age was then twelve, and those who stayed on after twelve (as some did, voluntarily) went into X7, where the instruction tended to be more advanced than in the usual elementary curriculum. To be in X7 marked one out as liking school.

much more boring and as soon as war ended I went back as secretary to the general manager of Hewlett and Blondeau's until their aeroplane works was closing down.

Love, Auntie Win.

Appendix C

Winifred Challis's account of VE Day celebrations in Bury St Edmunds

As war in Europe was ending in May 1945, Winifred reported in detail the celebrations planned and carried out in Bury St Edmunds, and her own opinions of them. The following are selections from her diary during these days.

Monday, 7 May

8.55 p.m. I saw flags from the Church Walks, where the poorer people live, as I came home. Later, when I went to post, I saw that the whole of the silly little town had its flags out. I shall have to keep indoors if I wish to evade this bloody war, it appears. Bills out ask the townsfolk to put out their flags and bunting *after* peace is announced. It has not been announced, but Abbeygate Street, dropping down to the Abbey Gardens, is wrapped and draped in flags and bunting. Aren't people idiots? Don't they ever read history and learn how other fools hung out flags and then in their turn were trodden underfoot? Or have I got that impression because at the cinema one always gets the pomp before the death, as a matter of contrast? Who knows?

I think at the office we were altogether more concerned about a holiday than about the end of the war. Actually, we don't feel the war is over. Planes still fly and the factory outside my window is going full pelt and nothing anywhere has changed. We have been unsettled over this holiday, through not knowing when it would start or its duration. I don't suppose any of us will do anything startling with it, but it will be a holiday. I think it ought to be two days. As a reward for 5½ years of war one day seems mean, especially when, as Joan remarked, we *may* be going about in bathchairs or on sticks when the next war ends. She was giving it its maximum time of 20 years between. I don't think anyone gives it longer, and the talk flickering about is that we shall be quarrelling with Russia and USA before many months, or even weeks.

I suppose the holiday is intended for people who want to get drunk. They would have taken a day off for that, in any case. Judging by the store set on it, getting drunk must be wonderful, but it is so beastly for the onlooker that I have never desired to try it and should never again recover my self-esteem if I did. Blast! That factory has stopped. Does it mean Churchill has said the war is over? Curse! I want two days off, not one. Everything seems deadly silent. Expect I'll have to wait until Joyce returns from the cinema and perhaps from a subsequent booze-up before I know. Church bells are supposed to ring, though. I *imagine* I hear them in the distance. Ah! That factory has started throbbing again, this time on a low note. Perhaps he won't break the news until morning, after all. It is now 9.15 p.m. Yanks were in the streets this evening and if it were announced now they would certainly not be confined to barracks. I don't know why they should be, but I suppose it is thought they would drink all the drink and perhaps the town would get its windows broken.

This is my clearest week at the office, meetings being only Mildenhall on Thursday and Bury on Friday, so the 'peace' should not fall on a day when I must attend a meeting. I am mending my raincoat, as I don't look like getting another this year or maybe ever. I simply must buy a winter's coat this winter, however, in case I have to go for an interview for a job. Actually, the end of this war makes me feel as if I'm going to a funeral and as if it is now time to bury all our dead, including the German dead. I am sorry for the slain Germans, and could not drink and make merry after committing such a slaughter, and reducing them to such degradation. I regret Martin has not written me. I've no idea whether he is sorry or intensely glad the war is over. He may, of course, be like myself over it, utterly phlegmatic and dull....

Tuesday, 8 May

... At 9.30 tonight several of us [from the Forces Study Group] went along to the Angel Hill. Such a crowd, and the Angel Hotel illuminated with red, white and blue fairy lamps. Dancing going on and all the children in the town dancing or in perambulators or on arms. Children and groups dancing. The men left us to go and get a feed, but as I am not in the Forces I could not accompany them, and Nancy [Roberts, ATS] wanted to see the Abbey Gardens illuminations under the mistaken idea that they were fireworks. The fairy lamps, however, were very pretty among the greenery. The Gardens were thronged with people and as we tried to get out again through the Abbey Gateway we found it a bottleneck. Eventually we moved with the crowd and after a few minutes intense squeezing and clinging together so as not to lose one another we were again on the Angel Hill.

I was getting hungry and still feeling half dead through the menstruation [and] felt that a meal would do me good. Where to go? Nancy said the Ten Bells hadn't a very good reputation but we agreed that no place had if Forces visited it, and they were all alike. She said also that last time they had only Spam, so that settled it. I suggested the St John Street place to which Regina had once taken me. Could not find it, so went in another about the same spot. Nobody would have known it was a little country town. The proprietors did not look bad. Tables covered with white oilcloth. Soldiers seated around. One young waitress and one little wizened woman who looked about 60 by face and arms but had a long mop of black frizzy hair loose with a bow of ribbon tied round her head and navy slacks (trousers). I thought of the dangers of infection and the dirt one might eat in such places, but we were willing to indulge in anything. Tea tasted rather awful and served in very thick, clumsy white cups and no saucers. Food was Spam and potatoes, which I ordered and Nancy refused. Then the girl returned to say no potatoes, only Spam sandwiches, so I said I too would have tea only. So I got no decent meal. Have just eaten a bit of chocolate instead.

One black-haired soldier was merrily drunk (all crowds tonight have been good-tempered) and shook hands in a pump-like fashion with a young American. He looked a wreck. Many of them looked a weedy, ill-nourished, undeveloped lot. The American gave the other a bottle of beer, so the proprietress said he must go outside to drink it as the police had warned her she would have to close if she allowed drinking. One fair girl sitting in a group of men looked blowsy. Nobody accosted us. The woman looked pleased as I gave her 6d. for two 2d. cups of tea and told her to keep the change. Then some Indians in turbans came in and shortly afterwards we came out.

Nancy thought everything seemed unreal and I marvelled how near to the old 'Merrie England' even one day's holiday could bring Bury St Edmunds. There is a certain grandeur about Angel Hill and the Abbey Gardens which aids the effect tremendously. I also felt life was unreal and we both could not realise that the war with Germany was over. We wondered if it would make any difference. I said for a week or two I hadn't cared what would happen to me. She suggested 'Live for the day' but that doesn't fit in because I do not live, I merely exist. She came to my house with me and we looked at its masses of chimneys and its odd shape and the little narrow house next door against this wide one, and again I said it was unreal and I ought to be leaving Bury. The house had been a refuge from bombs, but that was all. The only trouble was that I had nowhere to go to. I don't want to think of these years in Bury. And yet? Looking back, the house itself, or its furniture, and my correspondence with Martin gave it a soul, even if an anxious, weary, frustrated, sometimes clumsy, sometimes beautiful, soul. …

Wednesday, 9 May

I feel better in health today, though I just can't manage to sleep more than six hours even on holiday. Planes a bit noisy. The factory, thank God most fervently, is still.

At 1 p.m. Joyce came up, cigarette in mouth, to ask if I would cook dinner (lunch) of fish and chips as she had been having a drink and she and her sister were wanting to go to a pub for another with the cinema boys and her friend Mrs Tweed. She thought she might not see another victory day and at any rate hoped she wouldn't know another war like this one. So here am I, sitting on my bed writing while a lump of cod fries on the oilstove beside me. It will be cod and bread today and that's all. I am certainly not chipping potatoes. I do wish this war would end so I could get back to a decent standard of life!! But I can't see much prospect of that.

They say downstairs they don't like beer but one cannot buy gin and lime which anyway is at profiteering prices and after the first glass beer isn't too bad. They sip it. One said she could not drink the first glass without shuddering.

Evening, 11 p.m. Nancy Roberts and I went to Miss Westell's, then to Forces Group, and then here. I gave her lemonade and cake, and she went. Joyce came up and borrowed my gramophone. I went to bed again and she has just borrowed some tumblers as there are twelve cinema people downstairs. I hope not to see her again tonight but there doesn't appear much hope of going to sleep yet! Planes throbbing but factory still. Nancy wants to keep her civilian clothes in my wardrobe this summer. Another ring on the door. Several Yanks there in the party or perhaps cinema boys, or both.

Thursday, 10 May

7.50 a.m. Wish I were not so tired. Planes roar towards me and I cower under bedclothes in usual way. Later I remembered there were probably no bombs on the machines.

I gave a cheer last night – my first for months. Morrison gave out that 18B and imprisonment for alarm and despondency would no longer operate. Nancy, B.A., rejoiced with me, but everybody else at the Moral Welfare Home looked mildly surprised and from their expressions I quite think they had no idea at all what 18B was. Joan Burton didn't know either, when I mentioned it later.

Suppose I can wash my last bit of blackout though the attic may be glad of it occasionally. No good doing anything to the house or having wireless put on now, as of course I may be leaving at any time for my unknown destination on the dole. Brave new world!

INDEX OF PEOPLE AND PLACES

her niece (Shirley), 61–2, 68, 75, 142,
144–5, 160, 165
her pessimism, 59, 64–5, 108, 117,
126, 127–9, 137, 139, 142–3,
147–8, 150, 152, 152n–53n, 165
her relatives, 4, 86, 138, 143
her brother's family in Cambridge,
37, 46–7, 49–50
her sister's family in Staines, 4,
62–3, 68, 72–3, 74–5, 160, 161,
163
Chamberlain, Neville, 123
Chaucer, Geoffrey, 62
Chekhov, Anton, 58
Cheveley, 171
Chevington, 121
China, 83
Churchill, Winston, 7n, 35n, 47, 83, 84
(twice), 109, 124, 132, 133, 151
health of, 108, 110, 115, 116
Cragg, A.E. (public assistance committee
member), 35, 37, 112, 135, 156, 157
Cripps, Sir Stafford, 34–5, 132
Crowe, Mr and Mrs (Fabians), 119, 147n,
151

Dachau, 150, 152
Daladier, Edouard, 30
Dante Alighieri, 96
Darlan, Admiral François, 28–9, 30, 77–8,
90
Davies, Cecil, 64n
Davies, Emil, 100, 151
Day (relieving officer), 141
de la Chapelle, Bonnier, 77
de Gaulle, Charles, 44, 90, 96
Dorothy (typist), 60
Dovercourt, 67
Dumas, Alexander, 98
Dunstable, xvn, 178

East Suffolk, xvi, 3, 6
Eden, Anthony, 35n, 107n
Egpyt, 22
El Alamein, 20n
Eliot, T.S., 65
Ely, 142, 144–5

Flecker, James Elroy, 63
Foulger, Elsie (clerk), 101, 122, 141
France, 9, 27, 28, 28n–29n, 30, 44, 83,
90, 91

Franco, Francisco, 28, 97

Gandhi, Mahatma, 108, 110, 114
Germany, 24, 25, 26, 27, 43, 44, 77, 83,
90, 161
Gielgud, John, 107
Gollancz, Oliver, 131–2
Gooch (chief clerk), 8, 15, 17, 29, 30, 67,
109, 113, 120, 142
Grafton, Duchess of, 124
Granville, Edgar Louis, 28
Great Yarmouth, 37–8, 113
Greene, Mrs (public assistance committee
member), 12–13, 35
Greene King brewery, xvii, 16n, 57

Hadleigh, 43n, 57, 99
Hardwick Heath, 141
Harmer, Col. (public assistance committee
member), 135, 156
Harrison, William, 13
Harrison-Topham, Mrs, 135
Haverhill, 8n, 43n, 57
Heilgers, F.F.A., 53–4, 55, 82n, 83, 100,
113, 114–16, 118, 124, 132
Hill, 60, 55–6, 111
Hillcroft College, Surbiton, xviin, 170
Hitler, Adolf, 16, 28, 29, 110, 123
Hunt, W.H. (public assistance committee
member), 135, 136
Hunter, Ernest, 161
Hunter, Mrs, 135

India, 23, 27, 32n
Ipswich, xvi, 91
Isle of Man, xvi, 6, 17, 24, 25, 26, 29, 42,
44, 68, 85, 94, 102, 117, 152
see also internment, Hans Martin
Luther

Japan, 27, 83
Jarman, Harry, 41
Jarrold, Mrs (cinema and bar manager),
32, 36, 56
Jex, Mr (trade unionist), 118
Joyce, 180, 182–3

Kedington, 4n, 76, 103, 110n, 121, 153
Kiddy, Mr (relieving officer), 105
King, Captain H.R., 21
King's Lynn, 118n

INDEX OF SUBJECTS

contraception, 68
Co-operative Party, 103, 118, 134
Co-operative Societies, 103–4, 132, 162
Council for Education in Music and the
    Arts (CEMA), 41

De Havilland works, 73, 90
diary-writing, xi, 117, 123–4, 127, 149,
    169, 170, 173–5
drunkenness, 56, 77, 91, 121n, 147n, 180

electricity, 8, 16–17, 113, 150; *see also*
    wireless
Entertainments National Service
    Association (ENSA), 7
evacuees, 10n–11n, 20, 36, 72 plate 7, 73,
    74n, 120, 146, 157, 159, 164

Fabian Society, 73, 74, 82n, 83, 89, 96,
    100, 125, 126, 147n, 150–1, 163,
    164–5, 166
farming, 141
Finsbury Health Centre, 139
food, 8, 17, 19, 31, 32–3, 34, 39, 41–2,
    50–2, 54, 59–60, 70–1, 81, 88, 90, 96,
    101–2, 106, 111–12, 139–40, 145
    rations, 8, 18, 25, 96
    see also British Restaurant, potatoes
fuel overseer, 79

German Prisoners of War, 121n, 171
Gone with the Wind, 11, 119–20, 139

hats, 50
heating, 67–8, 85, 86, 136, 166
Home Guard, 32, 118
Home Office, 7, 29, 47, 62, 85, 94
    see also Herbert Morrison
hospitals, 17–18, 21, 39, 42, 51–2, 70, 71,
    86, 115, 153, 157
housework, 93–4, 101, 111, 146
housing, 52–3, 55–6, 106, 145n, 160
    see also heating, housing (at 62
        Guildhall Street), lodging houses
housing (at 62 Guildhall Street), 79
    Challis's rooms, 8, 12, 15, 21–3, 31,
        34, 37, 52, 61, 66–8, 75–6, 85–6,
        89, 101, 103, 150
        their furnishings, 58, 63, 85–6, 91,
            124–5
    rooms of other tenant (Mrs Nudds),
        75–6, 104–5

internee, *see* Hans Martin Luther
internment, 6n, 11–12, 24–6, 34, 38,
    130–31, 152
    see also Isle of Man
Irish, 27, 35–6, 52, 70, 77, 90–1, 100,
    120n
Italian Prisoners of War, 156

Jews, 25, 27, 58, 62, 68, 107, 110

Labour Party, 83, 104, 108, 123, 169
labourers, 28, 35–6, 53, 70, 80
local government employees, 20–1, 45,
    55, 80–1, 127; *see also* Blossom,
    Mrs Brown, Burchill, Day (relieving
    officer), Dorothy (typist), Elsie Foulger
    (clerk), Gooch (chief clerk), Joan
    Burton, Mr Kiddy (relieving officer),
    Lindsey (billeting officer), Arthur
    Mobbs (relieving officer), Mrs Osgood,
    Nelson (relieving officer), Ruth
    (typist), Mr Spencer (of NALGO),
    Frederick (*alias* 'Tommy') Thompson
    (public assistance officer) *see also*
    NALGO, wages and salaries
lodging houses, 35–6

marriage, xivn–xvn, 5, 22, 38, 43, 62,
    79–80, 129, 164
Mass-Observation, xi, 14, 24, 50, 58, 66,
    96, 123, 135, 163, 173–5
mayor of Bury St Edmunds, *see* Lake
medical doctors, 83–4; *see also* Drs
    Atkinson, Bett, O'Meara, Rae, Roger,
    Stork, Turner, Ware
menstruation, 34, 68, 86–7, 148, 157–8,
    158–9, 162, 181
'mental defectives'
    dealing with, 118, 151
    in an institution, 4, 103, 121
    people portrayed as, 6, 22, 106, 111,
        149, 150, 153–5 *passim*, 163
military exercises, 32, 146
Moral Welfare Home (St Elizabeth's), 23,
    24, 26, 63, 65, 80, 143, 156, 166, 167,
    183
    Challis's visits to, 23n, 131, 143,
        146
    see also Miss D.E. Westell (welfare
        worker, Moral Welfare Home)
music and musicians, 7, 19, 41, 58, 74,
    102, 107n, 113, 135, 146; *see also*